Making a Spectacle

A volume in
Curriculum and Pedagogy
The Curriculum and Pedagogy Group, *Series Editors*

Making a Spectacle

Examining Curriculum/Pedagogy as Recovery From Political Trauma

edited by

Megan Ruby
Oklahoma State University

Michelle Angelo-Rocha
University of South Florida

Mark Hickey
Oklahoma State University

Vonzell Agosto
University of South Florida

INFORMATION AGE PUBLISHING, INC.
Charlotte, NC • www.infoagepub.com

Library of Congress Cataloging-in-Publication Data

A CIP record for this book is available from the Library of Congress
http://www.loc.gov

ISBN: 978-1-64802-291-3 (Paperback)
      978-1-64802-292-0 (Hardcover)
      978-1-64802-293-7 (E-Book)

CONTENTS

SECTION II

ISSUES SURROUNDING AMERICAN GUN VIOLENCE
AND ITS NORMALIZATION IN SCHOOLS

SECTION III

HEALING POLITICAL TRAUMA
THROUGH ART EXPRESSION

SECTION IV

LIVED EXPERIENCES
WITH POLITICAL TRAUMA SURVIVORS

SECTION V

POLITICAL AFTERMATH AND CREATING SPACE
FOR RECOVERY/HEALING

SECTION VI

MORE THAN A LABEL: EMPOWERMENT
IN CREATING SPACE IN HIGHER EDUCATION

INTRODUCTION

Politically shameful situations affect education and turn places of healing such as homes, neighborhoods, enclaves, regions, and religious sites into places of shame. Diverse narratives of *political trauma* result, wherein marginalized groups are unable to use social and cultural resources to "protect themselves from the effects of chronic trauma" (Alford, 2016, p. 31). This edited book showcases critical perspectives engaged with political trauma that is socio-political and historical. Such trauma is associated with violence and collective efforts to dismantle it. Each contribution is an invitation to heal with students and educators, not to steal their pain (Razack, 2007). Powerful imagery and poignant words illustrate how educators are learning to interact while facing increased mass school shootings, the stress associated with climate change, and the rise of White nationalism. In the following sections, the authors confront political issues and incite reparative education (Tarc, 2011).

SECTION I: RECOVERY FROM POLITICAL TRAUMA THROUGH RESISTANCE

This first section introduces resistance in relationship to the state, educational institutions, and a pandemic. Authors in this section detail or model

Making a Spectacle, pages ix–xiv
Copyright © 2021 by Information Age Publishing
All rights of reproduction in any form reserved.

how arts and language support the examination of relationships between education and the nation-state. They document efforts to recover from political traumas. In "Performing Nepantla: Spanglish as Art Practice in the Rio Grande Valley Borderlands," the authors transcend the political borders between the United States and Mexico to perform nepantlando, weaving academic, narrative, and performative/visual writing together to bring an analysis of the merits of border pedagogy. The work that follows, "Six Poems With Images," chronicles the testimonios of local transformational resistance to the removal of the Mexican American Studies program from Tucson, Arizona, using art as a form of resistance to the decision to remove the program. The author supplements the works of resistance with poetry as a response to the movement. The third piece in this section, "Living Art Out Loud: Performances at the Texas Tech University (TTU) Public Art Collection," reflects on a series of performances composed from a collection of often untold stories that brought to light first-hand accounts of living through the AIDS crisis. The arts-based pedagogy affirms Laing's (2017) idea that while art cannot cure AIDS or bring back the dead, it does have the ability to foster an uncanny negotiating ability between people and to augment meaning-making and understanding through collaborative learning. The final chapter in this section calls attention to the relationship between compulsory education in Greece and the formation of political identity formed by the political values promoted in the state-sponsored school curriculum that reflects the ideological character of the governing authority.

SECTION II: ISSUES SURROUNDING AMERICAN GUN VIOLENCE AND ITS NORMALIZATION IN SCHOOLS

This section explores teacher and student responses to the trauma of gun violence in U.S. schools, such as routinized drills as a response to expected gun violence. Readers learn how school safety mandates reshape classroom concepts of safety, classroom practices, and school policies that surround school safety. This section opens with the poem "Only a Drill," which describes the witnessing of complex reactions to a routine lockdown drill at a community college in Colorado. Then in the chapter, "Caught in the Political Machine: Educators and Active-Shooter Drills," the audience further explores how the political argument around guns, freedom, and control creates trauma in Florida schools with the use of active shooter drills. This chapter explores the broader rhetoric around school shootings for how "gender and racial hierarchies define some people and act as threatening and others as *safe*." The poem, "So Used to Trauma," details a teacher's experiences with gun violence at various stages of their life and career. This section closes with "Grant, Martin, Garner, Rice, and Teaching On," which reflects on a teacher's responses to directives from their administration on the teaching of recent events involving gun violence.

SECTION III: HEALING POLITICAL TRAUMA THROUGH ART EXPRESSION

Starting this third section is a reflection by Varga and Flores, which provides an artistic process of working through trauma, pedagogically. It gives a glimpse of how educators and students are interacting with one another through curricular conversations. Similarly, Fisher situates art-making as a political process of sense-making to confront disastrous socio-political situations made possible by climate change and neo-colonialism. Fisher relates the pain of loss in New Orleans to the political aftermath of hurricane Katrina in the name of educational reform. In this section, displacement for Fisher and Newbery is part of the ongoing traumatization of students, families, communities, and cities. Newbery's work with middle-school youth integrates the arts and sciences as it gives attention to the chronic traumatization of neighborhoods. The place-based experience with political trauma echoes across the contributions in this section as each gives event traumas a historical narrative and offers creative ways of being here (now) and there (past, future).

SECTION IV: LIVED EXPERIENCES WITH POLITICAL TRAUMA SURVIVORS

This fourth section examines the strategies of care and pedagogies of families, teachers, and other school personnel when the political trauma of schooling affects students who have crossed borders as immigrants, as refugees, or as members of families who are mixed status. "Recently Arrived— Still Under-Served: Language Learning and Teaching in the Shadows" is a collaborative reflection of four educators and school leaders. They document struggles faced by emergent bilingual students learning English in the United States' public educational system. Collaboratively, they analyze how policies, educational programs, standardized testing, lack of resources, and trained educators influence students and families adjusting to schools where English is the hyper-dominant language. The authors share their experiences in the classroom, and how microaggressions, xenophobia, and systematic racism rooted in school policies influence in long-term the emotions of emergent multilingual learners and families. Next, "Intentional Caregiving Through Love and Cariño: Mixed Status Families Responding to Issues of ICE and Im/migration" explores the child-rearing practices of multigenerational mixed-status Mexican American families. Cariño, or love and care, are implicated in their resistance of oppressive politics, specifically regarding im/migration and Immigration and Customs Enforcement (ICE). These family stories, collected through a plática-based methodology, offer perspectives into how families protect and care for their children, although often through very different modalities situating families as the experts of providing care in the face of political trauma. In "A Testimonio of Political Trauma: Coyote Meets His Match," Paul Perez-Jimenez reflects on a striking moment of brutality that he experienced as a member of the Latinx minority that involved a situation of internalized oppression at the U.S–Mexico border. In "Patrick Stays Silent," Florida educators examine the effects of policies concerning English Language Learning (ELL) on the increasing number of students who are refugees from the Congo and Honduras. Finally, "Parent Café Reflections" reports on an elementary school's principal's efforts to lead in New South Wales, Australia. The rapid influx of refugee and asylum-seeking classified students created urgency not only to make sense of, but also to minimize, the political trauma affecting life within a rapidly changing community.

SECTION V: POLITICAL AFTERMATH AND CREATING SPACE FOR RECOVERY/HEALING

Turning to the fifth section in the volume, it comes as no surprise that the aftermath of the 2016 presidential election has left a wake of trauma for individuals who identify beyond the White, heteronormative structures of what society may find as "acceptable" (Sondel, Baggett, & Dunn, 2018). And since school mirrors the ideas and thoughts of society, this aftermath was bound to affect curriculum and pedagogy in educational settings. In the chapter "Neutrality as a Lightning Rod," the metaphoric title speaks to the inability for classrooms to be neutral spaces, especially after such a volatile election. Using interview data, teachers spoke of ways they grappled with tension with colleagues, administrators, and students while complicating the notion of neutrality in the classroom and school space in general. The idea of supposed neutrality echoes in the chapter on "Renegade Teachers," where queer and non-queer educators alike took a stance for their LGBTQ+ students and challenged ideas about what is appropriate to teach. Neutrality is problematic when it ignores how America has not been great for those who are Black or Brown people of color. The poem by Still, "Grappling With Current Politics: Make America Great For Once (MAGFO)," begs the question, great for whom? The difficulty of changing the politics of inequitable education is akin to pushing a boulder uphill as we see in Nadia Khan-Roopnarine's work on "Sisyphus With a Smile: On Finding Momentum Through Political Trauma in Education." Fending off chronic trauma is akin to conquering the mountain, and both require endurance and focus. The labor-intensive work of educating is labor-attentive, as the poem "Society Gate Keepers" illustrates as it gives attention to how educators manage political rhetoric and beliefs. Overall, this section brings the politics of education to the forefront and urges educators to reflect on how political trauma enters educational settings via curriculum and pedagogy.

SECTION VI: MORE THAN A LABEL: EMPOWERMENT IN CREATING SPACE IN HIGHER EDUCATION

In this last section of this book, we would like to draw your attention to how political trauma takes hold in education in matters of representation, combatting labels, and being able to speak back to the institution by creating safe spaces for Black scholars, students, and educators. One can see the glee and empowerment of a young child being able to see themselves in a book read to the class in the poem "A mirror" by Sarrah Grubb. The audience can feel the frustration surrounding labels and being a person of color in education today in "Inertia and *Pa' delante*," a reflection/poem by Freyca Berumen and Miryam Espinosa-Dulanto. These Indigenous Mexican women discuss their resilience in American culture that has given rise to White nationalism once again and their desire to carve out space not only to endure but to resist erasure for those seen as different. Furthermore, Asha Omar's powerful chapter, "Black Academic Resistance: A Visual Arts Approach to Empirical Research," combines the ideas of resilience, representation, and empowerment by evoking an arts-based approach to show Black educators' experiences at predominately White institutions (PWIs). Omar also gives implications on how PWIs can better serve Black students and educators. Altogether, this section shows that diversity in education goes beyond a political statement made in the press or a mission statement on a university website. It is about actions, showing up and creating space for Black, Indigenous, and students of color in and out of the classroom space to start to heal the political trauma of empty words and empty promises.

THE ROAD AHEAD UNDERSTANDING OUR TRAUMATIC PAST AND PRESENT

In the process of creating this edited volume on political trauma and recovery via curriculum and pedagogy, there have been many tumultuous events. A coronavirus pandemic (CoVid-19) struck at the end of 2019. In

2020, politicians (in the United States) battled over federal, state, and city-level responsibilities, and often overshadowed public health officials in the media and their advice on how to mitigate the spread of CoVid-19. Also, in 2020, the Black Lives Matter movement reignited as police brutality continued to take the lives of many cis and Trans Black men and women. Given these expressions of state-sanctioned White supremacy, people worldwide protested and demanded change. Political traumatization will undoubtedly continue and show up in curriculum and pedagogy. Educators will continue to reconcile the past as they mediate the politics of the present that create the future of education. Curriculum and pedagogy are two interrelated vehicles through which educators participate in educational future-making. Our aim with this edited book is to center healing and recovery from political trauma in readers' journeys to create a better tomorrow.

—**The Editors**
Megan Ruby, Oklahoma State University
Michelle Angelo-Rocha, University of South Florida
Mark Hickey, Oklahoma State University
Dr. Vonzell Agosto, University of South Florida

REFERENCES

Alford, C. F. (2016). *Trauma, culture, and PTSD*. New York, NY: Springer.

Laing, O. (2017). *The lonely city: Adventures in the art of being alone*. New York, NY: Picador.

Razack, S. H. (2007). Stealing the pain of others: Reflections on Canadian humanitarian responses. *The Review of Education, Pedagogy, and Cultural Studies, 29*(4), 375–394.

Sondel, B., Baggett, H. C., & Dunn, A. H. (2018). "For millions of people, this is real trauma": A pedagogy of political trauma in the wake of the 2016 U.S. Presidential election. *Teaching and Teacher Education, 70*, 175–185.

Tarc, A. M. (2011). Reparative curriculum. *Curriculum Inquiry, 41*(3), 350–372.

SECTION I

RECOVERY FROM POLITICAL TRAUMA
THROUGH RESISTANCE

CHAPTER 1

PERFORMING *NEPANTLA*

Spanglish as Visual Art Practice in the Rio Grande Valley Borderlands

Joellyn Sanchez
The University of Texas Rio Grande Valley

Ivan Cantu
The University of Texas Rio Grande Valley

Monica Varela
The University of Texas Rio Grande Valley

Maricela Casas
The University of Texas Rio Grande Valley

Maritzabel Salinas
The University of Texas Rio Grande Valley

Christen Sperry García
The University of Texas Rio Grande Valley

ABSTRACT

Rio Grande Valley native, Gloria Anzaldúa, refers to the U.S./Mexico border as "two worlds merging to form a third" (Anzaldúa, 2012, p. 25). Spanglish is a result of a *choque* or collision of Spanish and English. Engaging in neither fully English nor Spanish, Spanglish speakers inhabit *nepantla*, a Nahuatl word for living in-between worlds. *Nepantlando* is an active process of art making and teaching using the embodied experience of living in between worlds, a space that Anzaldúa (2012) describes as ambiguous, tense, and contradictory. In this chapter, we present artist and teaching practices of nepantla, or the act of living in between worlds. To begin, we discuss border pedagogy and borderlands pedagogies as a way to conceptualize nepantlando. Next, we present visual Spanglish as an art teaching practice of resistance on the South Texas/Tamaulipas, Mexico border. Together, we visualize and perform nepantlando using performative text and image. As artist-writer-teachers living in between worlds, in this chapter, we shift between academic, narrative, and performative/visual writing.

Vivo en este estado liminal entre mundos, entre realidades, entre sistemas
de conocimiento, entre sistemas de simbología. Este terreno fronterizo al umbral
de la conciencia, o pasaje, esta entretela, es lo que yo llamo nepantla.

[I live in this liminal state between worlds, between realities, between
systems of knowledge, between symbology systems. This liminal borderland
terrain, or passageway, this interface, is what I call *nepantla*.]

—Anzaldúa as cited in Codex Nepantla, n.d.).

Rio Grande Valley native, Gloria Anzaldúa, refers to the U.S./Mexico border as "two worlds merging to form a third" (Anzaldúa, 2012, p. 25). Spanglish is a result of a *choque* or collision of Spanish and English. Engaging in neither fully English nor Spanish, Spanglish speakers inhabit *nepantla*, a Nahuatl word for living in between worlds. *Nepantlando*[1] is an active process of art making and teaching using the embodied experience of living in between worlds, a space that Anzaldúa (2012) describes as ambiguous, tense, and contradictory. It is a space that is simultaneously breaking apart and coming together. Using nepantla in relation to making art and teaching is an approach to representing spaces of visual art and education on the U.S./Mexico border.

As *frontizera/os* [native border dwellers], we speak Spanglish. Some of us speak better Spanish than English, while others speak better English than Spanish. Regardless of our fluency levels in both languages, we all speak a mix of both. Language, or the mix of two, is not often addressed in art education scholarship, nor is the experience of living on a border, or in-between worlds. Our aim is to add our experiences of nepantla to the canons of art education that historically have represented White and Eurocentric perspectives. Moreover, nepantlando is an arts-based way of conceptualizing and representing experiences that are underrepresented and undertheorized in the field of art education.

Our author collective is comprised of five undergraduate art education students and a professor from the University of Texas Rio Grande Valley, a Hispanic-serving institution. We are from border regions of the United States including South Texas and the San Diego/Tijuana border. We all share lived experiences of nepantla regardless of our skin color, Spanish/English fluency, gender identity, or socioeconomic status. Our chapter came out of two socially engaged projects in the Fall of 2018 and 2019 that addressed a lived experience of nepantla. The common thread between both projects is the practice of Spanglish, a language that resides in between two worlds.

In this chapter, we present artist and teaching practices of nepantla, or the act of living in between worlds. To begin, we define border pedagogy and borderlands pedagogies that set the stage for nepantlando. Next, we present visual Spanglish as an art teaching practice of resistance on the South Texas/Tamaulipas, Mexico border. Together, we visualize and perform Spanglish from a nepantla (in-between worlds) perspective using performative text and image. As artist-writer-teachers living in between worlds, in this chapter we shift between academic, narrative, and visual/performative writing.

NEPANTLANDO: A FEMINIST BORDERLANDS APPROACH TO VISUAL ART PRACTICE AND TEACHING

As a way to situate our arts-based process of nepantla, we define border pedagogy (Giroux, 1991, 2005; Kazanjian, 2011) and borderlands pedagogies (de la Luz Leake, 2019) as two processes that use the geographical border in relation to theories and practices of teaching. Next, we put borderlands pedagogies and border pedagogy in conversation with an emerging process of nepantlando.

An inclusive teaching philosophy, *border pedagogy* (Giroux, 2005), uses the geographical borders as a way to look at difference and struggle from a democratic perspective. There are three aspects to border pedagogy. First, border pedagogy is a process used to understand the metaphorical and conceptual borders of underrepresented people, cultures, histories, and politics (Giroux, 1991; Kazanjian, 2011). The second aspect of border pedagogy is a call to action. Students learn to become perpetual border crossers and redefine the border in the process of constructing new identities. For example, "Students become border crossers in order to understand otherness in its own terms, and to further create borderlands in which diverse cultural resources allow for the fashioning of new identities within existing configurations of power" (Giroux, 1991, pp. 51–52). Third, border pedagogy gives voice to underrepresented histories, narratives, and identities as a way to reframe hegemonic canons of knowledge (Giroux, 2005). Border pedagogy offers a way to decenter and remap knowledge and power:

> [It] shifts the emphasis of the knowledge/power relationship away from the limited emphasis on the mapping of domination to the politically strategic issue of engaging the ways in which knowledge can be remapped, reterritorialized, and decentered in the wider interests of rewriting the borders and coordinates of oppositional cultural politics. (Giroux, 1991, p. 53)

A studio-based process, *borderlands pedagogies* draws from Paolo Friere's philosophy of decentering teachers to create an equitable learning process for all as way to "co-construct knowledge" (Menjivar, as cited in de la Luz Leake, 2019, p. 52) Borderlands pedagogies invites educators, students, and community members to examine migration in a social context. Communally, borderlands pedagogies use social art practice to learn through visual art. Culminating in multimedia artifacts such as drawings, photographs, text collages, published image, and text works, this "pedagogical style encourages thinking to extend beyond the 'us' versus 'them' ideology, pushing participants gazes toward the broader systemic complexities that perpetuate our contemporary narratives" (Borderland Collective, as cited in de la Luz Leake, 2019, p. 54). Utilizing borderlands pedagogies, the Borderland Collective is less interested in debating issues, but rather they welcome dialogue that requires one to listen, to question, and to be vulnerable.

Similar to border pedagogy and borderlands pedagogies, nepantlando uses migration and the geographical border as a viewpoint from which to teach. While border pedagogy does not focus on art making, borderlands pedagogies use the language of visual art to talk about embodied experiences of migration. What distinguishes border pedagogy and borderlands pedagogies from nepantlando is that the latter practices teaching and art making from a feminist and critical race theory perspective. Nepantlando uses borderlands theories of Gloria Anzaldúa including her feminist vision of a Chicana artist. Importantly, nepantlando centers on art practice and recognizes that most artists teach in K–12, university, museum, or community settings. Therefore, it does not distinguish between artist and art educator, because we view ALL visual artists as art educators.

Nepantlando uses Anzaldúa and Keating's (2015) feminist conception of a *border artist* as a way to center art practice on living in between worlds. They recognize and make productive the ambiguity, tensions, and contradictions that occur living in nepantla:

Border artists inhabit the transitional space of nepantla. The border is the locus of resistance, of rupture, and of putting together the fragments. By disrupting the neat separations between cultures, Chicana artists create a new culture mix, una mestizada. (p. 47)

Anzaldúa and Keating refer to *Chicana artists* in their discussion of border artists, and privilege them in the above statement as a group of underrepresented artists. In *Chicana/o Remix: Art and Errata since the Sixties* (2017), art historian and anthropologist Karen Mary Davalos argues that Chicana artists have been overlooked in Western art historical and art world contexts that have designated art associated with Chicana artists as exotic, primitive, "too female," or "too ethnic" (p. 11). Davalos exposes historical undercurrents that artists of color are perceived as separate or inherently different from White artists. Using a decolonial framework, Davlos argues that borderlands are under theorized within the fields of visual art and art history. This reflects Chicanx artists having been largely underrepresented within the American and Latin American art worlds. *Rhizomes of Mexican American Art Since 1848*, a future digital aggregating portal, brings to light that library science models are Eurocentric and do not categorize Chicanx artists as "American" artists.

Latina/o Critical Race Theory (LatCrit) addresses the invisibility of people of Latin American descent living in the United States. Historically, Latinx ownership of property and citizenship has been undermined. This is despite many having lived on U.S. lands prior to the treaty of Guadalupe Hidalgo in 1848, when parts of Mexico became U.S. territory. If U.S. Latinx ownership of land and property has been withheld, this idea conceptually extends to places on U.S. lands, including art institutions. The arts are considered White property and are "institutionalized within structures that protect the values of whiteness, such as schools, museums, and galleries" (Gaztambide-Fernandez, et al., 2019, p. 18). The arts as property of White people are evident in the absence of borderlands and Latinx issues in art and art education scholarship. Being that the U.S. population is nearly 20% Latinx, we believe that this is a huge disservice to artists/art educators, Latinx or not, who work within K–12, higher education, and art museums institutions. By representing *othered* or under-acknowledged bodies of knowledge, linking Latinx issues to art and pedagogy, both visual and written, artist scholar Leslie C. Sotomayor contends, we can then erase the silence:

No representation *is* representation, meaning that when we (marginalized people) do not see parts of ourselves, our histories, and contributions reflected in the society, the institutions, and the canons of knowledge in which we live, our realization of not being represented generates a silent loudness or a gaping hole. (Sotomayer, 2019, p. 134)

Nepantlando attempts to address underheard embodied experiences that explore the U.S./Mexico borderlands and other in-between emotional, geographical, and conceptual spaces. Nepantlando performs in both formal and informal spaces of education including art museums, community programs, schools, and places of public gathering that include social practices, which is a focus of borderlands pedagogies. Through the interconnected relationship between nepantla, art making and teaching, in this chapter we practice, ask, and question what does *nepantla* offer *art making* and *teaching*? How do the three interconnect? What are the results? This includes the relationship between theory and practice.

FIVE STUDENT ARTIST/TEACHERS PERFORMING NEPANTLA IN THE RIO GRANDE VALLEY

Deslenguadas. Somos las del español deficiente. We are your linguistic nightmare, your linguistic aberration, your linguistic mestizaje, the subject of your burla. Because we speak with tongues of fire we are culturally crucified. Racially, culturally and linguistically somos huerfanos—we speak an orphan tongue.

—Anzaldú, 1987, p. 58)

The Rio Grande Valley (RGV) is exceptionally rich in culture, history, and linguistic diversity. Situated north of Mexico at the southernmost tip of Texas, our languages blend to create a beautiful linguistic phenomenon. Our native Spanglish is commonly referred to as *pocho*, Spanglish, Border Spanish, Chicana/o Spanish/English, or Tex-Mex. In our experience, Spanglish is often invalidated by outsiders, people within our community, and by ourselves.

We are students at the University of Texas Rio Grande Valley (UTRGV), a Hispanic-serving institution (HSI). Our art education program places an emphasis on art practice and teaching as an embodied experience of nepantla and living on the border. Our curriculum includes the work of Gloria Anzaldúa and other Chicana and Latinx writers. In this section, we (students of Professor García) share the experience and outcomes of two projects that we created in our class, Art Education: Theory and Background. The first project is a visual dictionary created in the Fall of 2018 by Monica and Maritzabel. The second project, *The Carrito,* was created by Ivan, Mary, and Joellyn in the Fall of 2019. Both projects represent and reflect our lived experiences of nepantla. Though two projects in two different class sections, two common learning objectives were to (a) analyze the concept of nepantla, and (b) create a socially engaged project that explores nepantla.

A Visual Dictionary of the Rio Grande Valley According to Maritzabel and Monica

A dictionary is what you reach for when attempting to look for the *correct* word. It is considered a valid source. It is a factual book that legitimizes language. Our Spanish in the RGV is often looked down upon by native Spanish speakers as "Chicano Spanish is considered by the purist and by most Latinos deficient, a *mutilation* of Spanish" (Anzaldú, 1987, p. 35). Spanglish is often perceived as incorrect or inadequate. It has yet to be recognized as a "proper" way to speak Spanish by many Spanish speakers. This is coming from our own parents, our own blood. We seek validation from them. To be told by them that our way of speaking is wrong, leads us to believe that our language is invalid. Our mission is to create a dictionary that helps legitimize this language that many people deem as inept. Through this collaborative effort, we can defend our language and reduce the notion of incorrectness as "Chicano Spanish is not incorrect, it is a living language" (Anzaldú, 1987, p. 77). We believe that Chicana/o Spanish validates our culture that is constantly changing and growing.

What makes our Spanglish incorrect? We are constantly told in Mexico and the United States that our language is wrong because we mix them. Growing up, our Spanish speaking parents would scold us and tell us to speak *correct Spanish.* The belief that there is a superior Spanish creates a division within our community. The idea of a "pure" Spanish comes from fear of our Mexican culture being diluted by U.S. American culture. On the other hand, when we leave the Valley, we are perceived as having an *accent* and are criticized for not speaking *proper* English. We fear speaking incorrectly, and it sometimes impedes us from speaking our own first language, Spanish. It is as if we speak neither English nor Spanish *correctly.*

Our project goal was to validate our Valley language and identity. To realize this, we created a visual language dictionary that counters the misconception that our way of speaking *butchers* the Spanish/English language. Our assignment was to explore how border pedagogy and studying our experiences of in-betweenness can be art education in a public setting. We decided to focus on language as an everyday practice of our experience of living in nepantla.

Most of our Spanglish words are an amalgamation of an English word with a Spanish sound to it. For instance, *watcha,* to watch (see Figure 1.1),

Figure 1.1 Illustration of wachale and parquear by Monica Varela.

or *tocha*, to touch, are both English words with "a" (ah) sound at the end, common in Spanish words. These words are a natural phenomena, influenced by our environment and the constant merging of our worlds. This represents our feelings of not being American enough *or* Mexican enough. However, we are neither English nor Spanish. We are both!

Nepantla represents the potential for change or transformation within ourselves and our community. Our personal and cultural shifts arise through *conocimientos,* valuable lessons or understandings. "Conocimientos challenge official and conventional ways of looking at the world, ways set up by those benefiting from such constructions" (Anzaldúa & Keating, 2013, p. 542). English and Spanish dictionaries are conventional ways of looking at the world. *The Valley Dictionary* is a conocimiento that challenges traditional linguistic canons.

To gather the words for our dictionary, we prepared a large wooden chalkboard and took it to several locations across our campus when classes were in session (see Figure 1.2). We created a chalkboard space that enabled about 20 participants to write Spanglish words and doodle next to them. We wanted to create a memorable experience and have something interactive that would catch people's attention. Together, we discussed

Figure 1.2 A faculty member writing Spanglish words on our chalkboard.

their word and origins. The interactions with students and faculty were an important part of this project. Some people we interacted with disagreed with our idea that *our* Spanish should be legitimized. Some were set on the idea that the Spanish used on the board was incorrect. Some provided us with words they learned here, as they were not originally from the Valley. This is how diverse our language is in the Valley and why it is important that we create and give voice to this vault of words. Next, we collected the words on the board to begin our digital dictionary.

The Valley Dictionary validates and counters our language insecurities (see Figure 1.3). Before this project, we believed that our way of speaking was wrong because we were constantly being told so. We are not butchering languages, but rather we are creating a language out of our experiences living in the United States. Therefore, we accept ourselves for who we are.

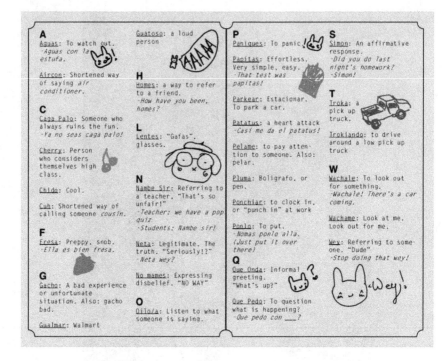

Figure 1.3 The start to our dictionary.

The Carrito [Cart] by Mary, Ivan, and Joellyn

Spanglish isn't just a mix of languages, it's an attitude.
—Alvarez, 2015.

We responded to our class assignment of creating a mobile space that addressed nepantla by designing *The Carrito*. Our goal of this project was to validate and present to our community a fluid language. We used a common object that we can relate to: a *carrito* [a mobile cart that sells foods] and *vendedores* [food vendors] to encourage people to share with us their way of speaking in the RGV. Prior to this assignment, we made *loteria* cards. One of us came up with a loteria card of the *vendedor*. With our carrito, we sold language instead of food. We displayed Spanglish words on *The Carrito* in a similar way that a *vendedor* displays items on their cart (see Figure 1.4).

The Carrito promotes the Spanglish language by having *Los Vendedores* (our group) define and communicate the diverse words we use everyday. These words are not in dictionaries. Each participant was invited to write a Spanglish word they knew on a ticket and hang it from our homemade umbrella. Our museum celebrates and validates the diverse languages of

Figure 1.4 Joellyn Sanchez, Ivan Cantu (dressed up as a vendedor), and Maricela Casas standing with their Carrito, December 4, 2019.

the RGV. Celebrating what we call Spanglish and Tex Mex slang, *The Carrito*'s role is to open and facilitate a community language space. Los Vendedores are those who are entrusted with the promotion and marketing of the Spanglish language by making known and representing words that we use. Our language is unique: *los que son de aquí*, but who have roots *de alla* (those who are from the valley, but have roots from across the border in Mexico). Our goal is to look at our language and celebrate it, rather than to be ashamed.

Living on the South Texas border has heavily influenced the way we live. Our Mexican culture is our roots. In addition, we embrace the U.S. American lifestyle. Out of this mix, our language is born. We feel like we do not belong. We are too *gringo* to be Mexican and too *pocho* to be American. This is what produces the Tex Mex/Spanglish we embrace in *The Carrito*. In the autobiographical film, *Selena*, her dad expresses how we feel:

Being Mexican American is tough . . . We got to be twice as perfect as everybody else! . . . Our family has been here for centuries, and yet they treat us as if we just swam across the Rio Grande. I mean we got to know about John Wayne and Pedro Infante. We got to know about Frank Sinatra and Agustín Lara. We got to know about Oprah and Cristina! . . . Japanese Americans, Italian Americans, German Americans: Their homeland is on the other side of the ocean. Ours is right next door . . . and we have to prove to the Mexicans how Mexican we are, we got to prove to the Americans how American we are. We got to be more Mexican than the Mexicans and more American than the Americans. Both at the same time! It's exhausting! Damn, nobody knows how tough it is to be Mexican American! (Navas, as cited in Sperry García, 2018, p. 50)

We traveled *The Carrito* to four places in the RGV in the Fall of 2019. Each place we traveled contributed to our mission: downtown McAllen, IDEA Academy, San Juan, the Edinburg Municipal Park, and our visual art building. On Halloween night, we traveled *The Carrito* to downtown McAllen and gave out candy. We quickly learned about some new Spanglish phrases none of us knew. People would come for the candy, but stay for discussions on language. At IDEA Academy San Juan Fall Festival, we received many words and phrases from students and staff. At the Edinburg Municipal Park (see Figure 1.5), we met a teenage couple that introduced us to a phrase that we Spanglish speaking *experts* did not know. *Cosa sad* is a term that is used to let someone know that they have had a bad experience with something. At our art building, many college students, professors, and visitors stopped by to contribute a word to *The Carrito*. We then displayed every word or phrase on our cart. We then celebrated Spanglish as many visitors came to view the cart. Below are some words that came out of our travels:

Cosa Sad—a term used when someone is feeling sad or depressed about something.
Los Shoos—this means "the shoes."
El Face—translates to "The Face"; this is used when people refer to Facebook.
El Parking—translates to "The Parking"; refers to the parking lot.
Janguear—to hang out or go out.

Living on the border, we have unique ways of pronouncing words and speaking. When we highlight the everyday words we use, we have a better understanding of our Spanglish/Tex Mex language. We are more creative than we think, when it comes to coming up with new phrases. Although they are not grammatically correct, these words are commonly used in the Valley. Many factors come into play in the development of Spanglish. A word comes to be because we have trouble pronouncing it. For example, we say *confleys* instead of *cornflakes*, or we learn *parquear*, to park a car, instead of the proper Spanish word, *estacionar*. Through *The carrito*, we accept our in-between language. We are proud of it, and we are not ashamed.

Our two projects are important because we document our regional language that has formed and represents our experience living in between worlds. Our Spanglish is true to us. It is a dialogue of our culture and our daily experiences in a country that tries so hard to uphold a monolingual ideology of "English-only." We believe that reclaiming our language

Figure 1.5   A close up of the Carrito at the Edinburg Municipal Park at night, Fall 2019.

unabashedly gives us power to challenge oppressive systems that try to dictate the way we should express ourselves. Our work is necessary because we feel accepted in our merging of two languages.

ACTS OF NEPANTLANDO: FRAGMENTED VISUAL AND PERFORMATIVE SPANGLISH EXPERIENCIAS

Exploring the active and practice-based process of nepantlando is important to us because we make visible our struggles of living in between worlds and shifting between languages. As a way to push against traditional Eurocentric and White canons of art education, we study and embody the concept of nepantla that is underrepresented in K–12 and higher education. Our Spanglish work gave us an opportunity to connect with others through our shared languages and cultural practices. Spanglish is our culture, it is a way we live our lives and celebrate. Despite Spanglish being looked down upon, it is our common language. For us, it is a unifying communal power in the RGV.

In the final section of our chapter, we use visual art and autohistoria-teoría[2] to theorize our experiences of nepantla, living in between worlds. Speaking Spanglish produces fragmented experiences as we inhabit and navigate multiple worlds. We (students and professor) have created a collaborative performance that is an extension of our nepantla work. Not only a language, we conceptualize Spanglish as an identity and state of being. Though creating images and arranging text, we share our testimonios of nepantla. We fluidly move between Spanish, Spanglish, and English. We spell some of the same words differently. However, all are valid. None are incorrect. These performative works serve as a conclusion or culmination of our nepantlando work.

Ivan
I know TWO languages . . . is there something WRONG with that?!?

Remember that one time in Mexico?!?

Aya en Mexico

We spent time with abuelo y abuela.   It was fun!

We came home . . . at the border . . . he got mad . . . dad was speaking Spanish

He made us feel like we did something wrong!   It's a language!

Most people at home speak it!

Why did he make us feel guilty!

"SPEAK ENGLISH. THIS IS AMERICA"

"ESPAÑOL ES MI PRIMER LENGUAJE"

"why do I NEED to speak ENGLISH?!?"

"I know BOTH languages!!!"

"Is it WRONG to know more than one language?!?"

"Is it RIGHT for me to change MY way of speaking?!?"

"I speak BOTH"

"WHY IS SHE SO MEAN"

"SHE PICKS ON US"

"SHE YELLED AT ME TODAY"

"if you are going to speak SPANISH here . . . go back to MEXICO"

Joellyn
Color.........*language*.........*family*

Color of my skin .... White ....
.... Moreno .... Dad ....

He is not your father

You are too white

Estoy Wera ....No estoy Gringa ....

You Speak Spanish

Color of my skin .... White ....
.... Dark .... Dad ....

Get away from him

.........SI ES MI DADDY!! ....

Maricela

You don't speak Spanish right

           You're too white to be Hispanic

Miran la portada... but they don't read the book... Experiencias fuera del valley...

Como se dice?   *Dilo bien!*

Where are you from?   *Where are your parents from?*

What are your traditions?   *Are we even Mexican?*

Hablamos Español con mama   *Only English between siblings*

Speak slowly...   *Speak Fast...*

Lo entiendo pero me da miedo hablarlo

You have an accent

Nos miran raro!

White boys laugh without knowing   *Los Españoles nos nombran gringas con vernos*

I know English   *Hablamos Español*

De donde son?

De donde somos?

No somos 100% Mexicanos

Ni el Español   *Nor English*

Maritzabel
:) :(:) :(

:) :(. . . así no se dice

           :) :(. . . como se dice?

                      :) :(. . . habla correcto

:(:) . . . that's not how it's said

           :(:) . . . how do you say?

                      :(:) . . . speak correctly

      Ama? Apa?~~~~~~~~~~~~~~~~~~~~~ Mom? Dad?

                       Practice your *English* !!

You don't know *Spanish* ??

    Disappoint

       Disappoint

          Disappoint

             Disappoint

                Disappoint

                  Don't Disappoint

                     Disappoint

                     Disappoint

Christen *performeando*

spanglish *entre*...

madison, wi...los angeles, ca...matamoros, mx...

milwaukee, wi...edinburg, tx...state college, pa...

san diego, ca...tijuana, mx

¡no hablas como eso!

learn it right!

wait, its estacionar and not parkear?

estoy en los angeles?

o estoy en brownsville?

no, *en* central pennsylvania

what language are you speaking?

Spanish

I thought you knew

no, *la frontera* is too far

english only

suddenly spanish becomes exotic

where are the *tortillas de maiz*?

y el pan dulce?

it's next to the penn state sweatshirts

what?

no,

not the dodgers

the frog hill stadium that I see from *mi casa*

no puedo ver nada—smog y haze

downtown LA

you'll get asthma is you're not careful

too many fumes on my commute

pregnant

but I had a reliable car

many *mujeres* don't

metro and buses take 4 plus hours to get there, LB

pinche LA metro!

mijo

adhd, asthma, and borderline autism

ya los tiene

just look at the toxins report in central LA

it's mainly in the barrios

money averts the poison

we're left with the rest

you know that touristy place—*olveras* street

by union station

where the red trolley used to go

that was their church
san juan la bautista
where gringos did not go
he said he would never buy a house
in our *barrio*
we're used to LA helicopter patrol and searchlights
latina/os (not hispanics in CA)
bodies
patrolled
from above
no me importó
art world job
*chicana*isms
don't fit
pero mi whiteness
doesn't fit
LA high profile artist studio
she said she doesn't like *comida mexicana*
what was I supposed to do?
always deficient from others around
didn't know how to eat
with a fork and knife simultaneously
gallery dinners
pero en tejas?
performing mexicana differently
they say *californianas* are *pochas*
victim of americanization in the 1940s
spreading white protestant practices
a los garcías
stripping our brownness, our cultural practices
and language
but wait
we might actually be from this side,
it's just the borders changed
green bay packer game radio
polish sausage or brats?
pero
donde están las tortillas?
wauwatosa didn't welcome *mexicanas*
they wanted the food but not the people
grandma sperry
which one do i hide
don't match

grandma garcia
sperry and garcia
hay tension
they don't match
which one to perform today?
pushing away WI hunting green bay packer
fan
with a nasally
accent
hispanic
the word imposed
what's a WI hispanic?
when we're hidden
in disguise
WI enchiladas
so bland
dad couldn't have spice
we suffered then
she was academically ignorant
he knew too much
?

university of wisconsin pwi
latina/os gravitated to one another like
como una isla
my only chicana profesora
knew
what it was like
other than that we were

como
una
isla

pero -
we are -
juntas -
y -
somas chingonas -

NOTES

1. At the College Art Association (CAA) Conference, Christen Sperry García (Sperry García & Cortez, 2020) referred to the convergence of art, teaching, and nepantla as *borderlands art pedagogy*. In conversation with the borderlands art pedagogy panel, Chicana Art historian Constance Cortez (Sperry García & Cortez, 2020) referred to "nepantla-ing" as an act of nepantla. Using a Spanish gerund (-ando), *Nepantlando* is a process that curator and art education scholar Leslie C. Sotomayor and Sperry García are conceptualizing as a Latina/x feminist, decolonial approach to teaching and art making.
2. Anzaldúa and Keating's (2015) term *autohistoria* as: [I]nterventions by women of color that transform traditional Western autobiographical forms. *Autohistoria-teoría*, then, encompasses critical self-reflection, lived experiences, transformations, creative acts, and historical contexts as well as a feeling of not belonging, intuition, reimagining, myth/symbology, and spirituality (Sotomayor, 2019, p. 138). Performing autohistoria-teoría is a way to "describe the genre of writing about one's personal and collective history using fictive elements, a sort of fictionalized autobiography or memoir: and autohistoria-teoría, is a personal essay that theorizes" (Anzaldúa & Keating, 2009, p. 578).

REFERENCES

Alvarez, A. (2015, June 1). 21 truths about speaking Spanglish. *BuzzFeed*. Retrieved from https://www.buzzfeed.com/alexalvarez/dale-que-you-can-do-this-meng

Anzaldúa, G. (1987). *Borderlands/la frontera: The new mestiza* (1st ed.). San Francisco, CA: Aunt Lute Books.

Anzaldúa, G. (2012). *Borderlands/la frontera: The new mestiza* (4th ed.). San Francisco, CA: Aunt Lute Books.

Anzaldúa, G., & Keating, A. (2009). *The Gloria Anzaldúa reader*. Durham, NC: Duke University Press.

Anzaldúa G., & Keating, A. (2013). *this bridge we call home, radical visions for transformation*. New York, NY: Taylor and Francis.

Anzaldúa, G., & Keating, A. (2015). *Luz en lo oscuro: Rewriting identity, spirituality, reality*. Durham, NC: Duke University Press.

Codex Nepantla. (n.d.). Retrieved from http://www.codexnepantla.net

Davalos, K. M. (2017). *Chicana/o remix: Art and errata since the sixties*. New York, NY: New York University Press.

de la Luz Leake, M. (2019). The social practice of borderland pedagogies. *Art Education, 72*(4), 50–58. https://doi.org/10.1080/00043125.2019.1602499

Gaztambide-Fernandez, R., Kraehe, A. M., & Carpenter, B. S. (2019). The arts as White property: An introduction to race, racism, and the arts in education. In R. Gaztambide-Fernandez, A. M. Kraehe, & B.S. Carpenter (Eds.), *The Palgrave handbook of race and the arts in education* (pp. 1–32). Cham, Switzerland: Palgrave Macmillan.

Giroux, H. A. (1991). Border pedagogy and the politics of postmodernism. *Social Text, 28*, 51–67.

Giroux, H. A. (2005). *Border crossing: Cultural workers and the politics of education.* New York, NY: Routledge.

Kazanjian, C. J. (2011). Border pedagogy revisited. *Intercultural Education, 22*(5), 371–380.

Sotomayor, L. C. (2019). Uncrating Josefina Aguilar: Autohistoria and autohistoria-teoría in feminist curating of a muñecas series. *Studies in Art Education, 60*(2), 132–143. https://doi.org/10.1080/00393541.2019.1600221

Sperry García, C. (2018). Borderlands art practice: Performing borderlands spaces through art///food///performative///writing///pedagogy (Doctoral dissertation). The Pennsylvania State University, State College, PA. Retrieved from https://etda.libraries.psu.edu/catalog/15630cxs5699

Sperry García, C., & Cortez, C. (2020). *Teaching on the margin: Nepantleros and borderlands art pedagogy.* Chicago, IL: The College Art Association (CAA) Conference.

CHAPTER 2

REFLECTING BACK

Kelly P. Staniunas
Mexico Solidarity Network

These images are from 35mm photographs captured around Tucson, Arizona—as a part of research that occurred between the end of 2017 and the beginning of 2019—with the help of six Tucson locals who, in their youth, rose up with their classmates and communities against the removal of the Tucson Mexican American Studies (MAS) program. Their willingness and urgency to share their stories extended beyond in-depth interviews as these *testimoniantes* guided me and my camera down the back roads and bustling intersections of their memories, emotions, and movement selves. The poems attempt to crack that lens wide open, as propagators of such a poisonous political climate would find their antidote in the abundant harvest of critical reflective praxis bursting well beyond the confines of school, where the movement itself would become a powerful pedagogical space.

Being from Massachusetts myself, I had no connection to the struggle for Mexican American Studies in Tucson. I came into contact via social media with the six individuals, who would later share their stories of resistance with me, after having seen them each appear in various forms of publicly available media sources related to their involvement in the

Making a Spectacle, pages 25–36
Copyright © 2021 by Information Age Publishing

movement. The Mexican American Studies Department, also sometimes known as Raza Studies, was created in 1998 (*Fisher v. United States*, 2008) as a long overdue portion of a broader desegregation mandate through which Ethnic Studies programs were developed in Tucson, Arizona. MAS came into being largely through the creative collaborations of community members and organizations (Terry, 2013), and may be understood to be deeply rooted in a long history of *Tucsonense* resistance, student/youth resistance, and the greater Chicanx movement. It was a program through and within which students were thriving, one which amplified the rhythm of their hearts, and whose success was overwhelmingly supported by substantial evidence (Cabrera, 2014; Cabrera, Milem, & Marx, 2012; Cambium Learning, 2011; Gómez & Jiménez-Silva, 2012). State lawmakers sought to, and eventually did, destroy the MAS program with the creation of Arizona House Bill 2281 (HB 2281), which was initially signed into law in 2010 (Romero, 2014), and had violently gutted MAS from the schools by 2012, including the banning and physical removal of books from the classrooms while class was in session. After an extensive legal battle in several phases, the eventual finding from a federal judge would vindicate the youths' original claims of xenophobia. The ruling stipulated that HB 2281 violated students' constitutional rights—having been motivated by "racial animus" and enacted with "discriminatory intent" (*González v. Douglas*, 2017). The case was decided only months before I would begin my research and more than five years after the program had already been completely dismantled.

In efforts to protect the program, youths engaged in forms of *transformative resistance* (Solórzano & Delgado Bernal, 2001) leading up to and directly following the program's destruction; the experience of such resistance served as the main focus for my dissertation research. As the research participants, or *testimoniantes*, clearly affirmed, the MAS classes adjusted their metaphorical cameras to a humanizing aperture; a responsibility to their communities, to their histories, to themselves, and to humanity found itself coursing through their veins. In this increasingly neoliberal world, there is not only an urgency on the part of the *testimoniantes* to have their *testimonios* be heard, there is also an urgency on our part for them to be heard, and for us to listen, to allow ourselves to be changed by them. Far exceeding anything that could be part of a formalized program, the field of education is operating with an unrecognized thirst for the kinds of knowledge that participants created and cultivated through their collective, and arguably revolutionary, movement actions outside of the classes. I created this poetry as I reflected on the *testimonios* communicated to me through our interviews. My hope is that it may help open spaces for further dialogue.

TAMBOR AGUACERO

THE MONSOON LASTED LONGER THAN EXPECTED
IN THE PUDDLES THEY COULD SEE THEIR OWN REFLECTIONS
AND THAT OF THEIR ANCESTORS AND GENERATIONS TO COME
A WINDOW TO THE PAST AND A DOOR TO BEYOND
IN A SEASON SHINING SO BRIGHT WITH LOVE AND COMMUNITY
IT NEVER SHOULD HAVE BEEN RAINING IN THE FIRST PLACE
BUT THE HARDER THE WIND THREW THEM
KNOCKING THEM DOWN, *EMPAPANDO SUS ALAS*
THE MORE THEY REMEMBERED HOW THIRSTY THEY WERE
THE COPAL SOOTHED THEIR SOULS, FLIPPING THE RAIN INTO *ÁNIMO*
COUNTLESS *HUITZILES* HOVERED NEARBY,
TURNING THE VOLUME UP AS THEY CRIED
ECHÁNDOLE GANAS MEDIANTE VOCES COLECTIVAS
RESISTING THE *TEMPESTAD OPRESIVA*, INTO THE SUNSET THEY FLY

Poem 2.1   *Tambor aguacero*

Might a heavy rain storm [*aguacero*] also be a percussion instrument [*tambor*], a collection of hearts beating together, something to refresh and grow in spite of it being intended to destroy? One can observe unexpectedness, resilience, and ingenuity; hot pink blossoms bloom out of prickly pear cacti, puddles form as slowly evaporating mirrors in the middle of the desert.

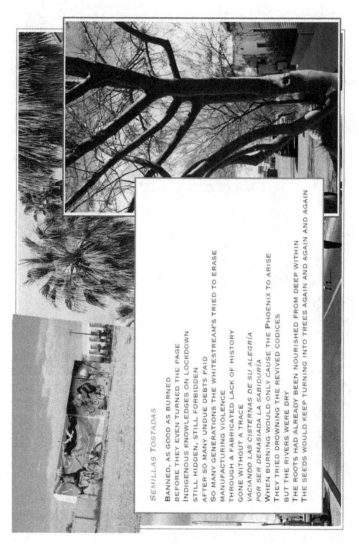

SEMILLAS TOSTADAS

BANNED, AS GOOD AS BURNED
BEFORE THEY EVEN TURNED THE PAGE
INDIGENOUS KNOWLEDGES ON LOCKDOWN
STILL HIDDEN, STILL FORBIDDEN
AFTER SO MANY UNDUE DEBTS PAID
SO MANY GENERATIONS THE WHITESTREAM'S TRIED TO ERASE
MANUFACTURING VIOLENCE
THROUGH A FABRICATED LACK OF HISTORY
GONE WITHOUT A TRACE
VACIANDO LAS CISTERNAS DE SU ALEGRÍA
POR SER DEMASIADA LA SABIDURÍA
WHEN BURNING WOULD ONLY CAUSE THE PHOENIX TO ARISE
THEY TRIED DROWNING THE REVIVED CODICES
BUT THE RIVERS WERE DRY
THE ROOTS HAD ALREADY BEEN NOURISHED FROM DEEP WITHIN
THE SEEDS WOULD KEEP TURNING INTO TREES AGAIN AND AGAIN AND AGAIN

Poem 2.2 *Semillas tostadas*

Palo verde trees across the street from El Casino Ballroom—where teach-ins occurred—on the south side of Tucson climb their way up into an image of palm trees on the University of Arizona campus at the Tucson Festival of Books. A downtown mural by Tucson artist Joe Pagac rides through the top left. In glaring irony, survival inside of tragedy, a legacy of sacrifice and resistance is juxtaposed with endless layers of wisdom feeding and fed by the deeply woven veins of the trees.

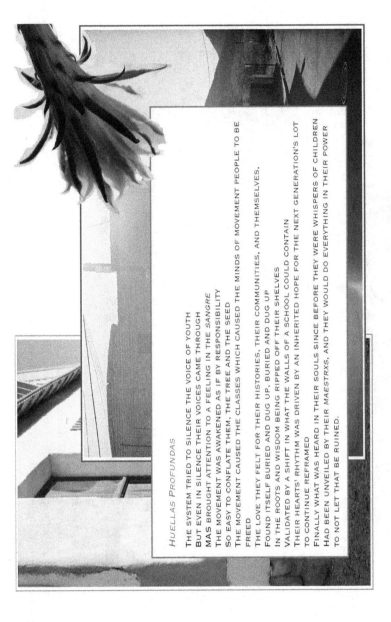

Poem 2.3 *Huellas profundas*

Old buildings on the south side of Tucson stand as reminders of the *Tucsonense* downtown. The movement brought *Testimoniantes* walking in deep footprints, a depth that enriched and was enriched by its connections to education through MAS.

HUELLAS PROFUNDAS

THE SYSTEM TRIED TO SILENCE THE VOICE OF YOUTH
BUT EVEN IN SILENCE THEIR VOICES CAME THROUGH
MAS BROUGHT ATTENTION TO A FEELING IN THE SANGRE
THE MOVEMENT WAS AWAKENED AS IF BY RESPONSIBILITY
SO EASY TO CONFLATE THEM, THE TREE AND THE SEED
THE MOVEMENT CAUSED THE CLASSES WHICH CAUSED THE MINDS OF MOVEMENT PEOPLE TO BE
FREED
THE LOVE THEY FELT FOR THEIR HISTORIES, THEIR COMMUNITIES, AND THEMSELVES,
FOUND ITSELF BURIED AND DUG UP, BURIED AND DUG UP
IN THE ROOTS AND WISDOM BEING RIPPED OFF THEIR SHELVES
VALIDATED BY A SHIFT IN WHAT THE WALLS OF A SCHOOL COULD CONTAIN
THEIR HEARTS' RHYTHM WAS DRIVEN BY AN INHERITED HOPE FOR THE NEXT GENERATION'S LOT
TO CONTINUE REFRAMED
FINALLY WHAT WAS HEARD IN THEIR SOULS SINCE BEFORE THEY WERE WHISPERS OF CHILDREN
HAD BEEN UNVEILED BY THEIR MAESTRXS, AND THEY WOULD DO EVERYTHING IN THEIR POWER
TO NOT LET THAT BE RUINED.

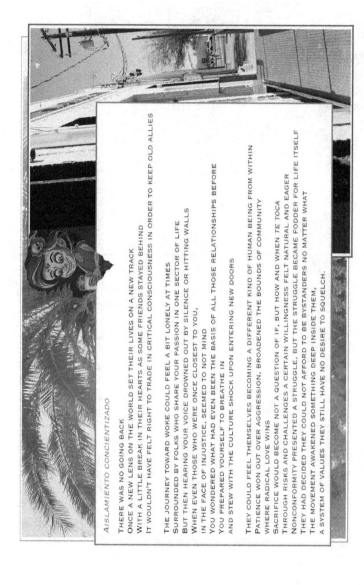

AISLAMIENTO CONCIENTIZADO

THERE WAS NO GOING BACK
ONCE A NEW LENS ON THE WORLD SET THEIR LIVES ON A NEW TRACK
WITH A LITTLE BREAK IN THEIR HEARTS AS SOME FRIENDS STAYED BEHIND
IT WOULDN'T HAVE FELT RIGHT TO TRADE IN CRITICAL CONSCIOUSNESS IN ORDER TO KEEP OLD ALLIES

THE JOURNEY TOWARD WOKE COULD FEEL A BIT LONELY AT TIMES
SURROUNDED BY FOLKS WHO SHARE YOUR PASSION IN ONE SECTOR OF LIFE
BUT THEN HEARING YOUR VOICE DROWNED OUT BY SILENCE OR HITTING WALLS
WHEN EVEN THOSE WHO WERE ONCE CLOSEST TO YOU,
IN THE FACE OF INJUSTICE, SEEMED TO NOT MIND
YOU WONDERED WHAT HAD EVEN BEEN THE BASIS OF ALL THOSE RELATIONSHIPS BEFORE
YOU PREPARED YOURSELF TO BREATHE IN
AND STEW WITH THE CULTURE SHOCK UPON ENTERING NEW DOORS

THEY COULD FEEL THEMSELVES BECOMING A DIFFERENT KIND OF HUMAN BEING FROM WITHIN
PATIENCE WON OUT OVER AGGRESSION, BROADENED THE BOUNDS OF COMMUNITY
WHERE RADICAL LOVE WINS
SACRIFICE WOULD BECOME NOT A QUESTION OF IF, BUT HOW AND WHEN *TE TOCA*
THROUGH RISKS AND CHALLENGES A CERTAIN WILLINGNESS FELT NATURAL AND EAGER
NONCONFORMITY PRESENTED A STRUGGLE. BUT THE STRUGGLE BECAME FODDER FOR LIFE ITSELF
THEY HAD DECIDED THEY COULD NOT AFFORD TO BE BYSTANDERS NO MATTER WHAT
THE MOVEMENT AWAKENED SOMETHING DEEP INSIDE THEM,
A SYSTEM OF VALUES THEY STILL HAVE NO DESIRE TO SQUELCH.

Poem 2.4   *Aislamiento concientizado*
Palm trees glow next to a young *huesuda* holding a candle, detail from the skeleton mural by Tucson artists Joel Valdez and Rock Martínez on the back of the 191 Toole building where youths would gather at a place called Skrappy's. *Testimoniantes* indicated that the classes and the movement as a whole transformed them in ways that could not be undone and have continued to impact their trajectories to this day.

Poem 2.5 *Sazón: Confianza*

On the right, a south side *Tucsonense* building; on the left, covered tables, where youths used to meet as they planned movement related actions, at the back of Revolutionary Grounds coffee shop on 4th Ave. *Testimoniantes* expressed that confidence was something that germinated as they became involved and through solidarity and collectivity. *Confianza* means both confidence and trust.

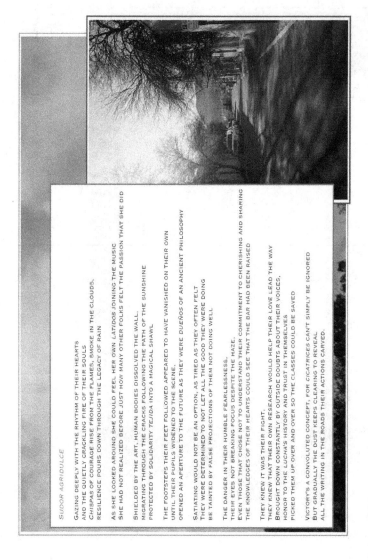

Poem 2.6 *Sudor agridulce*

Late afternoon and evening skies in downtown Tucson's southside; one can feel the warmth of the setting sun wrapping itself around the clouds. *Sudor agridulce* is a bittersweet sweat. *Testimoniantes* emphasized that it's difficult to view the overturning of HB 2281 as a win after they experienced so much loss; but their voices have been heard way beyond Arizona, and as one *testimoniante* put it, they're starting to notice the "ripples" in the pond.

SUDOR AGRIDULCE

GAZING DEEPLY WITH THE RHYTHM OF THEIR HEARTS
AND THE QUIETLY CRACKLING FIRE OF THEIR SOULS
CHISPAS OF COURAGE RISE FROM THE FLAMES, SMOKE IN THE CLOUDS,
RESILIENCE POURS DOWN THROUGH THE LEGACY OF RAIN

AS SHE LOOKED AROUND SHE COULD FEEL HER OWN *LATIDOS* JOINING THE MUSIC
SHE HAD NOT REALIZED BEFORE JUST HOW MANY OTHER FOLKS FELT THE PASSION THAT SHE DID

SHIELDED BY THE ART, HUMAN BODIES DISSOLVED THE WALL,
MIGRATING THROUGH THE CRACKS FOLLOWING THE PATH OF THE SUNSHINE
PROTECTED BY SOLIDARITY *TEJIDA* INTO A MAGICAL SHAWL

THE FOOTSTEPS THEIR FEET FOLLOWED APPEARED TO HAVE VANISHED ON THEIR OWN
UNTIL THEIR PUPILS WIDENED TO THE SCENE,
OPENED AN APERTURE TO THE FUTURE AS THEY WERE *DUEÑOS* OF AN ANCIENT PHILOSOPHY

SATIATING WOULD NOT BE AN OPTION, AS TIRED AS THEY OFTEN FELT
THEY WERE DETERMINED TO NOT LET ALL THE GOOD THEY WERE DOING
BE TAINTED BY FALSE PROJECTIONS OF THEM NOT DOING WELL

THE DANGER IN THEIR HUMBLE FEARLESSNESS,
THEIR EYES NOT BREAKING FOCUS DESPITE THE HAZE.
EVEN THOSE THAT CHOSE NOT TO UNDERSTAND THEIR COMMITMENT TO CHERISHING AND SHARING
THE KNOWLEDGES OF THEIR HEARTS COULD SEE THAT THE BAR HAD BEEN RAISED

THEY KNEW IT WAS THEIR FIGHT,
THEY KNEW THAT THEIR OWN RESEARCH WOULD HELP THEIR LOVE LEAD THE WAY
BROUGHT DOWN CONSTANTLY BY OUTSIDE DOUBTS ABOUT THEIR VOICES,
HONOR TO THE *LUCHA'S* HISTORY AND TRUST IN THEMSELVES
PICKED THEM UP OVER AND OVER SO THE CLASSES COULD BE SAVED

VICTORY'S A CONVOLUTED CONCEPT, FOR *CICATRICES* CAN'T SIMPLY BE IGNORED
BUT GRADUALLY THE DUST KEEPS CLEARING TO REVEAL
ALL THE WRITING IN THE ROADS THEIR ACTIONS CARVED.

RESPONSES FROM FIVE OF THE *TESTIMONIANTES* WHO INSPIRED THE POEMS

Julianna

"For some reason I feel like I needed to read them [the poems]. They bring me memories of struggle, but purpose and love at the same time. The first and last ones were my favorite, but I love them all. They brought me back down to earth and reminded me of why I am the way I am. They made me want to cry out of love. This work really reminds me that everything I did won't be forgotten. I may not have my name on any memorial or in history books, but I do have solace knowing that everything I did wasn't just for nothing. All the sleepless nights, crying with my friends, all the resources we put in, all the energy and love we gave was worth it" (Personal communication, May 25, 2020).

María Teresa

"The poem that meant the most to me was Poem 4: Fighting for Mexican American Studies was similar to us fighting for Black Lives Matter today! We have to stand in solidarity with one another to fight together on this injustice. And it does feel lonely at times when family and friends do not see it in the same way. But none of us can afford to be bystanders anymore. Your fight is my fight. It is amazing how you can make such tragedy, heartbreak, and endless crying nights into such beautiful poems" (Personal communication, June 2, 2020).

Alfred

The poems bring back real feelings. Reading the wording depicting emotions brings them back. The calm, chaotic, loving, confusingly grounded movement that was led by our heart" (Personal communication, May 27, 2020).

Mayra

"Although I have stepped down from a passion of mine, which has always been education and the right to learn, reading these poems made me think again of what I did with a community. I felt as if I had just been in the battle of taking back MAS classes and securing education again just yesterday.

Reading these words I felt various emotions. I felt happy, sad, nostalgic, but most importantly I felt proud. Reminds me again why I did what I did and why I fought with my community and how I don't regret meeting who I met and fighting the fight I fought" (Personal communication, June 3, 2020).

Crystal

"When I read the poem *Huellas profundas* it took me right back to the protests, vigils, and forums of *La Lucha*. I couldn't help but get emotional thinking of the moment when me and a few other classmates were giving a presentation on MAS, when our principal came in and began removing books during the presentation. It was an unbelievable time in my life, but it showed me just how strong I was. The movement allowed us to embrace the powerful and resilient Chicanxs we are. We fought for what we believed in no matter the cost. *En solidaridad*, our voices carried through the winds and were heard across all borders" (Personal communication, June 5, 2020).

GLOSSARY

Aguacero—a heavy rain, downpour
Aislamiento concientizado—conscientized isolation
Chispas—sparks
Cicatrices—scars
Confianza—confidence (and trust)
Dueños—owners
Echándole ganas mediante voces colectivas—giving it their all through collective voices
Empapando sus alas—soaking their wings
Huellas profundas—deep footprints
Huitzil—hummingbird (from Nahuatl)
Latidos—heartbeats
Lucha—struggle
Maestrxs—teachers (but more than teachers, also *compañerxs* in *la lucha*)
Sangre—blood
Sazón—seasoning
Semillas tostadas—toasted seeds
Sudor agridulce—bittersweet sweat
Tejida—woven, spun
Tempestad opresiva—oppressive storm
Tambor—drum
Testimonio—testimonial narrative, story/counterstory

Testimoniante—also sometimes called a *testimonialista* (Delgado Bernal, Burciaga, & Flores Carmona, 2012), refers to the person telling their story

Te toca—it's your turn

Vaciando las cisternas de su alegría por ser demasiada la sabiduría—emptying the wells of their happiness because of the wisdom being in excess

REFERENCES

Cabrera, N. L. (2014). Lies, damn lies, and statistics: The impact of Mexican American Studies classes. In J. Cammarota & R. Augustine (Eds.), *Raza studies: The public option for educational revolution* (pp. 40–51). Tucson: University of Arizona Press.

Cabrera, N. L., Milem, J. F., & Marx, R. W. (2012). *An empirical analysis of the effects of Mexican American Studies Participation on student achievement within Tucson Unified School District.* Retrieved from https://www.coe.arizona.edu/sites/default/files/MAS_report_2012_0.pdf

Cambium Learning. (2011, May 2). *Curriculum audit of the Mexican American Studies Department Tucson Unified School District.* Miami Lakes, FL: National Academic Educational Partners. Retrieved from https://www.tucsonweekly.com/images/blogimages/2011/06/16/1308282079-az_masd_audit_final_1_.pdf

Delgado Bernal, D., Burciaga, R., & Flores Carmona, J. (2012). Chicana/Latina testimonios: Mapping the methodological, pedagogical, and political. *Equity & Excellence in Education, 45*(3), 363–372.

Fisher v. United States. Case Nos. CV 74-90 TUC DCB, CV 74-204 TUC DCB, 549 F. Supp. 2d 1132 (United States District Court, District of Arizona, 2008, April 24).

Gómez, C., & Jiménez-Silva, M. (2012). Mexican American studies: The historical legitimacy of an educational program. *AMAE Journal, 6*(1), 15–23.

González v. Douglas. Case 4: No. CV 10-623 TUC AWT (United States District Court: District of Arizona, Filed 2017, August 22). Memorandum of Decision, Document 468.

Romero, A. (2014). The battle for educational sovereignty and the right to save the lives of our children. In J. Cammarota & A. Romero (Eds.), *Raza studies: The public option for educational revolution* (pp. 52–62). Tucson: University of Arizona Press.

Solórzano, D., & Delgado-Bernal, D. (2001). Examining transformational resistance through a critical race and LatCrit Theory Framework: Chicana and Chicano students in an urban context. *Urban Education, 36*(3), 308–342.

Terry, K. (2013). Community dreams and nightmares: Arizona, ethnic studies, and the continued relevance of Derrick Bell's Interest-Convergence Thesis. *New York University Law Review, 88*(4), 1483–1520.

FURTHER READING

Acosta, C. (2007, November). Developing critical consciousness: Resistance literature in a Chicano literature class. *The English Journal, 97*(2), 36–42.

Acosta, C., Castro, A., & Mejía, M. T. (2016). Young women in the movimiento: Chi-
can@ studies after the ban. In A. Butler-Wall, K. Cosier, R. Harper, J. Sapp, J.
Sokolower, & M. Bollow Tempel (Eds.), R*ethinking sexism, gender, and sexuality*
(pp. 175–184). Milwaukee, WI: Rethinking Schools.

Acosta, C., & Mir, A. (2012). Empowering young people to be critical thinkers: The
Mexican American Studies program in Tucson. *Voices in Urban Education,
34*(Summer), 15–26. Retrieved from http://vue.annenberginstitute.org/
issues/34/empowering-young-people

Cabrera, N. L., Meza, E. L., & Rodriguez, R. Dr. C. (2011, December 8). The
fight for Mexican American Studies in Tucson. *NACLA Report on the Ameri-
cas, 44*(6), 20–24. Retrieved from https://nacla.org/article/fight-mexican
-american-studies-tucson

Cabrera, N. L., Meza, E. L., Romero, A. J., & Rodriguez, R. Dr. C. (2013). "If there
is no struggle, there is no progress": Transformative youth activism and the
school of ethnic studies. *Urban Review: Issues and Ideas in Public Education,
45*(1), 7–22.

Cammarota, J., & Romero, A. (Eds.). (2014). *Raza studies: The public option for educational revolution.* Tucson: University of Arizona Press.

CHAPTER 3

LIVING ART OUT LOUD

Performances at the Texas Tech University Public Art Collection

G. Dean McBride
University of Texas at Arlington
University of North Texas

ABSTRACT

As a gay man, long-term survivor of HIV/AIDS and addiction, and educator, I am a dis/eased curricular being who has long practiced a pandemic pedagogy that troubles the enduring presence of an absent queer voice of survivorship and resilience. The words and gestures in this essay are a reflection on my production of *Living Art*: an interdisciplinary, site specific series of performances composed from a collection of often untold stories that bring to light first-hand accounts of living through the AIDS crisis. By risking transition of the internal dis/ease of long-term HIV/AIDS survivorship out into the potential learning spaces of Texas Tech University's (TTU) campus and its public art collection, *Living Art* exemplified Ellsworth's (2005) notion of radical, arts-based pedagogy and anomalous places of learning, and affirmed Laing's (2017) idea that while art cannot cure AIDS or bring back the dead, it does have the ability to foster an uncanny negotiating ability between people and to augment meaning making and understanding through collaborative learning.

Making a Spectacle, pages 37–47
Copyright © 2021 by Information Age Publishing
All rights of reproduction in any form reserved.

Figure 3.1   Living Art: Pink High Tops, performed at *Preston Smith* by Glenna Goodacre, TTU Administration Building, photo by Nataliya Sukhina.

PROLOGUE

As a gay man, long-term survivor of HIV/AIDS and addiction, and educator, I am a *dis/eased*[1] curricular being who has long practiced a pandemic pedagogy that troubles the enduring presence of an absent queer voice of survivorship and resilience. The words and

gestures that follow are a reflection on my production of *Living Art*: an interdisciplinary, site specific series of performances composed from a collection of often untold stories that bring to light first-hand accounts of living through the AIDS crisis. By risking transition of the internal dis/ease of long-term HIV/AIDS survivorship out into the potential learning spaces of Texas Tech University's (TTU) campus and its public art collection, *Living Art* exemplified Ellsworth's (2005) notion of a radical, arts-based pedagogy in which

> anomalous places of learning create topologies of relationality between self and others, inside and outside, inviting us to inhabit those topologies in ways that release potentiality for thoughts, feeling, and (inter)actions that in other old configurations are "captured" and not free to emerge. (p. 117)

Moreover, *Living Art* affirmed Olivia Laing's (2017) idea that while art cannot cure AIDS or bring back the dead, it does have the ability to foster an uncanny negotiating ability between people and to augment meaning making and understanding through collaborative learning. "Art has a way of healing wounds, and better yet of making it apparent that not all wounds need healing and not all scars are ugly" (p. 280).

ACT I: PROVOCATIONS

Today, just as it was in the early days of the AIDS crisis when President Ronald Reagan refused to acknowledge the epidemic's existence for more than five and a half years as almost 25,000 people died, there seems to be a desire to collectively "un-know" AIDS in the United States (Odets, 2019). In fact, as recently as Sunday, April 5, 2020, "U.S. Surgeon General Jerome Adams said on 'Fox News Sunday' that the next week will be 'the hardest and the saddest week of most Americans' lives'—calling it 'our Pearl Harbor moment, our 9/11 moment'—as the projected death toll from the coronavirus pandemic surges" (Knutson, 2020, para. 1). This is bewildering. Once again people with AIDS find ourselves in a sort of limbo; isolated in an alternate reality not shared by our fellows. We are here. We are among you. Don't get me wrong, I have a deep affinity for those who have lost loved ones to COVID-19 that is redoubled my remembrance of those I have loved and lost to AIDS. But, I find it hard to abide the collective amnesia that erases the trauma and grief that long-term survivors embody from the ongoing AIDS pandemic.

Although supposed "post-AIDS" discourses since the 1996 development of a three-drug cocktail to treat the virus have highlighted urgencies around the topics of race, gender, and economics, a disheartening consequence has been a conspicuous silence and disappearance of HIV/AIDS from cultural and political agendas. Queer memories and narratives about the virus have been suppressed, shifting attention away from HIV/AIDS in a race to assimilate to allegedly healthier mainstream norms (Campbell & Gindt, 2018).

LGBTQ+ people continue to live a historical present in which conservative fear of the erosion of civil institutions, including marriage and the military, is met by frustration with our own assimilation, which has been unwittingly brought about by neoliberal, mainstream queer activists who have spent their time and money vying for entrance into these very same repressive patriarchal structures. (Nelson, 2016). And, we long-term HIV/AIDS survivors find ourselves at a cultural crossroad where our voice is being dictated by these heteronormative societal shifts. I worry we have forgotten that the first great leaps toward liberation and pride since Stonewall emerged for

Figure 3.2 Living Art: Sylvania's Story, performed at *Run* by Simon Donovan and Ben Olmstead, TTU Sports Performance Center, photo by Sonora Ruelas.

us through the outcry from groups like ACT UP (AIDS Coalition to Unleash Power) and artistic media campaigns of resistance from organizations such as Gran Fury, Fierce Pussy, and many others. Our imaginations have been repressed primarily because of the annihilation of queers in the midst of the AIDS crisis (Schulman, 2012). And, because there are fewer of us left every day that were there to remember, it's hard to articulate our dis/eased queer voice to express just what happened and continues happening.

Larry Kramer (2015) recently wrote,

> There is no one else left alive to tell this history. So far as I know, I am the only person still here . . . I saw and heard and knew of much that others preferred not to see and hear and know, or, having seen and heard and known, declined to acknowledge. (Forward)

He is right. And, he is wrong. He's not the only one left alive to tell the history of HIV/AIDS. I'm still here. There are many of us still here that share the loneliness expressed by Kramer. Unfortunately though, for some of us who survived and lived to tell about it, there has remained a collective unspoken ban on delving into our experience. We have remained solitary, embodying the fear and shame and stigma that continue to shroud

HIV/AIDS. We have feared that an uncensored inquiry into our inner life and pasts might be too disturbing and overwhelming, exposing things that could be used against us (Halperin & Traub, 2009). Our unspoken and unheard voices, along with the spectral voices of those who perished, seem to be forgotten... it is devastating.

According to HIV/AIDS mental health specialists, most of us who survived the crisis are now considered to be suffering from what has come to be known as AIDS Survivor's Syndrome (ASS). ASS describes a psychological state of sustained traumatic survivorship resulting from having lived through the height of the AIDS pandemic (Anderson, 2016). Those of us who became HIV-positive during those early days, when having HIV/AIDS was a death sentence, are especially vulnerable to ASS. As AIDS spread, death appeared everywhere; we planned to die and buried many of our friends and loved ones. We live lives filled with the guilt of surviving when so many didn't. This has been the case for me. I often ask myself, why me? Like many of us, I have commonly experienced depression, anxiety, anger, survivor guilt, insomnia, hopelessness, substance abuse, sexual risk-taking, low self-esteem, avoidance, social withdrawal and isolation, lack of future orientation, and denial (Halkitis, 2015). How could this have happened?

According to the CDC, today there are more than 700,000 people with AIDS that have died since the beginning of the epidemic, and there are more than 1.1 million people living with HIV, of those over half of them aged 50 and older. Likewise, in 2018 there were 37,832 new HIV diagnoses of which nearly 8,000 were in young people under the age of 24 years old. (CDC, 2020). It's not over. The AIDS pandemic is both historical and contemporary, and as video artist, activist, and long-term AIDS survivor Gregg Bordowitz proclaimed with a banner installation in his recent retrospective at the Art Institute of Chicago: "The AIDS crisis is still beginning" (Well & Bordowitz, 2019). It is still beginning, and it's not just long-term survivors that are affected. Will it ever end?

▪

ACT II: INTERVENTION

Like Bordowitz, my own impulse as an artist and scholar is to understand and make meaning of what I and other AIDS survivors have experienced, and it was the genesis of *Living Art*. Conceived as a qualitative autoethno-dramatic inquiry into my own and others' unspoken dis/ease of long-term survivorship, my desire for *Living Art* was to create a space for hope within the queer politics of grief. Through the development of a dramatic text emergent and adapted from the intimate stories of surviving the AIDS crisis, *Living Art* incorporated Boal's (1985) newspaper theater and an original musical score to produce a theatrical performance event that gave collective

Figure 3.3   Living Art: John's Story, performed at *Riding Into the Sunset* by Electra Waggoner Biggs, TTU Memorial Circle, photo by Sonora Ruelas.

voice to diverse queer experiences of survivorship that uniquely embody the human condition under otherwise unimaginable circumstances.

Living Art was designed as performance autoethnography in order to give voice to what I and other AIDS survivors have seen, and heard, and known firsthand. As Denzin (2018) explains, performance autoethnography is a way to turn the personal into the political. It's a catalyst for democratic hope that places voice at the center of inquiry where it can be nurtured and heard. With performance autoethnography, our collective voice produces meaningful social criticism that helps us to endure and prevail as we align ourselves with others to make change for a better world.

Performance autoethnography proved an ideal tool for exploring questions that those of us who are long-term survivors of the AIDS crisis continue to ask: What happened? How can we give voice to that which until now has remained unspeakable? How can we give voice to those that left too soon? How can we confront and discover meaning in the seemingly unmeaningful chaos and uncertainty we continue to face? How can we begin to rethink that which is unthinkable? How can we understand that which is not understandable? How can we make sense of the senseless? How can we make meaning of what happened and continues to happen? How can we ensure that our history be taken into account?

The stories we tell reveal the relations we choose and expose ways we are held and undone by each other. With this in mind, I asked fellow long-term AIDS survivors and collaborators, drawn from HIV/AIDS social media communities, to write stories about those they lost to AIDS in hopes that it would reveal their own vulnerability and loneliness. I was not surprised when this was indeed the case. After all, giving voice to my own heretofore untold stories of precarious, seemingly isolated, survival was what was really driving the research to begin with. "Let's face it." Butler (2004) tells us, "We're undone by each other. And if we're not, we're missing something...One does not always stay intact. One may want to, or manage to for a while, but despite one's best effort, one is undone, in the face of the other..." (p. 24). Our stories, verbatim, became soliloquies that established the foundation of the dramatic text and were the inspiration for *Living Art*'s performance.

As Gaylon wrote, "The story I am about to tell is sad, some would say. I agree, but mostly it is a story of chosen families and lessons on living life in the time of plague." His sentiment epitomizes the storytelling represented in *Living Art* as it revealed important cultural practices and events, significant shared values and wisdom, and estimable, hard-won lessons learned from living in the eye of the storm.

Mike wrote,

> When your first date with a man involves tequila, Miller Lite, weed, and crystal meth, it's pretty likely that any relationship that follows will be rocky. And, yea, it was for us. Eleven years' worth, and then came great change. We got together in 1976. We were lovers; then partners. Husband came around much, much later and too late for us...

> A week or so after David's memorial it set in. It consumed me. A dark bottomless hole of depression. Suicide was on the table. There was no light. It was impossible to recall happiness.

> The next years were my darkest years sober. Simple survival one day at a time. The 1980s were a dull moan of sorrow as my friends continued to die.

ACT III: DÉNOUEMENT

Through *Living Art*'s production, I came to understand that the experience of finally giving voice to our personal stories is crucial to our learning selves in the making and our ongoing recovery. Not only were my collaborators willing to expose their vulnerability and eager to share, many even expressed sincere gratitude and a sense of relief at finally being asked to tell their long-held stories in an aesthetically meaningful way. As articulated in a personal letter to me after the event, Mike wrote,

It was a cathartic and overwhelming learning experience, affirming my own life and loss, David's lost life, and all our shared desires, hopes, and dreams that were cut short—but still remain. And to have our story performed for others was nothing short of transformative.

This heartfelt expression reminded me of just how much the presence of absence continues to leave a mark on all of us that must be voiced.

Living Art unearthed and helped to mitigate our far-reaching stigma, shame, and isolation—promoting renewed creativity and vitality for myself and my collaborators and enlightening young performers and audiences, insiders, allies, and strangers alike. *Living Art* emphasized that what happened to the HIV/AIDS community is not a secret and that silence about the decimation, oppression, and marginalization of any people, then and now, must be broken as a matter of survival for us all (Gould, 2009).

As survivors of the most devastating health crisis of the modern era, who have been forced to rely only on ourselves and have been shamed and marginalized into silence, we have been propelled into the future where, not unlike Benjamin's (1940) angel of history, we find ourselves facing the present looking back toward the past with a stunning desire to "awaken the dead and to piece together what has been smashed" (Part IX). We cannot afford

Figure 3.4 Living Art: David's Story, performed at *Park Place* by Glenna Goodacre, TTU Health & Human Services, photo by Sonora Ruelas.

to be silent. As Marlon Riggs, filmmaker and queer activist, proclaimed in the early 90s "Silence kills the soul; it diminishes its possibilities to rise and fly and explore. Silence withers what makes you human. The soul shrinks, until it is nothing" (Parmar, 2017, p. 81).

The time has come for us to tell our stories, for they are above all stories of hope and resilience, and not telling or hearing them does nothing to ease our ongoing marginalization, oppression, and injustice, nor to support the queer community's quest to be citizens, equal citizens. If we long-term survivors do not share our voices, our significant contributions to queer identity, culture, and heritage will continue to be erased through omission from the great heteronormative story of history. As people living with HIV and dying from AIDS-related illnesses, we must continue *Living Art* out loud, resisting insidious combinations of homo/transphobia, sexism, racism, ageism, and neocolonialism to make our predicaments known and our dis/eased queer voices heard. We have personal and collective experience coping with dis/ease that would be invaluable to most Americans, now more than ever, if they would only take time to notice.

Through *Living Art* my fellow long-term survivors and I took audiences on an emotional journey along a memorial pathway of survival that literally and figuratively represented our learning selves in motion. The events might be compared to a metaphorical prophylaxis that simultaneously both treats the dis/ease of long-term AIDS survival while at the same time exposes its pain and the hope of recovery. We turned our dis/eased learning selves inside out for audiences to see and hear and know. They were asked to risk contagion to our dis/eased queer truths and alterities as we removed our masks to be heard and to provoke them to regard themselves as another and another as themselves. We encouraged them to imagine what art can teach us about ourselves and others, and even how we treat each other in a historical present in which the dis/eased world seems to be falling down around us. As Sholette (2018) suggests, we have shared our own radical, uncanny pedagogy to create a rupture: "a discernable moment of alienation between subject and object, learning and doing, metaphor and thing, the very ground of both artistic study and social critique" (p. 292). Through *Living Art* we produced an artistic pedagogical intervention in which meaning and understanding in the making are always still beginning.

EPILOGUE

Finally, I have used the collective "we" throughout this reflection not because I wish to speak for my fellow HIV/AIDS survivors, but to reflect their support behind and around my lonely "I" in the production of *Living Art*;

Figure 3.5 Living Art: Sylvania's Memorial Installation, performed at Charles Maedgen Theatre, TTU, photo by Sonora Ruelas.

"I" became "we." And, I rally behind the "we" because it represents recovery and vitality that emerge as others join with me in *Living Art* out loud.

NOTE

1. The term dis/eased, as it is presented here and throughout, purposefully includes the "/." The backslash is used to indicate a binary coexistence between the concepts of ease—something less serious or severe and dis-ease—something that affects adversely. In my view, to be dis/eased is a particularly queer phenomenon.

REFERENCES

Anderson, T. (2016, August 8). What is AIDS survivor syndrome: And why you need to know (revised January 2020). *Let's Kick ASS.* Retrieved from https://lets-kickass.hiv/what-is-aids-survivor-syndrome-dc0560e58ff0

Benjamin, W. (1940). *Frankfurt school: On the concept of history by Walter Benjamin.* Retrieved from https://www.marxists.org/reference/archive/benjamin/1940/history.htm

Boal, A. (1985). *Theatre of the oppressed.* Theatre Communications Group.

Butler, J. (2004). *Precarious life: The powers of mourning and violence.* London, England: Verso.

Campbell, A., & Gindt, D. (Eds.). (2018). *Viral dramaturgies: HIV and AIDS in performance in the twenty-first century.* London, England: Palgrave Macmillan.

CDC. (2020). *Statistics overview: HIV surveillance report.* Retrieved from https://www.cdc.gov/hiv/statistics/overview/index.html

Denzin, N. K. (2018). *Performance autoethnography: Critical pedagogy and the politics of culture.* Abingdon, England: Routledge.

Ellsworth, E. (2005). *Places of learning: Media, architecture, pedagogy.* Oxfordshire, England: Taylor & Francis.

Gould, D. B. (2009). The shame of gay pride in early AIDS activism. In D. M. Halperin & V. Traub (Eds.), *Gay shame* (pp. 221–256). Chicago, IL: The University of Chicago Press.

Halkitis, P. (2015). *The AIDS generation: Stories of survival and resilience.* Oxford, England: Oxford University Press.

Halperin, D. M., & Traub, V. (2009). Beyond gay pride. In D. M. Halperin & V. Traub (Eds.), *Gay shame* (pp. 3–40). Chicago, IL: The University of Chicago Press.

Knutson, J. (2020, April 5). Surgeon general says this week will be "our Pearl Harbor, our 9/11 moment" in the U.S. *Axios.* Retrieved from https://www.axios.com/surgeon-general-coronavirus-april-3bba39f2-87b6-45a7-a1f4-7ecb7fa6e7a7.html

Kramer, L. (2015). *The American people: Volume 1: Search for my heart.* New York, NY: Farrar, Straus and Giroux.

Laing, O. (2017). *The lonely city: Adventures in the art of being alone.* London, England: Picador.

Nelson, M. (2016). *The argonauts.* Minneapolis, MN: Graywolf Press.

Odets, W. (2019, July 22). Ronald Reagan presided over 89,343 deaths to AIDS and did nothing. *Literary Hub.* Retrieved from https://lithub.com/ronald-reagan-presided-over-89343-deaths-to-aids-and-did-nothing/

Parmar, P. (2017). Affinities. *OUT/LOOK & the Birth of the Queer, 10,* 80–82. Retrieved from http://www.queeroutlook.org/portfolio/pratibha-parmar/

Schulman, S. (2012). *The gentrification of the mind: Witness to a lost imagination.* Berkley: University of California Press.

Sholette, G., Bass, C., & Social Practices Queens. (2018). *Art as social practice: An introduction to the principles and practices of teaching social practice art.* New York, NY: Allworth Press.

Well, G., & Bordowitz, P. (2019). *Gregg Bordowitz: I wanna be well.* Chicago, IL: The Art Institute of Chicago. Retrieved from https://www.artic.edu/exhibitions/9170/gregg-bordowitz-i-wanna-be-well

CHAPTER 4

PLURIBUS VS. UNUM AS VALUES IN CITIZENSHIP EDUCATION

Eleni Mousena
University of West Attica, Athens, Greece

ABSTRACT

Constructing political identity and values is a key goal of education. This paper aims to explore the political values promoted in compulsory education in Greece. In particular, it addresses the questions: Which values are promoted in citizenship education textbooks, and what is allegedly its relationship with otherness in general? The values of *Pluribus* or *Unum* as analytical categories emerge from the theoretical framework and the research questions. Given that Greece, in the last decades, has been receiving vast flows of migrants and refugees, it is worth considering the political values that characterize the relevant school curriculum. The analysis essentially involves the textbooks of citizenship education curriculum for the last 50 years, split into two historical periods: The Dictatorship and the Metapolitefsis. The qualitative content analysis shows significant differences in the frequency by which these values are promoted in each of the two periods. During the Dictatorship the value of homogeneity, or *Unum*, appears most frequently, while the value of heterogeneity, or *Pluribus*, is further promoted during the historical period of the

Making a Spectacle, pages 49–62

Metapolitefsis. It is concluded that political values in education change in favor of accepting students' diversity and healing their political trauma.

The formation of citizens out of individuals is a major objective of contemporary education systems. The content of citizenship education today focuses on the development of an autonomous personality which is characterized by democratic political identity and understanding of and respect for diversity and otherness. *Education for democratic citizenship* means education, training, awareness-raising, information, practices, and activities which aim, by equipping learners with knowledge, skills and understanding, and developing their attitudes and behavior, to empower them to exercise and defend their democratic rights and responsibilities in society, to value diversity and to play an active part in democratic life, with a view to the promotion and protection of democracy and the rule of law (Council of Europe, 2010).

Citizenship education may sound as an issue that has already been analyzed, a "déjà vu" concept, as has been observed by some scholars. However, its dynamic nature and its connection to actual circumstances seem to provide a way out of the impasse caused by this statement. It is the cultural pluralism of modern societies that takes citizenship education out of the dead end of an already reviewed and resolved research subject. Greece in recent decades accepts huge numbers of immigrants and refugees, to whom the right of education and of induction to profession and society has been recognized by the UN Convention on Human Rights.

Immigrant and refugee students have experienced difficult situations, such as war, danger, and the death of relatives. Many arrive in Greece unaccompanied by parents or relatives and are likely to suffer political trauma. The way they get into school may heal this trauma or make it worse. "As an influx of immigrant students pours into local schools—some traumatized, some without formal schooling—schools reach for ways to support them" (Zimmerman-Orozco, 2015, p. 48). Political trauma refers to the inability of marginalized groups to use the social and cultural resources (Alford, 2016). The concept of political trauma focuses on the context to which the individual belongs and not on himself. In other words, it is the responsibility of the competent institutions and persons to heal it, and not the "patient's" individual ability (Goodwin, 2015). As Razack (2007) notes, we do not wish to further pathologize students and educators or steal their pain.

The aim of the paper is to explore the political values promoted in compulsory education in Greece in the last 50 years, in which two different ideological regimes governed, the Dictatorship 1967–1974 and the Metapolitefsis 1974 to date. In particular, our concern focuses on the following questions:

- Which values are promoted in citizenship education in textbooks?
- What is allegedly its relationship with otherness in general?

The qualitative content analysis essentially involves data from the citizenship education textbooks.

There are two main factors in the educational process, the curriculum and the teacher who implements the curriculum. In this paper we will look at the first factor. However, it would be worthwhile to consider how teachers are challenging the integration of immigrants and refugee students into the school, as most of them are prepared for the profession at a time when the principle of homogeneity was paramount. Teaching through the lens of equity requires looking closely at curriculum and culture. According to Gorski and Swalwell (2015), "Schools can commit to a more robust multiculturalism by putting equity, rather than culture, at the center of the diversity conversation" (p. 34).

Designing a curriculum that can lead to the establishment of a democratic citizenship identity is the desideratum. The traditional curricula, promoting the 3Rs, do not seem to suffice to respond to current challenges. Cultivating multiculturalism in students and promoting innovation are crucial. According to Reimers (2016), the content of such a curriculum should place emphasis on environmental studies, world history, and public health. In addition to helping students develop knowledge of critical global challenges, educators must also address the range of skills that global competency requires, from foreign-language study and religious literacy to curiosity about the world and an understanding of personal agency, empowerment, and leadership.

LITERATURE REVIEW

Ethnocentrism and Political Identity

One of the most significant elements of modern educational systems is the formation and, more importantly, the appropriation of the public self by the nation-state. It is this fact that defines school cognitive content as ethnocentric. Given that the development of modern education systems occurred in parallel with the establishment of nation-states, the formation and appropriation of individuals' political identity seems to be a matter of course. Dewey (1916) stresses that

> the importance of education for human welfare and progress was captured by national interests and harnessed to do a work whose social aim was definitely narrow and exclusive. The social aim of education and its national aim were identified, and the result was a marked obscuring of the meaning of a social aim. (p. 97)

This is the time when Max Weber defines state as an institution which has a monopoly on legitimate violence, while Ernest Gellner (1992) defines it as the institution which has a monopoly on legitimate education, which Gellner regards as more significant and central than legitimate violence (p. 70).

However, ethnocentricity is not the only aspect of bourgeois education systems which attracted criticism since their overall constitution was not democratic. The ethnocentric curriculum plays a crucial role in shaping future social identities and it is regarded as a major tool for developing nationalism. An immediate outcome of ethnocentric school knowledge is the development of negative national stereotypes for other nations through instruction in false statements. However, this process is also seen from a positive perspective as it enhances social cohesion. It has been argued that national governments have serious reasons to act in this manner (Russel, 1971, p. 19). Today, a broader approach should be taken to school knowledge for the reason that, as Ross (2000) points out, social identities and cultures are no longer secure and static. According to him,

> Social mobility, migration, increased awareness of gender, environmental concerns, social exclusion, and class all continue to contribute to a general challenge to traditional verities. Even if there was once a national stability—and what stability and coherence there was may have been at best an invention—it does not continue today. (p. 97)

The viewpoint has been expressed that an ethnocentric curriculum is only legitimate as a response to the *nation at risk* theory, according to which a general impression exists of the nation-state in economic decline (Goodson, 1994). However, images and stereotypes tend to persist and finally crystallize the emotional reactions of hatred and contempt, a fact which should not be underestimated (Gadoffre, 1951). On the other hand, serious objections have been voiced with regard to ethnocentric curricula. The most notable of these focuses on the discrepancy between the fact that pedagogical work cultivates a humanitarian culture while, at the same time, it promotes views on separate races, chosen nations, friendly and barbarian peoples (Pring, 1999).

The same contradictions of the ethnocentric curriculum are also discussed in the collective work Τι είναι η Πατρίδα μας; which discusses the Greek curriculum. According to the authors, the strong pacifistic message and the promotion of peace as a moral value in history textbooks is undermined by the praise to the Greek revolution, which is a hymn to bravery and heroism. This promotion of bravery, as the authors stress, "stands in contrast to today's peace-loving message about the priority of human life" (Φραγκουδάκη, Δραγώνα, 1997, p. 366), but also to democratic values as a whole.

It has been proposed that the emphasis placed on one nation's virtues as opposed to those of other nations should be abandoned. An essential argument is the one in favor of developing a political, rather than a national, identity. Two approaches have emerged in political theory regarding national identity. The first, known as *communal nationalism* concerns the establishment of national identity on the basis of nation, while the second, which is referred to as *constitutional patriotism, civic nation* (Smith, 2000, p. 24), or *civic nationalism* (McLaughlin & Juceviciene, 1997), claims that political identity should be based on respect for the constitution. Civic nationalism is democratic in nature. It envisions nation as a community of equal citizens who have rights and who are patriotically attached to a common set of political practices and values. The place occupied by law in civic nationalism is taken by local popular culture, especially language and customs, in communal nationalism. It should be noted that while in civic nationalism, political identity is built according to law and reasoning, in communal nationalism, it is based on sentiment.

The merit of political identity lies in creating a sense of belonging as well as in cooperation, loyalty, stability, and social solidarity. The political identity formed in the context of civic nationalism is flexible and, therefore, capable of covering many different political views and of being open to cultural pluralism. Thus, since the cultivation of political identity through the education system is necessary, this identity should be based on law, reason, political values, loyalty to and support of the constitution.

Social Pluralism and Education

The term *social pluralism* refers to the different cultural identities mainly distinguished in terms of ethnic origins, race, gender, and religion. That is, reference is made not only to the traditional social class relationships, but also to the ethnic-cultural categories (predominantly related to migrants) which are becoming increasingly common within national territories. Traditional pedagogical discourse was aimed at homogenization while marginalizing or concealing the existence of cultural specificities. Nowadays, such practices are disputed on the grounds that they are incompatible with the conventions on human rights and that they seem to produce the opposite effects.

Coexistence with other cultures is not an occurrence of the past decades. Many great civilizations of the past were characterized by heterogeneity. What has changed is that today travel and communications take place at a much faster rate. The existence of diverse population categories can be the cause of conflict but it can also instigate blending. What needs to be done is find ways to prevent conflicts and use heterogeneity in a favorable way. It has been proved that closed societies are condemned to decline. For this reason, pluralism should be hailed rather than regarded as a misfortune. As Παπαγεωργίου (1997) characteristically notes,

There is no better mirror in which to see ourselves than the carrier of an ethno-cultural otherness coexisting with us. Being obliged to live with others is not a misfortune, as we are injudiciously accustomed to believe, but a unique opportunity to recognize and to reflect on ourselves. (p. 22)

It would seem that education systems which persist with integrative practices similar to those adopted in the formation phase of nation-states have no place in today's world, in which heterogeneity and multi identity features predominantly. Diversity is perceived as an alternative educational idea or rationale which can become a key concept of a dynamic "social" approach to pedagogy. At the same time, education is called upon to transform itself from a mechanism for controlling and reproducing inequality to an institution which will confront and restrict it. "This shift from deficit perspectives to asset-based approaches should be at the heart of any school improvement effort" (Irizarry, 2015, p. 70).

The main goal of a multicultural citizenship dimension in education is socialization and learning on the basis of tolerance for diversity. Young individuals should learn to tolerate "the other." This cannot be achieved unless they gain an insight into what causes this difference between "the other" and themselves. A multicultural dimension in education means that all social or cultural groups should be addressed in general education curricula, particularly in textbooks content. Varro (1999) stresses that diversity has no place in the integration model of the bourgeois democratic school. This model changed and, from 1981 onward, references to the "locals" gradually decreased, while elimination of diversity has been replaced by the "right to diversity." However, researchers note that school curricula lack such flexibility, thus impeding the academic and social success of "foreign" students (Gough, 1999; Sears, 1994; Varro, 1999).

The question arises, then, as to whether the different sources of diversity should be included in school content or concealed as if they did not exist. If a people's heritage is passed down through education, the key issue of the multicultural dimension is *whose* heritage is transmitted when this people consists of several subcultures (Callan, 1997; Gorski & Swalwell, 2015; Pratte, 1988; Rothstein, 2015). Establishing an acceptable boundary between majority rule and the principle of justice clearly relates to the proper functioning of democracy. Citizenship education scholars are faced with the challenge of establishing acceptable boundaries between these competitive forces and transform this into educational practice. Instilling in children the political virtues of tolerance and mutual respect does not homogenize children, nor does it negate the existence of genuine differences. Rather, it supports uniqueness and autonomy more effectively than any other learning process (Dill 2015; Zunnernab-Orozco, 2015).

Whether curricula should support the principle of *Unum* or that of *Pluribus* has become a major concern in the United States, where this is an issue intrinsic to the composition of society. Freeman Butts, advocates a reform of curricula based on pluralistic integration. In their work, *The Revival of Civic Learning*, Butts (1980) observes an increasing tension between the values of uniqueness (*Unum*) and those of pluralism (*Pluribus*), suggesting that both should be evaluated and promoted by civic educators. Patrick (1986), in the *Immigration in the Curriculum*, dismisses the two views of monolithic integration and proposes that of pluralistic integration. The pluralistic integration approach, on the other hand, acknowledges social complexity in societies in which ethnicity may vary significantly between groups as well as between individuals. Pluralistic integration is more compatible with education on democratic citizenship as it combines majority rule with minority rights. It is the most compatible approach with the western theories on democracy.

Population diversity, as formed in European countries over the past decades, raises concern about the problems caused by the "inconsistency" between school culture and the culture of daily life. New pedagogical views and practices persist in the necessity of cohesion between the knowledge provided in schools and the cultural traits of beneficiaries. This can lead to a school which no longer resembles, in Forquin's (1996) words, "a monastery or a fortress" (p. 188; Yeager, 1998, p. 207). In conclusion, since citizenship education aims to produce well-informed and responsible citizens who respect the laws of the political community to which they belong, it follows naturally that these citizens will respect, tolerate, understand, and treat their fellow citizens on equal terms, even when some of them are "different."

METHODOLOGY

The ultimate goal of citizenship education is the development of a democratic personality which is characterized by autonomy, by a democratic political identity, and by the exhibition of feelings and behaviors of understanding of and respect for everything perceived as *different*. As indicated, in a previous unit, two views on nation have been developed. The ethnotic perception is based on cultural elements and the national integration is not considered to be complete, while blood ties take precedence. The second view expresses a political unity for which law is a point of reference. In this case, citizenship is founded on the right to territory.

Based on the above, this study aims to explore the political values promoted in compulsory education in Greece in the last 50 years, in which two different ideological regimes governed, the Dictatorship 1967–1974 and the Metapolitefsis 1974 to date. In particular, our concern focuses on the following questions:

• Which values are promoted in citizenship education in textbooks?
• What is allegedly its relationship with otherness in general?

The sample of textbooks is:

A: Τσιρίμπα, Α. (1969). Αγωγή του Πολίτου, ΣΤ´ Τάξη.
B: ΟΕΔΒ (1989). Κοινωνική και Πολιτική Αγωγή, ΣΤ´ Τάξη.

The textbooks analysis employs the qualitative content analysis method that provides scope for analyzing more complex topics, where meanings are based on the sum of the meaning, and it suits small or incomplete samples. Moreover, qualitative analysis focuses on the text producer's intentions and motivation, while it is interested in content as a reflection of deeper phenomena. In other words, it is concerned with other facts and meanings which remain latent in the explicit content. During the analysis process, the existence, or the absence, in the content of a characteristic is significant. Interpretation is part of the analytical process, that is, it occurs simultaneously, rather than following analysis (Bardin, 1977; Berelson, 1971; Neuman, 1994).

The analytical categories selected do not correspond to the thematic units of the textbooks contents. Rather, they emerge from the sum of the material. A major element of distinction of the analytical categories is the recorded ideological content, perceptions, ideas, views, which are spread across all thematic units. We have, in other words, a kind of restructuring of the text which leads to the identification of themes and the formation of categories. This means that analytical categories constitute new units, which emerge from the groupings of excerpts from the texts. This process is a kind of condensed analytical code.

CONTENT ANALYSIS AND DISCUSSION

A. Dictatorship Era (1967–1974)

The citizenship education textbook of the Dictatorship era does not contain any political or law-related elements concerning the establishment of the concept of nation. Ethnic and cultural features are prevalent, along with references to racial elements, and blood ties are particularly stressed. Moreover, religion occupies the most prominent place in terms of citations over all other cultural features, a trait which is less common in the books of the next period.

"Its soil is sacred because it has been watered with the blood of Saints and heroes. In mountains, in the flatlands and in its waters ancestral bones are scattered, of fathers and brothers, who fell fighting for its freedom, its glory and its honor." (A, p. 71)

"Greek society consists of members belonging to the same race, the Greek race. Its members have the same origins, the same religion, they speak the same language, have the same morals and customs, the same traditions, the same history, the same longings and the same ideals." (A, p. 185)

It becomes clear from the above quotations that political identity is sought to be established according to a race-related perspective of nation. Although it would be worth analyzing and interpreting these elements with the aid of racial theories, such a task is beyond the scope of the present study.

Tradition maintains the dominant position and morals, customs, and traditions are approached through a Christian/religious perspective.

"Christian traditions, such as those regarding worshiping God, honoring the dead, adoring the Saints etc., are maintained and practiced with reverence and faith." (A, p. 12)

"The Greek Polity displayed and [still] displays an interest in ensuring all the means which are necessary for an unobstructed, civilized and Greek-Christian coexistence of its inhabitants." (A, p. 14)

Once again, a distinction is drawn between good and bad morals. Characterizations are not related to qualitative aspects of behavior as much as they are to superficial elements. To the textbook's author, for example, the way in which individuals dress takes priority; it must not be "modernized" as this would signify a relaxation of morals. At the same time, issues of social conduct do not seem to be considered equally important:

Dress today, both male and female, has become one of the most serious problems in society. This is because it keeps changing form and, day by day, it is becoming ostentatious and provoking. [...] Nor should we imitate ways of dress which do not befit the Greek character or the ideals of Greek-Christian civilization. (A, p. 191)

In addition, only boni mores are considered legitimate; in other words, the ones which are consistent with the Greek-Christian spirit and which should be officially recognized by the state. "Greek legislation recognizes them, as long as they are good, that is, as long as they accord with the teachings of Greek-Christian civilization" (A, p. 187).

The urban environment is seen as a threat which can cause the adulteration of Greek-Christian morals. City dwellers, it is stressed, should be polite and decent and they should transact in honesty and sincerity (A, p. 17).

This is an obvious implication that the inhabitants of cities do not actually behave in the desired manner. In contrast, the author has more sympathy for the "Greek village," whose inhabitants do not "directly fall under the influences of the social life of the cities, but they preserve the morals, customs, traditions and all the other institutions exactly as they received them from their fathers..." (A, p. 15). For these reasons the Greek village is rewarded by the regime:

> Dedicated and loyal to the Greek-Christian traditions, it remains an inexhaustible source of strength for great and heroic actions to the glory of our Country, despite having been neglected for many years. Today, however, for the first time since our nation's regeneration, it receives the warm affection and the impartial support of the new Greek State which was founded by the National Revolution of 21st April 1967. (A, p. 15)

Extracts such as this indicate that the military regime seeks to be legitimized by addressing the conservative provincial population. The Greek nation's historical past is long and glorious. At the same time, the nation's aspirations are signs of a future which is brighter and even more glorious than its past. To the author of the citizenship education textbook of this era, the materialization of the Great Idea was not buried in the ruins of the Asia Minor Catastrophe. Rather, it remains the prime goal of the Greek nation, which shall be followed by the dissemination of Greek and Christian ideals to the whole world. It is the destiny of the Greek nation to conquer other peoples. The Greeks' homeland is "the homeland of heroes and the Homeland of Homelands of the whole world" (A, p. 161).

> The Greek Nation is the oldest Nation in the world...it constitutes a wonder in the history of humanity...Various studies have shown that contemporary Greeks have the same virtues and the same faults as their ancestors [...] [Greece] gave the world the finest intellectual creations. (A, pp. 82–83)

The "national anniversary of April 21," which was added to the other national anniversaries, occupies a large part of the teaching content. It is the date of establishment of the dictatorship regime. The Greek army, with the aid of which the Greek people conquered their "freedom," is also praised.

> The holidays which the entire Nation celebrates in memory of important events during their anniversary are called national [holidays]. March 25, October 28, and April 21 are considered National holidays. (A, p. 77)

> April 21 is the third great National holiday [...] it is the anniversary of the Revolution of our heroic Army... (A, p. 80)

A reversal of values is discerned in these texts. The meaning of freedom and legality is explained outside established views on these values. Clearly, this is an explicit ideological subversion. When compared to other nations, the Greek nation always was superior and it remains so. The prevalence of the ideals of Hellenism and the Greek Orthodox Christian Church have contributed to this.

B. Metapolitefsis Era (1974–to date)

In citizenship education textbooks of the Metapolitefsis era, references to the concept of nation are not void of the ethnocentric perspective which dominated the books of the previous period. In other words, there are references to the formation of nation on the basis of purely political and legal characteristics which presuppose the existence of a strong rule of justice. At the same time, the idea of an endangered nation is emphasized: "All the struggles of the Greeks sought to repel attacks by other peoples who wished to conquer them (B, p. 17).

The element of race as a concept of nation, which dominated the dictatorship era textbooks, is now withdrawn. Post-dictatorship textbooks do not endorse a racial/racist approach to nation. "Nation" is now defined as an "idea" on which all ethnic and cultural features such as common origins, common language, religion, and culture are based:

> This idea, the sense shared by all, that we belong to the same union and that we have the same origins, language, religion and culture, and which urges us to aspire to live in an organized way in the same free state, is the nation." (B, p. 17)

The presentation of the notions of territory and of the establishment of the Greek nation-state is extremely obscure. The assertion that many Greeks who live and work abroad have a strong Greek national consciousness is frequently repeated: "Not only have we Greeks who live in Greece belonged to the Greek nation. Expatriate Greeks also belong to it. The millions of Greeks who live and work in all five Continents" (B, p. 17).

A distinction is drawn between the Greeks who act within the country and expatriates, who have a heightened sense of their national origins: "In their second homeland, Greek expatriates feel strongly about the national idea. They cultivate the Greek language, our national traditions, and the orthodox Christian religion. All this fortifies their national origins (B, p. 17)."

The unique allusion to a politically-oriented concept of nation is made in relation to other countries: "There are states, only few as a matter of course, whose people belong to more than one ethnicities, without this meaning that they wish to be divided into separate nations" (B, p. 19). It is obvious that population heterogeneity and the likelihood of territory-based citizenship is recognized.

School contents of this period are differentiated from those of the previous periods in two ways. Firstly, references to Greek tradition and to the alleged necessity of keeping this tradition free from foreign influences have been removed. Secondly, ideas on the superiority of the Greek nation are absent. In conclusion, the views expressed in the Metapolitefsis textbooks on the concept of nation keep their distance from the profoundly ethnocentric views of the previous period and they begin to focus more on theories of the citizens' nation.

CONCLUSIONS

Citizenship education aims to produce autonomous and active citizens with democratic political identity, who understand and respect social and cultural pluralism. This study explored the political values promoted in compulsory education in Greece in the last 50 years. The qualitative content analysis of school textbooks shows significant differences in the frequency by which these values are promoted in the two parts of this period.

During the Dictatorship the value of homogeneity or *Unum* appears most frequently. It was found that the goal of the respect and tolerance to diversity is distorted due to the ethnocentric nature of the content. The dimension of social pluralism is not reflected in the contents of school materials. Indeed, only the dominant types of social subjects are included, which are traditionally regarded as accepted and legalized. In other words, the contents support the development and cultivation of a strong Greek national identity, rather than of a democratic political identity, during the period of Dictatorship. The formation of a political identity concerns the consequences arising from the interference of religion in this process. The religious institution appears to intervene in the development of consciousnesses, in parallel with political institutions.

In the Metapolitefsis period, which is also called the period of the restoration of democracy, the philosophy of education is changing. The same goes for textbooks. The analysis shows that the ethnocentric character in the program is less intense and the value of heterogeneity or *Pluribus* is further promoted. During this period, fundamental international political changes also affected Greece. With the collapse of the Soviet regime, many Greeks repatriated. In addition, economic migrants from Eastern European and Balkan countries entered Greece in search of a better life. Immigrant reception programs have been set up in education, while teachers have been trained on intercultural education. In addition, in the last decade, refugees and migrants from Asian and African countries have arrived in Greece. The analysis of the textbooks of political education shows that the respect of the diversity and the inclusion of foreign students in education has passed into their contents. This is an optimistic element for the healing of the political trauma of foreign students, but also for the cultivation of social cohesion through education.

However, as we have argued, curriculum is a key factor in cultivating political values. The other very critical factor is the teachers themselves, their beliefs and the mentalities they express. It would be particularly interesting to investigate their attitude towards the healing of the political trauma of their students.

REFERENCES

Alford, C. F. (2016). *Trauma, culture, and PTSD*. New York, NY: Macmillan.

Bardin, L. (1977). *L' analyse de contenu* [Content analysis]. Paris, France: PUF.

Berelson, B. (1971). *Content analysis in communication research*. New York, NY: Hafner Press.

Butts, R. F. (1980). *The revival of civic learning: A rationale for citizenship education in American schools*. Bloomington, IN: Phi Delta Kappa.

Callan, E. (1997). *Creating citizens: Political education and liberal democracy*. Oxford, England: Oxford University Press.

Council of Europe. (2010). *Recommendation CM/Rec(2010)7*. Retrieved from https:// search.coe.int/cm/Pages/result_details.aspx?ObjectID=09000016804ec3a9

Dewey, J. (1916). *Democracy and education*. New York, NY: The Free Press.

Dill, V. (2015). Homeless–And doubled up. *Educational Leadership, 72*(6), 42–47.

Forquin, C. J. (1996). *Ecole et culture* [School and culture]. Bruxelles, Belgium: De Boeck University.

Gadoffre, G. (1951). Images nationales francaises et stereotypes nationaux [French national images and national stereotypes]. *Bulletin International des Sciences Sociales, III*(3), 622–630.

Gellner, E. (1992). Έθνη και Εθνικισμός [Nations and nationalism]. Αθήνα: Αλεξάνδρεια.

Goodson, I. (1994). *Studying curriculum: Cases and methods*. Buckingham, England: Open University Press.

Goodwin, B. (2015). Simple interventions boost self-esteem. *Educational Leadership, 72*(6), 74–76.

Gorski, P. C., & Swalwell, K. (2015). Equity literacy for all. *Educational Leadership, 72*(6), 34–41.

Gough, N. (1999). Globalization and school curriculum change: Locating a transnational imaginary. *J. Education Policy, 14*(1), 73–84.

Irizarry, G. J. (2015). What Latino students want from school. *Educational Leadership, 72*(6), 66–71.

McLaughlin, T. H., & Juceviciene, P. (1997). Education, democracy, and the formation of national identity. In D. Bridges (Ed.), *Education, Autonomy and democratic citizenship* (pp. 23–35). London, England: Routledge.

Neuman, L. W. (1994). *Social research methods: Qualitative and quantitative approaches.* Boston, MA: Allyn & Bacon.

ΟΕΔΒ. (1989). Κοινωνική και Πολιτική Αγωγή [Social and political education, 6th grade]. Athens, Greece:Textbook Publishing Organization.

Παπαγεωργίου, Κ., (1997). Περί πολυπολιτισμικότητας. Πρόλογος στο: ΤΑΙΗΛΟΡ Τ., Πολυπολιτισμικότητα [Multiculturalism and "the politics of recognition"]. Αθήνα: ΠΟΛΙΣ.

Patrick, J. J. (1986). Immigration in the Curriculum. *Social Education, 50*(3), 172–176.

Pratte, R. (1988). *The civic imperative: Examining the Need for Civic Education.* New York, NY: Teachers College Press.

Pring, R. (1999). Political education: Relevance of the humanities. *Oxford Review of Education, 25*(1/2), 71–87.

Razack, J. S. (2007). Stealing the pain of others: Reflections on Canadian humanitarian responses. *The Review of Education, Pedagogy and Cultural Studies, 29*(4), 375–394. https://doi.org/10.1080/10714410701454198

Reimers, F., & Chung, C. (2016). *Teaching and learning for the twenty-first century: Educational goals, policies, and curricula from six nations.* Cambridge, MA: Harvard Education Press.

Ross, A. (2000). Curricula for citizens and for their teachers: Processes, objectives or content. In *Developing identities in Europe: Citizenship education and higher education* (pp. 89–100). Huddersfield, England: CiCea.

Rothstein, R. (2015). The story behind Ferguson. *Educational Leadership, 72*(6), 28–33.

Russel, B. (1971). *Education and the social order.* London, England: George Allen and Unwin.

Sears, A. (1994). Social studies as citizenship education in English Canada: A review of research. *Theory and Research in Social Education, 22*(1), 6–43.

Smith, A. (2000). Εθνική Ταυτότητα [National identity]. Αθήνα: Οδυσσέας.

Τσιρίμπα, Α. (1969). Αγωγή του Πολίτου, ΣΤ΄ Τάξη [Education of the citizen, 6th grade]. Athens, Greece: Textbook Publishing Organization.

Varro, G., (1999). La désignation des élèves étrangers dans les textes officiels [The designation of foreign students in official texts]. *Mots, 61,* 49–66.

Φραγκουδάκη, Α., Δραγώνα, Θ., (Επιμ.). (1997). Τί είναι η πατρίδα μας; Εθνοκεντρισμός στην εκπαίδευση [What is our homeland? Ethnocentrism in education]. Αθήνα: Αλεξάνδρεια.

Yeager, A. E. (1998). Democracy, social studies, and diversity in the elementary school classroom: The progressive ideas of Alice Miel. *Theory and Research in Social Education, 26*(2), 207.

Zimmerman-Orozco, S. (2015). Border kids in the home of the brave. *Educational Leadership, 72*(6), 48–53.

SECTION II

ISSUES SURROUNDING AMERICAN GUN VIOLENCE
AND ITS NORMALIZATION IN SCHOOLS

CHAPTER 5

ONLY A DRILL

Emily Marie Passos Duffy
Red Rocks Community College

The alarm goes off about twenty minutes into my second class as a newly hired adjunct in the English Department at Red Rocks Community College, Lakewood Campus. 15.3 miles from Columbine High School via West Bowles Ave and CO-470 W. 11.5 miles via S Union Blvd.
Two voices blare through the PA system in alternating syncopation. The first voice tells us we are in LOCKDOWN and the second reminds us that this is a drill.

I turn off the lights and attempt to lock the door. I discover the door does not lock. Something is broken or   out of   alignment. One of my students gets up and tries to lock the door   it still doesn't lock.

Not knowing what to do, I say well, good thing this is a drill. My students laugh. I wonder if my joke is in poor taste.

I keep my body there, by the door. I peer through the small   rectangular window. I take slow,   measured breaths. I don't know why I stand there. I want   to keep an eye on things. Watch   the

Making a Spectacle, pages 65–67

blank fluorescence of the hallway.   Maybe, subconsciously, I want to gesture to my students: I would be willing to put myself   between you and harm's way.

I notice the teacher in an adjacent classroom continues teaching through the drone of the alarm. Lights on. It's my first semester so I am wont to follow the procedures outlined in an email sent to all faculty and staff.

The email outlined procedures and not demeanor. How should I—how should I... Should I be   irritated by the interruption to   my instruction? Grateful for a disruption in   linear, packaged minutes, this moment we all have to   breathe together in the dark as adrenaline surges?

My students seem unfazed. They are low income first generation college students, parents, concurrent enrollment high schoolers. Some put their heads down and nap, others scroll on their phones   faces lit by screens

This isn't their first lockdown drill.

My hopes for this group: I want to build community against a backdrop of white nationalism   detangle   power lines   feel joy

This class   most are white bodies. a Native body, a Trans body, & 4 Latinx bodies, including mine. Week 1, I say look, I want to share that my mother is   Afro-Brazilian and an immigrant   I say this because I know my body   is read as white   in so many spaces.

I do not tell them that I am also a sex worker but I include a piece by one on the syllabus Week 13 because assigned readings are one way I share more about myself   and what I value in learning. Teaching, on good days, feels like music. I am a haphazard conductor holding melody in one hand and an expo marker in the other. Many years ago I underwent an active shooter training as an undergraduate RA.

I remember nothing of use but terror.

The repetitive drone of the loudspeaker begins to feel like a beat. Could we make   music out of this noise. Breathe over institutional time. Spill through the windows.

This is only a drill.

Before the alarm, we were
discussing exigence

rhetorical appeals
audience awareness

this is only a drill . . .

another rhetorical situation

CHAPTER 6

CAUGHT IN THE POLITICAL MACHINE

Educators and Active-Shooter Drills

Jessica O'Brien
University of South Florida

Vonzell Agosto
University of South Florida

Concern about safety from human acts of violence was not the initial concern of *safety (emergency) drills*. School fires preceded school violence as the public's major concern. Then, in 1851, after a false alarm left 40 killed and others injured due to the mob-like exodus, educators took it upon themselves to practice orderly exiting to reduce panic during an evacuation (Perkins, 2018). Today, groups of students are entrusted to the leadership of a few adults whose responsibility is to ensure school safety (Brock et al., 2001; Perkins, 2018). Today, the human-made disasters caused by mass shooters using assault weapons poses a newer kind of threat resulting in schools operating with locked or blockaded doors and educators preparing to run, hide, or fight if attacked. Increasingly, they are expected to lead emergency/safety/

Making a Spectacle, pages 69–84
Copyright © 2021 by Information Age Publishing
69

school drills such as the active-shooter drill (A-SD), which is used to prevent or diminish the harm that active-shooters could cause.

We argue that this particular iteration of drills, the A-SD, is an extension of racialized and gendered political trauma that gets animated within schools. As such, educators are caught in the political machine of multiple and conflicting strands of discourse that pertain to safety/danger and their roles are being redefined using *safety-related* titles such as guardians, marshals, and first responders (O'Toole & Friesen, 2016). To illustrate this argument, we trace A-SDs historically and politically through news articles, policy documents, and guides (i.e., district emergency management or safety plans) with attention to the political machine in the state of Florida. Along the way, signal the need for a framework to sustain educators through political trauma.

The purpose of this chapter is to offer an educator sustainability framework that mediates and ameliorates political trauma, past and present. It is intended to support educators to engage one another with care during politically charged interactions that occur, whether in schools or public life (Britzman, 2009; Tarc, 2011). We ground this sustainability framework in reparative curriculum and pedagogy that makes use of digital technologies and mentoring networks to aid in self and collective care. This approach to educator sustainability supplements district-level leadership teams who (should, do, will) shoulder the responsibility of embedding such practices in schools (Thomas, Crosby, & Vanderhaar, 2019). We first introduce ourselves and the theories of trauma informing our treatment of A-SDs and then integrate reflective *vignettes,* literature, and analysis.

POSITIONALITY AND THEORY: WHO/WHERE WE ARE, HOW WE GOT HERE/WILL GO FORTH

Jessica: As an educator in Florida completing my first year in a doctoral program and my eighth consecutive year of teaching, I was questioning my future as a teacher and how I could deepen my pedagogical content knowledge and professional tie to educational technology focused on virtual learning experiences. During the academic year, 2019–2020, course assignments allowed me to bring interest in technology and teaching as mentorship together with sustainability to address professional development and leadership (mine and others'). In these assignments and in conversations with Dr. Agosto (Author 2), which began when I was a master's student, I identified A-SDs as a significant stressor.

> **Dr. Agosto:** Jessica and I realized we had common interests in mentoring women in education and using technology pedagogically

to sustain others/ourselves who are educators. When Jessica (Author 1) expressed her uncertainty about continuing to teach in a K–12 setting, I was challenged to comprehend why emergency drills were a source of her anxiety. At that time, I had not seen the 16th episode of *New Amsterdam* from Season 2 (Schulner, Shireen Razack, & Zisk, 2020) or realized some drills were using faked deaths, actors, and blood. I speculated, perhaps the threat of becoming a victim to gun-related violence seemed more probable given the recency of the Marjory Stoneman Douglas shooting (2017) and its proximity to where she works and studies (in the Tampa area). Our conversation led us to ponder what it means to be an educator in Florida post-Stoneman Douglas with A-SDs in place. While this question is particular to one state, the personal reflections that follow echo political tensions in state legislatures, presidential rhetoric, and broader politically charged debates over safety, rights, risks, health, and well-being.

Jessica's experiences with, and our orientation to, such drills are best understood from a critical sociopsychological view of individual/collective trauma as that which is instigated by political trauma. According to Alford (2014, 2016), trauma is politics and is political when it prevents socially marginalized groups from appropriating the defensive resources of the culture to mediate the connection between them and the trauma over time (*chronic trauma*). Political trauma captures the idea of trauma as a product of violence and violation (i.e., human right violations, state violence against individuals or groups) that can be experienced as an ongoing interaction between the psychological state and its social environment (Donoso, 2018).

Jessica: It was a month after the Stoneman Douglas school shooting. I sat in a faculty meeting, still shaken by the events, as the administrative team informed us (educators) there would be a lockdown drill with evacuation drills every month for the foreseeable future. I reflected on the previous school years, where I struggled to summon the courage to even drive myself to school before the tragedy at Stoneman Douglas. Since the Las Vegas concert shooting, certain times of the year (especially around the holidays) have left me anxious. Now I struggle to find peace despite constant reminders that a mass shooting is probable, if not imminent.

According to the Substance Abuse and Mental Health Services Administration (SAMSHA, 2014 p. 7; definition of trauma), trauma results from "an event, series of events, or set of circumstances that is experienced by an individual as physically or emotionally harmful or life-threatening and that has lasting adverse effects on the individual's functioning and mental, physical, social, emotional, or spiritual well-being" (p. 1). However, more pronounced in our engagement with A-SDs is a critical social-psychological framing of trauma and a psychoanalytical/existential framing of reparation (curriculum/pedagogy) as in helping to restore who/what was wronged.

> **Jessica:** At school, my colleagues and I guided 11-year-old students through a survival tactic—the administration's advice was this: Stay calm, and your students will too. I exhaled, but I couldn't shake my anxiety. To get myself prepared mentally for the students and the drill, I reviewed the materials from the school district and the administration for the fourth time. I knew our students would have questions, and as a teacher, I needed to feel as if I could answer and put their fears at ease. I felt lost, unsure, and emotionally unable to present myself as a protector—someone my students would look to in a crisis. I pushed these existential thoughts down—only to have them appear at another time.

Centering political trauma does not preclude the combined study of, for instance, sociopolitical or historical traumas associated with violence (Tarc, 2011). The framework of political trauma helps to acknowledge national responsibility for the past, which does not necessarily address its ongoing lived effects on survivors and communities (Henderson & Wakeham, 2009; Tarc, 2011). Also implicated are the materials (i.e., guides) that are reviewed, or in Jessica's case reviewed again and again. The contextual backdrop that follows introduces the responsibility of the state (FL) and nation-state (United States) in fueling political traumatization leading to the development of A-SDs.

FLORIDA, ONE OF THE UNITED (AND DIVIDED) STATES OF AMERICA

In recent decades (2000–2020), several forces have converged to link guns to schools in Florida: (a) political lobbying (e.g., national rifle association, NRA) and (b) campaigning (e.g., *Make America Great, Again,* MAGA) to advance the policy agendas that get taken up by the Florida Legislature and influence education policy. The political machinations are also being mediated by movements in support or opposition. One person in particular, Florida's NRA lobbyist, Marion Hammer, stands out as having been successful in advancing policies to the extent that Florida's gun owners hold a uniquely privileged status (Spies, 2018).

In the eighties, Hammer crafted a statute allowing anyone who can legally purchase a firearm to carry a concealed handgun in public, after paying a small fee for a state-issued permit and completing a rudimentary training course. With her support came the 2005 implementation of Florida' revised (stand your ground) self-defense laws. In addition, these laws provide legal immunity to individuals using lethal force in self-defense. Not only was there a significant increase in homicides and homicides by firearm between 2005 and 2014 (Humphreys, Gasparrini, & Wiebe, 2017), one in particular set off public outcry and the *Black Lives Matter* movement.

The Black (17-year-old) youth Trayvon Martin was shot and killed in Florida (2012) by a man who claimed it was an act of self-defense. His delayed arrest (44 days after the shooting) was followed by an acquittal. Then in 2020, the incident returned to the political headlines when the shooter threatened to sue presidential candidates Elizabeth Warren and Pete Buttigieg for defamation of character after they posted a social media message attributing Martin's death to White supremacy and racism. Their comments, the influence of the NRA, and the protests associated with the Black Lives Matter movement illustrate the role of nation-state (i.e., police departments, court system) and political campaigns and movements have linked gun related violence to White supremacy.

The participation of educators in movements against White supremacy and gun-related violence that affects schooling is constrained by the laws governing collective action. In Florida, a *right to work* state (McGuire, 1973), educators comprise a marginalized group with limited opportunity to collectively resist harmful policies since the state restricts labor strikes (FL Stat. Sec. 447.13). According to Orta (1993), "As a result of this statutory scheme, many public employees feel that they lack sufficient power to effectively bargain for the benefits which they desire" (p. 280). The same restrictions do not apply to students. The following case is one example where students have publicly protested to increase attention to guns as a safety threat.

Soon after the Marjory Stoneman Douglas High School mass shooting in Parkland, FL (2018), when a 19-year-old entered his former school, opened fire, and killed 17 people (students and faculty members), students attending the school started a national campaign against gun violence, the *March for Our Lives* movement. They publicly demanded increased school safety measures, as some of them complained that as Black students they were being excluded by the student organizers and the media (Sanchez & Gallagher, 2018). Eventually, students' recommendation for a mobile reporting system, *FortifyFL* was adopted into the Marjory Stoneman Douglas Public

Safety Act of Florida (FL Senate Bill 7026, Chapter 2018-3, Laws of Florida), which became law in Florida in 2018.

The law addresses gun violence by restricting firearm access to those undergoing a mental health crisis and enhancing "coordination between education and law enforcement entities at the state and local level" (SB 7026, p. 1). Among other things, SB 7026 bridged concerns about mental health, gun violence, gun safety, general safety, and diversity in schools.

- It mandated A-SDs to be included in schools' safety plans.
- It (Section 5) amended Florida Statute 30.15 regarding the power, duties, and obligations to: "Establish requirements including concealed carry permit, firearms, and other training, psychological evaluation, drug test, diversity training, ongoing training, and firearm qualification" (p. 1). In other words, school districts in Florida could permit teachers to carry a concealed weapon in schools (Rogers et al., 2018).
- It established the Coach Aaron Feis Guardian program. Guardians are armed personnel (school employees) who volunteer to help prevent or abate an active assailant incident on school premises. School administrators (not teachers) can participate and undergo training in the use of firearms and diversity (content unspecified) and are responsible for formulating individual school safety plans.
- It asked for a "Florida Safe School Assessment Tool to be used by each school district and public school in conducting security assessments to identify threats and vulnerabilities" (p. 3).

According to *SB 7026 (4) EMERGENCY DRILLS; EMERGENCY PROCE-DURES.–1860 (a): Drills for active shooter and hostage situations shall be conducted at least as often as other emergency drills.* Although the frequency of drills is ambiguous in the law, they are to occur no less often than other drills. Thus, multiple drills are to be conducted multiple times during a school year.

EXPERIENCE WITH SAFETY BILLS AND DRILLS

Jessica: [Drill Day] Before the drill, I told the students exactly what is going to happen: Someone will come over the speaker and say LOCKDOWN, LOCKDOWN, LOCKDOWN. We will silently stand and move to the side of the room and wait quietly until the fire alarm sounds. I told them I was nervous too and I hoped nothing would ever happen to our school. I also hoped they would trust me and my ability to keep them safe. What I didn't share with the students was this—I cannot plan for the real thing. The windows were already covered. I closed the blinds, turned off the Smartboard, moved the desks so the students could fit against the wall, and checked to make sure the doors were locked. These are the steps I might not get to do during an actual emergency.

As Jennings and Greenberg (2009) explain about teachers,

They are supposed to provide a nurturing learning environment, be responsive to students, parents, and colleagues, juggle the demands of standardized testing, coach students through conflicts with peers, be exemplars of emotion regulation, handle disruptive behavior and generally be great role models. (p. 1)

My co-teacher Lauren, (pseudonym), had worked for the crisis hotline before becoming an educator. Her expertise and training in a high-stress work environment assisted in the classroom. As Lauren and I prepared for the day, I told her I was concerned about the drill and how (although I reviewed the process and I planned on talking with the students about why we are doing it) I did not feel I could guide the students through it well. I asked her to guide us through the drill. She calmly did so by using a grounding exercise. She asked the students how they were feeling. Then she whispered they were safe, and it was okay to be afraid even when we don't understand why. Her confidence and calm disposition lowered the anxiety in the room, including my own. She emphasized that if we prepare, we could be empowered and not just victims. This drill could be looked upon as a positive exercise. Lauren has since left the school. I wondered why Lauren had not created a lesson on de-escalating fear among students and educators since her words were soothing and validating.

In a study of job-related stress, researchers found educators were more likely to be resilient and experience well-being around their professional peers when they had access to personal resources (e.g., motivation, efficacy), contextual resources (e.g., trusting relationships with leaders, fellow teachers, and students) and strategies such as problem-solving, exercising self-care, managing a healthy work–life balance, and practicing mindfulness (Mansfield, Beltman, Broadley, & Weatherby-Fell, 2016).

COPING WITH THE FEAR OF (ANTICIPATED) DANGER AND VICTIMIZATION OR THEIR AFTERMATH

Implicated in school-based shootings, in anticipation of them and their aftermath (Armstrong & Carlson, 2019), is emotional/mental health (i.e., post-traumatic stress disorder, PTSD) related to survival (i.e., *survivor guilt*) and suicide-related death (Silman, 2019). Preparation whether to deter such violence in schools or recover in its aftermath reproduces the conditions or memories of calamity and brings attention to the mental health effects of school shooting pre- and post-shooting incidents.

> **Jessica:** [Present Day] Today, the school has two points of entry. We utilize a gate where we buzz in twice before entering the main office. It is not uncommon for the school to go into a lock-in, where the school locks everyone inside the building. A lock-in means there is a crisis in the vicinity of the school but not actually on site. Classes continue, students can leave the room with a buddy. These drills range from minutes to hours under an even more watchful eye of teachers and administration. We receive an ALL CLEAR announcement once the threat has subsided. Since we already operate on a modified lock-in, our doors remain closed and locked throughout the day. When mandatory ID badges are visible, educators are vigilant of any suspicious behavior. There is no general feeling of reprieve, just more checking and double-checking to make sure my doors are locked, so the kids feel safe.

Educators entering schools may respond to demands to lead A-SDs and feel as if, "I did not sign up for this!" The mounting demands can contribute to their stress and burnout, which are often attributed to personal and professional variables (Stauffer & Mason, 2013). These variables may be difficult and slow to change without extensive individual psychological change along with comprehensive political or educational reform (Brasfield, Lancaster, & Xu, 2018).

> **Jessica:** A lock-out occurs when an emergency could pose an immediate threat to the campus. With this drill, the doors are locked, educators take account of all students in the room, no one leaves the room, instruction suspended, changing from one to another is halted, all access points secured, and everyone is expected to keep calm and quiet. We have been in lock-out status for an armed robbery on two different occasions. During one, an SUV drove by the school with

someone waving a gun at students outside the gym class. The threat seems unrelenting since the drill response to threats not just on campus, but also in the neighborhood. The continuity of threat can be challenging for readers inexperienced with these drills to comprehend.

Related to the anticipation of gun-related violence in schools is the topic of coping with the *fear of crime* or *fear of being victimized* (Johnson & Barton-Bellesa, 2014). In a study examining the connection between school policies and *fear of victimization,* Ricketts (2007) found that school violence reduction policies did not mediate anxieties among school personnel since their fear of victimization emanated from the perceived risk of crime in the community. Anxiety-related fear of crime and/or victimization associated with the threat of violence or aggression may provoke educators to psychologically distance themselves from others (Galand, Lecocq, & Philippot, 2007; Johnson & Barton-Bellesa, 2014). To counter psychological distancing, is to connect through relationships of support. As such, mentoring relationships can be forged as a social-coping mechanism to manage anxiety that comes with the anticipation of violence or its recurrence. To that end, we next describe a sustainability framework based on the idea of a reparative curriculum and two areas that have sustained us in our work to become politically astute and supportive educators: mentoring and technology.

REPARATIVE CURRICULUM FOR EDUCATORS: SUSTAINED BY MENTORS AND TECHNOLOGY

The reparative curriculum framework we advance herein responds to the political trauma, steeped in racialized and gendered discourses around safety/danger, that manifests A-SDs. The framework responds to two gaps in professional preparation and development: (a) educators (except for school psychologists or counselors) rarely receive specialized professional development training to identify students with nonacademic difficulties such as emotional or social problems (Fox & Harding, 2005; Swezey & Thorp, 2010); and (b) educators rarely receive opportunities to develop a critical sociopolitical awareness of trauma as a phenomenon (beyond their psyches) affecting their attitudes, practice, and organizational culture or ethos.

William F. Pinar (2006) advances reparative curriculum in the preparation of educators, one that dissolves White racism and White masculinity (Pinar, 2006). He and others (e.g., Kimmel & Mahler, 2003) connect race/gender and age to sexuality and religion to understand looming discourses in education past and present. Drawing on religious narratives, Pinar (2006) points to how a surplus of desire rather than scarcity provided the religious backdrop for the development of racial–sexual hierarchies. Applied to the current context with A-SDs in mind, a surplus of desire translates into having educators, of whom the majority are women, *protect and serve* on the one hand and cower on the other. In the A-SD scenario, like sacrificial lambs, educators are expected to remain with students and protect them even if they could escape. At the other end, sainthood is projected onto them in the hope they will disarm (castrate) those (who are often) pubescent men—*gunboys* (Glick, 2020), who tend to be White males and former students (Katsiyannis, Whitford, & Ennis, 2018; Lee, 2013).

The need for a reparative curriculum for educators as described by Pinar (2006), as offering analysis combining sociopolitical categories (i.e., White male/masculinity, racial–sexual hierarchies), is exemplified in the comments made by the 19-year-old shooter (Cruz) in the Marjory Stoneman massacre. He echoed broader political–presidential rhetoric of the time with references to potential threats, fear of crime, and anti-immigrant bias in a letter he wrote while in jail.

> "I feel like there is a reason why we're trying to stop immigrants," Cruz writes. "They attack people, destroy property, and spread disease. It's a big issue. I'm waiting for the moment when society collapses because of one of these issues." (Norman, 2019, p. 5)

According to Norman (2019), a reporter from the Miami News, it was known that the 17-year old was racist. School shooters who are former students and ideologically affiliated with racist/White supremacist rhetoric blur the geographic boundaries of racialized fear and victimization. Active-shooter drills can be interpreted as an extension of White male dominance operating primarily from a distant perch.

Both interpretive concepts, scarcity and surplus, are used widely in discussions about planetary sustainability. They help anchor issues of safety and violence in debates about the surplus or scarcity of guns (in schools) to racialized/gender desires (political agendas) that result in practices such as A-SDs, and link our interest in sustainability to a reparative curriculum through which educators can be supported/sustained when facing existential questions about life/death. What is needed is a reparative curriculum that sustains educators who are aware of trauma-related anxiety and in communication/dialogue through mentoring networks conducted virtually/digitally using technology.

Mentoring to Foster Sustainability

Reparative curriculum, as we envision it, brings awareness to how ideas about *safe,* un*safe,* or threatening are politically determined by broader gendered-racialized discourses. Reparation, as advanced by Tarc (2011), is both politically and pedagogically responsible for learning from the past and reconciling estranged communities and wounded social states through public learning, thinking, participation, dialogue, and action. Forging a reparative curriculum can be a painful and painstaking process, one that compels careful support of educators with one another as they tentatively enter into the public life that comes with the role (Tarc, 2011). The context for this work can be enhanced through mentoring as an expression of and conduit to sustainability.

Salas-Zapata and Ortiz-Munoz (2018) define sustainability as a goal of humankind expressed as ideas, social expectations, and human actions as well as "the integration of the application of social-ecological criteria or qualities to the planning, designing and/or functioning stages of reference systems" (p. 155). Reference systems of concern here would be *safety* and *danger*. In the context of A-SDs and political traumas from which they spring, the base of the word sustainability, *sustain*, has two meanings that apply. It means to suffer through something as well as to strengthen or support physically or mentally as in to promote continuity (Lexico, n.d.). Mentoring is an avenue for building networks of professionals who sustain one another to operate maximally even in less than ideal circumstances.

By the concept *mentor*, we mean one who guides another/others with the aim to have a positive influence (Olaolorunpo, 2019, p. 144). The mentorship relationship often involves a seasoned professional who can redirect and affirm the growth of the mentee into their respective fields (Bell-Ellison & Dedrick, 2008). In contrast, is a collaborative peer-mentoring network composed of educators (e.g., Jessica and Laura) who help one another harness their skill sets and provide social/emotional support to ensure their sustainability in ways that are healthy and healthful—or reparative. Mentoring, as we conceive of it within a sustainability framework, would bridge care with political action (Britzman, 2009), through the following six attributes: serving as a role model, nurturing, building a friendship, learning from an experienced person, interacting regularly, and developing an enduring relationship (Olaolorunpo, 2019). We recommend the development of peer-mentoring networks in the context of A-SDs that bridge preventative and responsive care, with recovery from political, physical, and psychical traumatizing circumstances.

Educators can learn to develop mentoring networks akin to the transdisciplinary teams and their smaller groups (hubs) involved in sustainability research and education across nations. One in particular is the *Pathways* transformative knowledge network (TKN), which uses a process model in which each hub works as a transformation lab in response to their ecological–political–social moments. The same way the TKN acknowledges the ways science can be reconfigured is political, so too can education, safety, and drills. Like members of the TKN, educators can also emphasize sustainability and mentor, "punctuated by moments for data collection, sharing and co-learning and collaborative reflection" (Ely et al., 2020, p. 5).

Tech Support

Responding to natural or human-made disasters in a timely and effective manner can reduce deaths and injuries, contain or prevent secondary disasters, and reduce the resulting economic losses and social disruption. Appropriate information technology solutions can improve response time and quality. Educators surveyed about their preparation for various drills, including A-SDs, felt the need for drills that were more authentic or realistic (Allen, Lorek, & Mensia-Joseph, 2008; Perkins, 2018). However, simulated drills lack realism and are expensive while more realistic drills can induce trauma (Balasubramanian, Massaguer, Mehrota, & Venkatasubramanian, 2006).

An alternate solution to commonly used simulation tools allows for the dynamic creation of what-if scenarios and the capacity to determine the response to the changing disaster landscape (Balasubramanian et al., 2006). A simulation framework for crisis response activities must address the modeling of human behavior (and decisions made by humans) in a changing environment. DrillSim is a simulation framework, a multi-agent system for crisis response activities, that mainly (a) embodies agents that drive the simulation in different roles and make decisions and (b) captures the environment under which agents make decisions through the use of a pervasive infrastructure (Balasubramanian et al., 2006). Pedagogically, simulated "safety-trainings" could be paired with electronic-mentoring (e-mentoring) networks similar to the use of telehealth to triage patients or telemarketing to conduct surveys. In these cases, health and satisfaction are central. A reparative curriculum in efforts to maintain *safety* would also center health and (employee) satisfaction while exposing the politically traumatizing histories and events unfolding outside of schools.

Platforms and applications that allow virtual interactions (i.e., e-mentoring) and the quick and easy development and use of communication channels (i.e., forms or polls) can support immediate and long-term data generation through which educators can check in on one another or debrief after drills. This online approach to data collection allows educators to interact and respond to the emotions that drills provoke. It could also allow the administration to conduct a pulse check on their faculty's emotional state and overall mental wellness and inform meaningful discussions during faculty meetings. If conducted in ways that allow educators to sense they are safe among their colleagues, sharing their emotions and others' experiences with anxiety or stress, such activities could bolster morale.

CONCLUDING REMARKS AND RECOMMENDATIONS
FOR FUTURE INQUIRY

Education is a professional field increasingly shaped by political spectacles in which educators are increasingly expected to guard, shield, hide, or sequester themselves and students from injury due to calculated threats. What it means to be an educator in Florida today is informed by political traumatization whereby competing discourses and ideologies concerning safety and guns (control, freedom) are racialized and gendered. Active-shooter drills prepare them to sustain the impact of the threat in order to sustain students first, and themselves second, from physical and mental harm. As such, such drills may induce a greater need for organizational and self-care (SAMSHA, 2014).

Organizations such as the *National Child Traumatic Stress Network*, the *Treatment and Services Adaptation Center*, and the *National Center on Safe Supportive Learning Environments* offer support. However, they emphasize secondary or vicarious trauma that comes with educating underserved learners. Suggesting that trauma is brought on by working with students experiencing trauma, rather than the politics and policies that have underserved them and their students, risks promoting a deficit narrative about students. Instead, information from such organizations can be paired with the lessons that youth provide on collective responses to trauma: how to network, organize, and use communication technologies to make their demands public, raise alarms, and confront racial exclusion within their ranks.

Also needed is a research base on fear and drills: the extent to which policies and practices such as A-SDs ameliorate or exacerbate educators' anxieties and what restrains them from internalizing political trauma (resisting it), and how over-preparation can minimize fear and desensitize educators to the horror of gun-related violence. We recommend researchers examine educators' ethno-racial experiences, attitudes regarding gun violence, and fears regarding potential threats in connection to the premises of culturally relevant pedagogy (Ladson-Billings, 1995; Thomas et al., 2019): to advance *cultural competence, sociopolitical consciousness, and achievement.*

The framework of educator sustainability offered above is intended to mobilize rather than victimize educators. This framework advances a mentoring network through which caring others support recovery and reparation (Bessell, Medina, Pilonieta, Pacheco-Plaza, & Kloosterman, 2007; Prilleltensky, Neff, & Bessell, 2016). Sustaining educators and communities through A-SDs is not only a matter of surviving, but also a matter of recognizing what relationships and practices are not sustainable. This includes attending to how relationships and practices based on gendered and racial hierarchies define some people and acts as threatening and others as *safe.*

REFERENCES

Armstrong, M., & Carlson, J. (2019). Speaking of trauma: The race talk, the gun violence talk, and the racialization of gun trauma. *Palgrave Communications, 5*(1), 1–11.

Alford, C. F. (2014). *Trauma and forgiveness: Consequences and communities.* Cambridge, England: Cambridge University Press.

Alford, C. F. (2016). *Trauma, culture, and PTSD.* London, England: Palgrave Macmillan.

Allen, K., Lorek, E., & Mensia-Joseph, N. (2008). Conducting a school-based mock drill: Lessons learned from one community. *Biosecurity and Bioterrorism: Biodefense Strategy, Oractice, and Science, 6*(2), 191–201.

Balasubramanian, V., Massaguer, D., Mehrotra, S., & Venkatasubramanian, N. (2006, May). DrillSim: A simulation framework for emergency response drills. In S. Mehrotra, D. D. Zeng, H. Chen, B. Thuraisingham, & F.-Y. Wang (Eds.), *International conference on intelligence and security informatics* (pp. 237–248). Berlin, Germany: Springer.

Bell-Ellison, B. A., & Dedrick, R. F. (2008). What do doctoral students value in their ideal mentor? *Research in Higher Education, 49*(6), 555–567.

Bessell, A. G., Medina, A. L., Pilonieta, P., Pacheco-Plaza, M., & Kloosterman, V. I. (2007). *The support network for novice teachers: An evaluation.* Coral Gables, FL: University of Miami, School of Education.

Brasfield, M. W., Lancaster, C., & Xu, Y. J. (2019). Wellness as a mitigating factor for teacher burnout. *Journal of Education, 199*(3), 166–178.

Britzman, D. P. (2009). Love's impressions: A psychoanalytic contribution. *British Journal of Sociology of Education, 30*(6), 773–787.

Brock, S. E., Sandoval, J., & Lewis, S. (2001). *Preparing for crises in the schools: A manual for building school crisis response teams.* New York, NY: Wiley.

Donoso, G. (2018). "I have never worked with victims so victimized": Political trauma and the challenges of psychosocial interventions in Ecuador. *Journal of Social and Political Psychology, 6*(2), 420–448. https://doi.org/10.5964/jspp.v6i2.928

Ely, A., Marin, A., Charli-Joseph, L., Abrol, D., Apgar, M., Atela, J., . . . Yang, L. (2020). Structured collaboration across a transformative knowledge network—learning across disciplines, cultures and contexts? *Sustainability, 12*(6), 1–20.

FL Stat. Sec. 447.505. (2019). Labor Organizations.

Fox, C., & Harding, D. J. (2005). School shootings as organizational deviance. *Sociology of Education, 78*(1), 69–97.

Galand, B., Lecocq, C., & Philippot, P. (2007). School violence and teacher professional disengagement. *British Journal of Educational Psychology, 77*(2), 465–477.

Glick, S. (2020). How colonization fostered public mass gun violence in the US (and what Education and Society can do about it). *The International Journal of Critical Pedagogy, 11*(1), 105–129.

Henderson, J., & Wakeham, P. (2009). Colonial reckoning, national reconciliation? Aboriginal peoples and the culture of redress in Canada. *English Studies in Canada, 35*(1), 1–26.

Humphreys, D. K., Gasparrini, A., & Wiebe, D. J. (2017). Evaluating the impact of Florida's "stand your ground" self-defense law on homicide and suicide by firearm: An interrupted time-series study. *JAMA Internal Medicine, 177*(1), 44–50.

Jennings, P. A., & Greenberg, M. T. (2009). The prosocial classroom: Teacher social and emotional competence in relation to student and classroom outcomes. *Review of Educational Research, 79*(1), 491–525.

Johnson, B. R., & Barton-Bellessa, S. M. (2014). Consequences of school violence: Personal coping and protection measures by school personnel in their personal lives. *Deviant behavior, 35*(7), 513–533.

Katsiyannis, A., Whitford, D. K., & Ennis, R. P. (2018). Historical examination of United States intentional mass school shootings in the 20th and 21st centuries: Implications for students, schools, and society. *Journal of Child and Family Studies, 27*(8), 2562–2573.

Kimmel, M. S., & Mahler, M. (2003). Adolescent masculinity, homophobia, and violence random school shootings, 1982–2001. *American Behavioral Scientist, 46*(10), 1439–1458.

Ladson-Billings, G. (1995). Toward a theory of culturally relevant pedagogy. *American educational research journal, 32*(3), 465–491.

Lee, J. H. (2013). School shootings in the US public schools: Analysis through the eyes of an educator. *Review of Higher Education & Self-Learning, 6*(22), 88–119.

Lexico. (n.d.) *Sustain.* In *Lexico.com dictionary*. Retrieved from https://www.lexico.com/en/definition/sustain

Marjory Stoneman Douglas Public Safety Act of 2018, SB 7026, Chapter 2018-3, Laws of Florida. Retrieved from https://www.flsenate.gov/Session/Bill/2018/7026/BillText/er/PDF

Mansfield, C. F., Beltman, S., Broadley, T., & Weatherby-Fell, N. (2016). Building resilience in teacher education: An evidenced informed framework. *Teaching and Teacher Education, 54*(2), 77–87.

McGuire, R. G. (1973). Public employee collective bargaining in Florida-past, present, and future. *Florida State University Law Review, 1*(1), Article 2.

Norman, B. (2019, April 9). Jailhouse letters show school shooter Nikolas Cruz remains a staunch Trumper behind bars. *Miami New Times*. Retrieved from https://www.miaminewtimes.com/news/from-parkland-school-shooter-nikolas-cruz-writes-of-support-for-donald-trump-ron-desantis-and-gun-rights-11143077

Olaolorunpo, O. (2019). Mentoring in nursing: A concept analysis. *International Journal of Caring Sciences, 12*(1), 142–148.

Orta, D. M. (1993). Public employee collective bargaining in Florida: Collective bargaining or collective begging. *Stetson Law Review, 23*, 269.

O'Toole, V. M., & Friesen, M. D. (2016). Teachers as first responders in tragedy: The role of emotion in teacher adjustment eighteen months post-earthquake. *Teaching and Teacher Education, 59*(1), 57–67.

Perkins, J. C. (2018). Preparing teachers for school tragedy: Reading, writing, and lockdown. *Journal of Higher Education Theory & Practice, 18*(1), 70–81.

Pinar, W. (2006). *Race, religion, and a curriculum of reparation: Teacher education for a multicultural society.* New York, NY: Springer.

Prilleltensky, I., Neff, M., & Bessell, A. (2016). Teacher stress: What it is, why it's important, how it can be alleviated. *Theory Into Practice, 55*(2), 104–111.

Ricketts, M. L. (2007). K-12 teachers' perceptions of school policy and fear of school violence. *Journal of School Violence, 6*(3), 45–67.

Rogers, M., Lara Ovares, E. A., Ogunleye, O. O., Twyman, T., Akkus, C., Patel, K., & Fadlalla, M. (2018). Is arming teachers our nation's best response to gun violence? The perspective of public health students, *American Journal of Public Health, 108*(7), 862–863.

Salas-Zapata, W. A., & Ortiz-Muñoz, S. M. (2018). Analysis of meanings of the concept of sustainability. *Sustainable Development, 27*(1), 153–161.

Sanchez, R., & Gallagher, D. (2018, March 30). Black students at Marjory Stoneman Douglas High School want to be heard. *CNN.* Retrieved from https://www.cnn.com/2018/03/29/us/parkland-school-black-students-trnd/index.html

Spies, M. (2018, February 23). The NRA lobbyist behind Florida's pro-gun policies. *New Yorker.* Retrieved from https://www.newyorker.com/magazine/2018/03/05/the-nra-lobbyist-behind-floridas-pro-gun-policies

Schulner, D. (Writer), Shireen Razack, Y. (Writer), & Zisk, C. (Director). (2020, March 10). Perspectives [Television series episode]. In D. Foster, P. Horton, D. Schulner & M. Slovis (Executive Producers). *New Amsterdam.* Pico Creek Productions, Mount Moriah, Universal Television.

Substance Abuse and Mental Health Services Administration. (2014). *SAMHSA's concept of trauma and guidance for a trauma-informed approach.* Rockville, MD. Author. Retrieved from https://www.nasmhpd.org/sites/default/files/NCTIC_Final_Report_3-26-12(1).pdf

Stauffer, S. D., & Mason, E. C. (2013). Addressing elementary school teachers' professional stressors: practical suggestions for schools and administrators. *Educational Administration Quarterly, 49*(5), 809–837.

Silman, A. (2018, March 26). What happens to the mental health of school-shooting survivors? *New York Magazine: The Cut.* https://www.thecut.com/2019/03/understanding-the-parkland-shooting-survivor-suicides.html#_ga=2.201074342.964742376.1585509451-465099285.1585509451

Swezey, J. A., & Thorp, K. A. (2010). A school shooting plot foiled. *Journal of Research on Christian Education, 19*(3), 286–312.

Tarc, A. (2011). Reparative curriculum. *Curriculum Inquiry, 41*(3), 350–372.

Thomas, M. S., Crosby, S., & Vanderhaar, J. (2019). Trauma-informed practices in schools across two decades: An interdisciplinary review of research. *Review of Research in Education, 43*(1), 422–452.

CHAPTER 7

so used to trauma, so calm

Samuel Jaye Tanner
The Pennsylvania State University–Altoona

1

you should've seen me,
so calm while getting robbed,
      in a fast-food restaurant,
the other night manager blubbers,
      "i have a wife and kids," he says,
      "open the fucking safe," the gun says,
      "i'll do it," i say,
the gun presses against my skull,
it's 1999 and i'm 19,
      so used to trauma,
      so calm,
open the safe, hand him a burlap sack, $2000,
      "come with me," the gun says,
      "you've got the money," i say,
      "i don't want to die,"
he leads us to the backroom,

tells us to get on our knees,
the gun presses against my skull,
       "i'll kill you if you move,"
and then he's gone,
the other night manager blubbers,
i pray with him,
later, after midnight, i get home,
i wake dad up,
       "subway was robbed," i say,
       "oh," he says,
       "i almost died,"
       "oh,"
oh—

2

you should've seen me,
so calm during the lockdown,
       in a public high school,
the principal's voice is metallic,
       "this is a code red," the loudspeaker says,
       "is this real, mr. tanner?" a student says,
       "i think so," i say,
i move quickly, grab my keys, think of Columbine,
       the doors to the blackbox don't lock,
       (i teach drama in a theater),
it's 2004 and i'm 24,
       so used to trauma,
       so calm,
i gather 60 students in a dressing room,
       "be quiet," i say,
       "somebody's been shot," a cell phone says,
       "fuck,"
i stand near the unlocked door with brandon,
       we use silent gestures to plan,
       what would we do if a gun comes through the door?
a metal rod from a set of drawers,
       a 10th grader holds it like a knife,
time passes in a crowded dressing room with
       60 blubbering students,
linoleum anxiety, linoleum death,
and then the principal's metallic voice,
       "the lockdown is over," the loudspeaker says,
and then they're gone,

later, in the hallway, i'm leaving school,
i see the choir teacher,
      "that was scary," i say,
      "yes," she says,
      "i don't get paid enough for this,"
      neither of us laugh,
oh—

3

you should've seen me,
so calm during class,
      in a public university,
kids learning to be adults,
the students are wide-eyed,
      "we should be armed," one says,
      "i don't want to be a teacher," another says,
      i shrug,
the gun presses against my skull,
it's 2019 and i'm 39,
      so used to trauma,
      so used to teaching,
      so calm,
tell them my stories, we talk, etc.,
      "that's fucked up," or
      "mental health," or
      "i don't want to die,"
      or something,
we sit together with this stuff,
      nothing to say or do,
i don't like guns,
and then these future teachers are gone,
later, i'm talking with my wife,
      (my son solomon has just started kindergarten)
      "they had a fight, run, or hide drill today,"
      "oh," i say,
      we're both silent,
oh—

CHAPTER 8

GRANT, MARTIN, GARNER, RICE, AND TEACHING ON

Brian Gibbs
University of North Carolina at Chapel Hill

You aren't quite sure what to do. You've arrived a bit later at school this morning and so the main office is actually fairly crowded. The office secretaries are busy typing and answering the incessantly ringing phone, the random squawk of a walkie-talkie as a security guard goes past, and teachers in their early morning haze, coffee in one hand, hair still wet, check their mailboxes as well, as you stand there, legs unable to move, breath tight, as your right hand grips the memo severely, crinkling at the edges as your left hand steadies yourself against the mailbox and the wall. You're late because you haven't slept well for several nights, the news causing you to lay down with tension and bolt awake.

Through endless hours of conversation with your wife you try to find a place for the consistent killing of young Black men by police across the country. You organized teachers across discipline, but mostly social studies and English teachers to think through how to teach through this, how to help students to understand, to process, to connect it to skills of empowerment. It

Making a Spectacle, pages 89–91
Copyright © 2021 by Information Age Publishing

led to breakthrough and breathtaking conversations. Teachers shared their misunderstandings, their fears, and their plans. Resisting a uniform curriculum you encouraged teachers to connect with their students and to engage them in a way that was comfortable, comforting, and truthful for them. Some teachers worked in teams, others alone, all sharing, giving and getting feedback, bonding, struggling to understand and develop ways that students could understand, and digest, to gain wisdom and empowerment, to not feel victimized, cornered, or hopeless. Hours of free time spent. Hours of unpaid time spent connecting the murders to curriculum. 29 teachers spent over 30 hours of their own time ... precious time ... expectant time.

You slept for the first time last night soundly and deeply dreaming of what you would teach today. You'd gone to an event that had gone late. At a church with a mostly African-American membership. An outsider you sat alone, your wife with your child listening to the congregation and other outsiders like you struggle to make sense but to then commit to struggling on.

Now in the central office the memo that ended it all.

"To: All Teachers and Staff
From: Principal Rangel
Re: The Teaching of Recent Violent Events

In consultation with our area superintendent and the assistant superintendent in charge of psychological services it has been decided that the teaching of the shooting deaths of Black youth by police officers is not to be taught. If students bring it up in class expressing a need to talk about it please refer them to counseling or psychological services. As our school is a multiethnic school it has been determined that teaching about or discussions of recent events could serve no greater purpose than to sew dissension, suspicion, and rage amongst the students along racial and ethnic lines. We therefore encourage you to teach on. District wide assessments are coming sooner than you think. This is to be considered a directive not from me but from our area superintendent Dr. Benjamin Johnson. He, his administrative staff as well as ours will be making impromptu classroom visits to make certain this directive is carried out. Anyone found to be teaching or discussing this subject with students can be written up for insubordination. Please teach well."

The paper has been involuntarily crushed in your right hand.

The students are talking about it amongst themselves, unfiltered, unfacilitated, unguided. A recipe for anger ... for aggression ... and for misunderstanding.

The room, which had been spinning, stops and suddenly becomes clear.

In that moment a student's voice enters your mind. A student from a long time ago. What he said seemed so cliché at the time, but suddenly it has a powerful resonance.

"Only you can stop you," he had said.

"Only you can stop you."

SECTION III

HEALING POLITICAL TRAUMA
THROUGH ART EXPRESSION

CHAPTER 9

RESTORATIVE (RE)CREATION(S)

Releasing Thoughts and Perspectives Through Counter-Cartography

Bretton A. Varga
California State University, Chico

Kiara Flores
Booker High School

Art is a wound turned into light.

—Georges Braque

On September 16, 2017, Hurricane Maria unleashed 175-mph winds across the islands of Dominica, the U.S. Virgin Islands, and Puerto Rico. Widely acknowledged as the most devastating natural disaster to hit the clutch of islands, the road to recovery has been challenging on various levels. Along with the physical trauma inflicted by the superstorm on multiple non/living landscapes, residents of these islands have been forced to endure an (unnecessary) added layer of affectual/emotional anguish. Several weeks after the winds retreated and the flood waters subsided, President Trump

Making a Spectacle, pages 95–98
Copyright © 2021 by Information Age Publishing
All rights of reproduction in any form reserved.

visited Puerto Rico to survey the damage and distribute supplies. While it is common for presidents to promote a sense of activism and communal empathy by visiting devastated localities (Skidmore, 2013), the people of Puerto Rico—arguably hit the hardest by the hurricane—endured a visit by Trump fraught with mockery and jest.

Upon arriving in the battered—albeit affluent—town of Guaynabo, Trump began his televised visit by minimizing the loss of life from Maria— misquoted as 16 fatalities, which would eventually rise to 2,975 (The George Washington University, 2018)—to that of a "real storm" like Hurricane Katrina which hit New Orleans, Louisiana in 2005 causing 1,833 deaths (Brunkard, Numuland, & Ratard, 2008). Then, noticing a stack of solar-powered flashlights, Trump quipped that the flashlights were no longer needed on the island, despite nearly 90% of Puerto Ricans clinging to life *without* electricity. Perhaps the most visceral display of Trump's impudence came later that day when his motorcade stopped at a local church in San Juan. With a hundred or so people in attendance, Trump began chucking supplies into the crowd, exaggerating the extension of his right hand outwardly as if he were shooting a basketball into a hoop with each toss. This abhorrent performativity of disrespect was not lost on those in attendance, nor on those watching abroad.

One such onlooker, Kiara Flores, a sophomore in Northwestern Florida high school, continues to grapple with the image of President Trump denigrating her fellow Puerto Ricans. During a pilot study conducted by the lead author, Kiara was given the opportunity to select a theme related to an issue of personal bearing. As the study was structured around the creation of artistic/material counter-cartographies, Kiara leveraged this specific (shameful) memory into an (abstract) work of art depicting spatial relationships between centers of racism/hate and her community (see Figure 9.1).

Underpinned by Soja's (2010) notion of consequential geographies, counter-cartographies draw upon art/abstraction as a means for visually/ materially disrupting common approaches/uses of maps in classroom settings (Varga & Agosto, 2020). Inspired by the artistic methodology of celebrated abstract artist Mark Bradford (e.g., identifying, layering, and excavating), counter-cartographies seek to become an "articulation of resistive action: [holding] the capacity to escape categories, identities, and role of normative order" (Kuntz, 2019, p. 11). Specifically, after identifying an issue, participants were asked to (aesthetically) display the spatial relationship of two or more entities by layering assorted materialities. Once created, map-makers were encouraged to dig/rip/tear into their counter-cartography in an attempt to unveil temporal/historical considerations pertaining to their issue/topic. While reflecting on the process she describes as "vigorous" and the title of her artwork, Kiara Flores said:

Figure 9.1   Needle in the haystack [paint, paper on cardboard].

My map represents the different hate groups that are in our area. Having moved here from Connecticut last summer, I was just really surprised at how many racist things I would hear, so I was interested in learning more about local racist organizations. Within my artwork there are terms and ideas that are covered up that represent the ways society and history has tried to cover-up racism. I will never forget seeing the President of the United States throw toilet paper and paper towels at the crowd in Puerto Rico after Hurricane Maria. It was so demeaning and this was especially hurtful considering that my grandmother was badly injured during the storm. It seemed like he was above us and was making a joke of the situation. But, it makes me want to learn more about why racism happens. There was certainly a sense of healing through putting together a piece of art because I could, in a sense, release my thoughts and perspectives regarding this memory and systemic racism in America.

Regarding the title of this work of art, I thought about the true source and controversy of why racism exists, going all the way back to when humans first roamed the Earth. Racism is something that is taught and we, as humans, are not born racist. It is an idea. It is something breakable, we can break the cycle. The needle in the haystack usually symbolizes something that is impossible to find and when looking at my piece, there is a lot going on. However, it is clearly expressed that the problem is right in front of us. So, it is actually the opposite. There are too many needles in the haystack, or too many problems in the word racism alone when it comes to the world. But ultimately, I feel, we have pulled many needles from this haystack.

Artistic/material expression holds the capacity to help people articulate physical/emotional experiences that can be challenging to convey through textual measures (Stuckey & Nobel, 2010). Engaging with artistic/material means also offering imaginative ways to confront and (emotionally) heal from (politically) reprehensible situations through self-reflection (Camic, 2008). Although traditionally maps are used (pedagogically) to arrange, demarcate, and (re)order, when (re)conceptualized through an (abstract) artistic/material lens, maps can transcend static, normative approaches to teaching/learning and provide spaces for teachers/students that "create congruence between their affective states and their conceptual sense making" (Yorks & Kasl, 2006, p. 53). While Donald J. Trump is not likely to change his slanderous rhetoric or pejorative behavior, perhaps teachers/students can artistically/materially alter the way they confront politically shameful situations while congruently tapping into individual reservoirs of healing.

REFERENCES

Brunkard, J., Numuland, G., and Ratard, R. (2008). Hurricane Katrina deaths, Louisiana, 2005. *Disaster Medicine and Public Health Preparedness, 2*(4), 215–223.

Caminc, P. M. (2008). Playing in the mud: Health psychology, the arts and creative approaches to health care. *Journal of Health Psychology, 13*(2), 287–290.

Kuntz, A. M. (2019). *Qualitative inquiry, cartography and the promise of material change.* London, England: Routledge.

Skidmore, M. J. (2013). Anti-government is not the solution to the problem—anti-government is the problem: The role of ideology in presidential response to natural disasters from San Francisco to Katrina. *Risk, Hazards, & Crisis in Public Policy, 3*(4), 1–17.

Soja, E. W. (2010). *Seeking spatial justice.* Minneapolis: University of Minnesota Press.

Stuckey, H. L., & Nobel, J. (2010). The connection between art, healing, and public health: A review of current literature. *Framing Health Matters, 100*(2), 254–263.

The George Washington University. (2018). *Ascertainment of the estimated excess morality from hurricane Maria in Puerto Rico.* Washington, DC: Milkin Institute School of Public Health.

Varga, B. A., & Agosto, V. (2020, April). *Material counter-cartographies: (Un)mapping (in)justice, social complexities and re-creative reticulations.* Paper presentation at the annual meeting of the American Educational Research Association, San Francisco, CA. https://convention2.allacademic.com/one/aera/aera20/ (Conference canceled)

Yorks, L., & Kasl, E. (2006). I know more than I can say: A taxonomy for using expressive ways of knowing to foster transformative learning. *Transformative Education, 4*(1), 43–64.

CHAPTER 10

WHEN THE AIRBORNE TOXIC EVENT BROKE NEW ORLEANS' LEVEES

David R. Fisher
Independent Researcher

ABSTRACT

In the aftermath of 2005's Hurricane Katrina, those in power chose to implement policy that would destroy cultural milieu, community schools, and terminate teachers and administrators. This chapter presents a critical arts-based inquiry approach that uses artistic vignettes as a means of practicing empathy with victims of disastrous environmental and political agenda—Airborne Toxic Events. Informed by a critical pedagogy of place and Crocco's (2007) *Teaching the Levees* as a place-based curricular model for democratic dialogue and civic engagement, I offer a tangible guide to experiencing different interpretations of similar events in order to foster cultural synthesis and political consciousness.

Making a Spectacle, pages 99–109
Copyright © 2021 by Information Age Publishing
All rights of reproduction in any form reserved.

THE AIRBORNE TOXIC EVENT

Hurricanes, like other (un)naturally or fictitiously occurring disasters, tend to foster a fear of the unknown and a questioning of the (un)natural, perhaps supernatural, reasons behind them (Stern, 2007). Using creative devices such as metaphors, visual art, and song lyrics to relate human activities to these (un)natural disasters is not uncommon. In the novel *White Noise* (1985), Don DeLillo raises concerns about the toxic nature of media. During the dystopian story, a toxic chemical cloud leaks out of an overturned railroad car, leading to a mandatory evacuation of a nearby town. DeLillo calls it "The Airborne Toxic Event." Some describe the toxic event as a metaphor for media dissemination calling it a "ritual delivery of alarmist information and data that perpetually proclaims itself as essential for the lives of its recipients" (Baya, 2013, p. 160). In this way, toxins are released into the air and airwaves to enter the minds and bodies of unsuspecting individuals.

Analogous to education is the treatment of students and their minds as receptacles to be filled with information. This approach reflects Freire's (1970/2000) banking metaphor and his argument that pedagogy of this type dehumanizes students. As such, education can contribute to and suffer from airborne toxicity. The airborne toxic event discussed herein is the story of Hurricane Katrina (2005) and its aftermath on New Orleans' educational system. I draw on curriculum and arts as a way to promote empathy with the educators, students, and families who lived in the wake of Katrina and the associated perplexing politics and media messages. This approach to empathy is undergirded by critical (place-based) pedagogy and offers a critical arts-based approach to education that fosters meaningful political action informed by critical reflection (Finley, 2008). Through critical arts-based inquiry one can practice empathy by remembering the past and attempting to rectify the present for the benefit of the future.

SOCIAL AND ECOLOGICAL SUSTAINABILITY

The failed levee system in New Orleans, whether destroyed by human conspiracy or the destructive force of nature, represents the impact of humanity on the environment simultaneously with its opposite, the impact of the environment on humanity. The preservation of the New Orleans landscape through the use of levees was a desperate, perhaps naive, attempt to challenge the formidable power of nature. There was a massive displacement of New Orleans' residents due to Katrina. In Spike Lee's 2006 documentary *When the Levees Broke*, Michael Dyson likened the moving of poor Black people from New Orleans during the mandatory evacuation to the forced removal of Africans from their homeland during times of slavery. The Data

Center (2019) found that the Black population of New Orleans fell by 92,245 between 2000 and 2018.

When forced to leave our places, the results can be devastating. "The importance of the loss of a sense of place to an individual or a people's sense of themselves cannot be over-estimated" (Graham, 2014). In other words, where we live is entirely ingrained into our sense of being. DeLillo (1985) described the displaced residents of his postmodern novel as a tragic army of the dispossessed. The dispossession of those fleeing Hurricane Katrina and the destruction of their homes, schools, and places of cultural significance was exacerbated by the political trauma of gentrification and charter schools. Similar to Indigenous ideas of place that focus on social and ecological sustainability (Seawright, 2014), the dispossessed residents had been preserving their culture and place through their history of lived experiences. Settler colonialist philosophy, on the contrary, views place through capitalist and neoliberal ideas of individualism, ownership, and private property (Seawright, 2014); in New Orleans, the removal of Black people provided an opportunity for elite profit. After the storm, "Richard Baker, a prominent Republican congressman from [New Orleans], said, 'We finally cleaned up public housing in New Orleans. We couldn't do it, but God did'" (Klein, 2007, p. 4).

Gruenewald (2003) calls the combination of the social aspects of critical pedagogy with the ecological aspects of place-based pedagogy *socio-ecological*. Both, he explains, must be considered in order for "teachers and students to reinhabit their places, that is, to pursue the kind of social action that improves the social and ecological life of places, near and far, now and in the future" (Gruenewald, 2003, p. 7). Humankind has a "responsibility to restore and conserve our shared environment for future generations" (Gruenewald, 2003, p. 6). The place-based knowledge of New Orleans' residents about levees, the delicate relationship to nature, and the treatment of Black residents as second-class citizens created a sense of distrust in the social psyche of the city. They resisted as long as they could. Through the practice of empathy with those forced out of New Orleans by Hurricane Katrina or the gentrification occurring in its aftermath, students will recognize that "all Americans are vulnerable to disasters of one form or another" (Crocco, 2007, p. 1).

CRITICAL ARTS-BASED PEDAGOGY OF PLACE

In 1929, Memphis Minnie and Kansas Joe McCoy recorded "When the Levee Breaks," one of many songs written about the Great Mississippi River Flood of 1927. Though the music of the classic blues tune appears to be lilting and upbeat, there is an ominous quality to it. The idiosyncratic seventh chords and falling melodic riffs seem metaphoric to the sounds of toppling levees, the whooshing of wind and water, and the swaying of cypress trees on the bayou. The almost prophetic lyrical line, "If it keeps on rainin', levee's goin' to break," paints the dreary picture of anxiety felt by residents along the Mississippi River as they wondered if the levees would hold up to the relentless thrashing of mother nature.

Later the line, "Cryin' won't help you, prayin' won't do you no good," portrays the inevitable trouble to come. Finally, the words "Yeah, the mean old levee taught me to weep and moan, told me leave my baby and my happy home" describes the migration of many people affected by the Great Mississippi River Flood, not unlike the forced evacuation of New Orleans' residents in the days during and following Hurricane Katrina. A majority of displaced residents from New Orleans stayed displaced. Sastry and Gregory (2014) found in their study of displacement locations of Hurricane Katrina victims that just under one third of the displaced residents of New Orleans actually returned to the dwelling in which they resided prior to the hurricane.

In the days following Katrina, many were critical of the Bush Administration's handling of the recovery effort. On September 2, rapper Kanye West famously went off script during a live Katrina charity show and said, "George Bush doesn't care about Black people." This quote prompted Houston-based hip hop duo K-Otix (The Legendary K.O.) to release a politically charged protest song just a few days later titled "George Bush don't like Black people." The group utilizes a Kanye sample in this upbeat song reminiscent of East Coast hip hop. Among themes K-Otix criticizes in their lyrics are the length of time it took for the recovery effort to get underway ("Since you taking so much time we surviving ourself [*sic*]") and the inability of desperate residents to get food and water without retribution from police

(Well, swam to the store trying to look for food. Corner store's kinda flooded so I broke my way through. I got what I could but before I got through, the news said police shot a Black man trying to loot).

In a historic photograph of the Great Mississippi River Flood, taken in 1927, (see https://louisianadigitallibrary.org/islandora/object/state-lhp%3A2783), the labeler described the displaced residents as refugees. Displaced Black residents are seen sitting on a levee with flooding in the background. The term refugee is generally used to refer to people who flee their home country due to war, famine, persecution, natural disaster, and so on, and seek safe haven by crossing borders into other lands. The media disseminated the same airborne toxic moniker for Black people fleeing the rising waters on the tops of houses and bridges in the wake of Hurricane Katrina's wrath. Inquiring pedagogues can find many examples of photographs on the internet depicting the aftermath of Katrina to use in critical arts-based inquiry projects. Particularly poignant are photographs of armed police blocking Katrina victims from crossing the Gretna Bridge into Whiter suburban areas (Crocco, 2007; Kopp, 2005).

Some condemned the usage of the term refugee, believing it was used erroneously to describe displaced Black Americans as second-class citizens (Petrucci & Head, 2006). Although the media described a city within the United States as the third world (DeGravelles, 2009; Giroux, 2006) and its supplanted residents as refugees (DeGravelles, 2009), Petrucci and Head (2006) found this was not the first example in U.S. history of Black Americans being described as refugees. Runaway enslaved people on the Underground Railroad, for example, were labeled as such (Petrucci & Head, 2006). It was not until after the Second World War that consensus developed among nations as to the interpretation of refugees (Petrucci & Head, 2006).

The toxic employment of the terms refugee and third world in describing the displaced people and place of New Orleans after Katrina raised serious questions of what it meant (and still currently means) to be a citizen of the United States. Simply being born on American soil or to citizen parents does not seem to be enough, especially if the person is born Black and poor. The othering of New Orleans' residents was conceivably a way to clear the conscience of White America. If the "foreign" city was believed to be un-American, our Freedom Fries culture could wipe its hands clean of a pitiful recovery effort and the uncomfortable awareness of American inner city life in general. Calling into question the citizenship of Black people, see Obama, helps maintain the supremacy of settler culture. Cresswell (2013) suggests challenging the binary between citizen and noncitizen through descriptors such as shadow, barely, and insurgent citizens. There are people that are legally citizens of a nation state or brought in with little choice as children, the Dreamers[1] come to mind, yet through their lived experiences are othered as some entity in the spectrum between citizen and noncitizen.

Many agree that the system of education in New Orleans prior to Katrina was in a dire state (Akers, 2012; Alijani, Kwun, & Yu, 2014; Beabout, Stokes, Polyzoi, & Carr-Chellman, 2011; Buras, 2011; Garda, 2011; Holley-Walker, 2007; Jabbar, 2015; Johnson, 2012; Parsons & Turner, 2014; Ralston, 2010; Tuzzolo & Hewitt, 2006; Wolf, 2010). This was partly due to a history of racial inequity in educational spending. After the civil war, New Orleans integrated schools only until the Union soldiers left in 1877 at which time the schools were quickly segregated again and would remain so for almost 100 years (Ralston, 2010). Ralston (2010) mentions that White schools in New Orleans received almost four times as much tax dollars than their Black counterparts. Before integration, the White population in New Orleans' schools was around 50%. By 2004, the year before Katrina, New Orleans' schools were 94% Black (Ralston, 2010).

In the aftermath of Katrina, the secretary of wducation allocated a large sum of money to specifically build charter schools, not rebuild traditional public schools in New Orleans (Parsons & Turner, 2014). The governor of Louisiana, Kathleen Babineaux Blanco, used the money to create a new charter school district and enacted several laws concerning charter schools in New Orleans (Parsons & Turner, 2014). Of the most striking toxic changes to educational legislation were Acts 35 and 42, which, among other things, allowed for the firing of all public school employees in New Orleans and changed "the state's original ruling that required charter schools, like public schools, to serve the same or greater percentage of students qualifying for free or reduced lunch" (Parsons & Turner, 2014, p. 106). The neoliberal practice of privatizing public schools into charter schools turns education into a commodity or product (Apple, 2005; Saltman, 2009). This hasty resolution that swept over the city wreaked havoc on the already struggling Black population. Klein (2007) refers to "these orchestrated raids on the public sphere in the wake of catastrophic events, combined with the treatment of disasters as exciting market opportunities, 'disaster capitalism'" (p. 6). "This conservative movement threatens the development of public schools as necessary places that foster engaged critical citizenship" (Saltman, 2009, p. 28). Because charter schools are not zoned like traditional public schools, the sense of community created when students living next to each other attend the same school is lost. The "No Excuses" charter schools founded in buildings of formerly community-based schools, disregard the importance of place and cultural milieu, the practice of empathy, and community engagement. In addition, all 7,500 employees of the Orleans Parish School District, a majority of whom were Black, were terminated and "replaced by young and predominantly White transplants from 'education reform' organizations like Teach for America, New Leaders for New Schools, and the New Teacher Project" (Dixson, Buras, & Jeffers, 2015, p. 289). As Wolfe (2006) argued, societies based on the structure of settler colonialism destroy to replace. While nature helped destroy in the case of New Orleans, it was an event influenced by the toxicity of consumer capitalism (Ladino, 2012).

AN ARTISTIC PATH TO EMPATHY

I might argue that in order to rebuild community ties and increase cultural synthesis in New Orleans, a good start would be to dissolve charter schools and reopen the lost community schools closed in the trail of the disaster. However, even if this idealistic idea came true, bringing the displaced students, families, teachers, and administrators back to their former neighborhoods and schools would prove difficult at best. This notion is not exclusive to New Orleans. The airborne toxic devastation caused by charter schools in general has caused amnesia to placed-based knowledge; the standardization of curriculum has helped this amnesia as well, but with community and place-minded pedagogues in schools, standardization can be stretched to cover local issues of significance. In general, however, charter schools and standardization fail to promote community and, therefore, preserve alienation and hinder the emergence of consciousness and critical intervention (Freire, 1970/2000).

Crocco (2007) brings to the fore something I believe wholly lacking in "standard" curriculum—the pedagogy of empathy. In the case of New Orleans, there are at least two strands possible in discussing the empathic practice: (a) the erasing of schools, community, and culture as a tragedy that could befall anyone, and (b) having compassion for and offering grace to individuals in danger even if they chose to stay (Klopfer, 2017) through a hurricane or any other calamity or situation. No one has the foresight to know what kind of catastrophe will fruit. For example, I have personally lived through a share of hurricanes while living in Florida. During 2018's Hurricane Irma, the eye passed almost right over my house; many in the nearby city of Lakeland were without power for over a week. Although there is always premonition of the unknown, the majority of us do not expect a catastrophic disaster.

It is one thing to speak of empathy, to practice empathy, and to discuss how we might need more of it in the world, but to teach it to children and adults is formidable. Especially, as Gruenewald (2003) mentions, "In place of actual experience with the phenomenal world, educators are handed, and largely accept, the mandates of a standardized, 'placeless' curriculum and settle for the abstractions and simulations of classroom learning" (p. 8). Seventeen years after Gruenewald's concern, teachers are literally reprimanded for straying from scripted curriculums. Is it even possible, then, to incorporate Crocco's (2007) curriculum on Hurricane Katrina in today's K–12 classrooms? Using critical arts-based inquiry as a way of understanding subjectivity and emotion might help. In order to have an aesthetic experience, "one's interest and reactions must be absorbed by or immersed in the expressive qualities being attended to" (Reimer, 1989, p. 103). During my educational leadership internship, my "project" was to lead several teachers in integrating the arts into their classrooms. Although I am an adherent of both the formalist view of art, that is, art for art's sake, and the expressionist view or art, that is, the meaning of art is both inside and outside the piece, I had to settle on the idea that using the arts in non-arts classrooms could offer supplemental material and present information in differing ways for those students needing further application of concepts. Educators sometimes use the buzzwords differentiation and scaffolding to represent extra support for students struggling with new ideas. Within the tightly scripted curriculums of our current educational scene, there is a miniscule space to present information using the subjective, empathic nature of the arts. For example, my usage of literature, music and lyrics, and photography in this chapter is not in vain. My goal is to substantiate the idea that every individual experiences the world differently. In showing these slight differences by using artistic examples, I am hoping that the emotions of readers and students might be reached and they are able to identify with or self project "into the qualities of the thing to which [they are] responding" (Reimer, 1989, p. 103). "Because the arts are conducive to thick descriptions and detailed multivoiced narratives about everyday experiences, they provide useful formats for conducting inquiry that is dialogic and portrays 'truths' in flexible dynamic forms" (Finley, 2008, p. 144). In showing contrasting interpretations of one toxic event, I hope the experiencer makes the connection that the people who endured Hurricane Katrina (or any hardship really) and chose to stay (Klopfer, 2017) may have interpreted the world differently than those of us who stood back and watched from the safety of our living rooms and coffee shops. Critical arts-based inquiry emphasizes and enhances skills such as creativity, imagination, critical analysis, empathy, experimentation, synthesis, and voice (Power, 2014); skills that are vital for advocating a social justice worldview and resisting political oppression.

WHITEWASHED FENCES

In the satirical *New Orleans Education Reform: A Guide for Cities or a Warning for Communities? (Grassroots Lessons Learned, 2005–2012)* Buras (2013) quips, "It is time to recognize that the New Orleans model is a guide for white education entrepreneurs (and select allies of color) to racially reconstruct the city, including its schools, for their profit" (p. 150). New Orleans' horrific recovery in the name of opportunity and prosperity further exacerbated the educational debt that had been accrued "by the historic, economic, socio-political, and moral inequities [against African Americans] that had been allowed to persist since the founding of the nation" (Ladson-Billings, 2011, p. 1453). Like the concept of settler colonialism in which destruction is a means to replace, the New Orleans that once was would never be again; a once missed opportunity for Manifest Destiny became realized (Calderon, 2014; Tuck & Gatzambide-Fernández, 2013; Wolfe, 2006).

Fifteen years after Katrina, it appears as if little has been resolved. The perplexing questions the storm raised, questions of oppression, questions of citizenship, while brought into prominence for a short while, have been painted onto the pages of history using mostly White hues. The airborne toxic event the hurricane trawled across the Louisiana swamp uncovered a hemophilic wound deeper and older than the roots of America. The superficial explanation of toxic events provided by the government and media was enough for some. To the residents of New Orleans, the residents that could never truly inhabit their whitewashed home city again, the appalling treatment left much to be desired. Communities, students, and others involved in educational environments can learn to empathically engage one another in civil dialogue by using curricular ideas from models like Crocco's (2007) *Teaching the Levees* and employing critical arts-based inquiry as a means of furthering humanistic understanding.

NOTE

1. The Dreamers are individuals protected under the Deferred Action for Childhood Arrivals (DACA) legislation introduced in 2012 under the Obama Administration. The Trump Administration has been trying to end the program since 2017 citing government overreach. Deferred Action for Childhood Arrivals safeguards individuals brought to the United States "illegally" as children from deportation and allows them to live, work, and be educated in the United States. The status must be renewed every 2 years. While DACA is universally applied to children from all foreign nations, those whom it benefits are largely from Mexico (Dickerson, 2020; Walters & Holpuch, 2020).

REFERENCES

Akers, J. M. (2012). Separate and unequal: The consumption of public education in post-Katrina New Orleans. *International Journal of Urban and Regional Research, 36*(1), 29–48.

Alijani, G. S., Kwun, O., & Yu, Y. (2014). Effectiveness of blended learning in KIPP New Orleans' schools. *Academy of Educational Leadership Journal, 18*(2), 125–141.

Apple, M. W. (2005). Education, markets, and an audit culture. *Critical Quarterly, 47*(1/2), 11–29.

Baya, A. (2014). "Relax and enjoy these disasters": News media consumption and family life in Don DeLillo's. *White Noise. Neohelicon, 41*(1), 159–174.

Beabout, B. R., Stokes, H., Polyzoi, E., & Carr-Chellman, A. (2011). Social upheaval and school reform. *International Journal of Educational Reform, 20*(1), 57–82.

Buras, K. L. (2011). Race, charter schools, and conscious capitalism: On the spatial politics of whiteness as property (and the unconscionable assault on black New Orleans). *Harvard Educational Review, 81*(2), 296–331.

Buras, K. L. (2013). New Orleans education reform: A guide for cities or a warning for communities? (Grassroots Lessons Learned, 2005–2012). *Berkeley Review of Education, 4*(1), 123–160.

Calderon, D. (2014). Speaking back to manifest destinies: A land education-based approach to critical curriculum inquiry. *Environmental Education Research, 20*(1), 24–36.

Cresswell, T. (2013). Citizenship in worlds of mobility. In O. Soderstrom, D. Rue-din, G. D'Amato, & F. Panese (Eds.), *Critical mobilities* (pp. 105–124). London, England: Routledge.

Crocco, M. S. (Ed.). (2007). *Teaching the levees: A curriculum for democratic dialogue and civic engagement.* New York, NY: Teachers College Press.

Data Center. (2019, October 10). Who lives in New Orleans and metro parishes now? *The Data Center.* Retrieved from https://www.datacenterresearch.org/data -resources/who-lives-in-new-orleans-now/?utm_source=newsletter&utm_ medium=email&utm_content=http%3A//www.datacenterresearch.org/data -resources/who-lives-in-new-orleans-now/&utm_campaign=Who%20Lives

DeGravelles, K. H. (2009). The global meets the local: The third world-ing of New Orleans. *Journal of Curriculum and Pedagogy, 6*(1), 139–155.

DeLillo, D. (1985). *White noise.* New York, NY: Viking Press.

Dickerson, C. (2018, June 19). What is DACA? And how did it end up in the Su-preme Court? *The New York Times.* Retrieved from https://www.nytimes.com/ article/what-is-daca.html

Dixson, A. D., Buras, K. L., & Jeffers, E. K. (2015). The color of reform: Race, edu-cation reform, and charter schools in post-Katrina New Orleans. *Qualitative Inquiry, 21*(3), 288–299.

Finley, S. (2008). Critical arts-based inquiry. In L. M. Given (Ed.), *The SAGE encyclo-pedia of qualitative research methods* (Vol. 1; pp. 142–145). Thousand Oaks, CA: SAGE.

Freire, P. (2000). *Pedagogy of the oppressed.* New York, NY: Continuum. (Originally published in 1970)

Garda, R. A. (2011). The politics of education reform: Lessons from New Orleans. *Journal of Law & Education, 40*(1), 1–42.

Giroux, H. (2006). *Stormy weather: Katrina and the politics of disposability.* Boulder, CO: Paradigm.

Graham, M. (2014). Place and spirit-spirit and place. *EarthSong Journal: Perspectives in Ecology, Spirituality and Education, 2*(7), 5–7.

Gruenewald, D. A. (2003). The best of both worlds: A critical pedagogy of place. *Educational Researcher, 32*(4), 3–12.

Holley-Walker, D. (2007). The accountability cycle: The recovery school district act and New Orleans' charter schools. *Connecticut Law Review, 40*(1), 125–163.

Jabbar, H. (2015). 'Drenched in the past:' The evolution of market-oriented reforms in New Orleans. *Journal of Education Policy, 30*(6), 751–772.

Johnson, K. A. (2012). The myth and rhetoric of the new birth of excellence and opportunities for African American students in New Orleans. *PowerPlay, 4*(1), 1–35.

Klein, N. (2007). *The shock doctrine: The rise of disaster capitalism.* New York, NY: Macmillan.

Klopfer, A. N. (2017). "Choosing to stay:" Hurricane Katrina narratives and the history of claiming place-knowledge in New Orleans. *Journal of Urban History, 43*(1), 115–139.

Kopp, C. (2005, December 15). The bridge to Gretna: Why did police block des-perate refugees from New Orleans? *CBS News.* Retrieved from https://www .cbsnews.com/news/the-bridge-to-gretna/3/

Ladino, J. K. (2012). *Reclaiming nostalgia: Longing for nature in American literature.* Charlottesville: University of Virginia Press.

Ladson-Billings, G. (2011). Race to the top, again: Comments on the genealogy of critical race theory. *Connecticut Law Review, 43*(5), 1439–1457.

Lee, S. (Director). (2006). *When the levees broke: A requiem in four acts* [Film]. United State: HBO Documentary Films.

Parsons, E. C., & Turner, K. (2014). The importance of history in the racial inequality and racial inequity in education: New Orleans as a case example. *Negro Educational Review, 65*(1/4), 99–113.

Petrucci, P. R., & Head, M. (2006). Hurricane Katrina's lexical storm: The use of "refugee" as a label for American citizens. *Australasian Journal of American Studies, 25*(2), 23–39.

Power, S. (2014, September 4). Arts-based inquiry: The natural partner for social justice. *Teacher Magazine.* Retrieved from https://www.teachermagazine.com. au/articles/arts-based-inquiry-the-natural-partner-for-social-justice

Ralston, S. (2010). Adding autonomous schools to New Orleans' menu of school choice. *Loyola Journal of Public Interest Law, 11*(2), 389–439.

Reimer, B. (1989). *A philosophy of music education* (2nd ed.). Englewood Cliffs, NJ: Prentice Hall.

Saltman, K. J. (2009). Schooling in disaster capitalism: How the political right is using disaster to privatize public schooling. In S. Macrine (Ed.), *Critical pedagogy in uncertain times* (pp. 27–54). New York, NY: Macmillan.

Sastry, N., & Gregory, J. (2014). The location of displaced New Orleans residents in the year after Hurricane Katrina. *Demography, 51*(3), 753–775.

Seawright, G. (2014). Settler traditions of place: Making explicit the epistemological legacy of white supremacy and settler colonialism for place-based education. *Educational Studies, 50*(6), 554–572.

Stern, G. (2007). *Can God intervene? How religion explains natural disasters.* Westport, CT: Greenwood.

Tuck, E., & Gaztambide-Fernández, R. A. (2013). Curriculum, replacement, and settler futurity. *Journal of Curriculum Theorizing, 29*(1), 72–89.

Tuzzolo, E., & Hewitt, D. T. (2006). Rebuilding inequity: The re-emergence of the school-to-prison pipeline in New Orleans. *The High School Journal, 90*(2), 59–68.

Walters, J., & Holpuch, A. (2020, June 18). What is Daca and who are the Dreamers? *The Guardian.* Retrieved from https://www.theguardian.com/us-news/2020/jun/18/daca-dreamers-us-immigration-explainer

Wolf, N. L. (2010). A case study comparison of charter and traditional schools in New Orleans recovery school district: Selection criteria and service provision for students with disabilities. *Remedial and Special Education, 32*(5), 382–392.

Wolfe, P. (2006). Settler colonialism and the elimination of the native. *Journal of Genocide Research, 8*(4), 387–409.

CHAPTER 11

THE CRITICAL, POSTHUMANITIES AS A LENS FOR CURRICULUM THEORIZING

Trauma-Informed Curriculum in a More-Than-Human, More-Than-Critical World

Mary Newbery
Quinnipiac University

PROLOGUE: RE-MEMBERING AN ARTIST RESIDENCY

Over the past several years, I have participated in a middle school, artist residency that takes place in a small city in the northeastern United States. A multi-year endeavor and part of an emergent STEAM[1] initiative in the school, each spring an exhibiting or alumni artist from a regional contemporary art museum and the museum's educational team come to the school and spend a week thinking, imagining, and creating with our seventh grade students. During this time, adults and youth collaborate to design a project that is meaningful and reflective of the ideas, aspirations, and creative

Making a Spectacle, pages 111–124

energies of the participants. Resisting the adoption of a traditional, prede-termined concept or theme-based approach, a central feature of the pro-gram is that the students' and artist's collaborative project will hatch amidst planning conversations and emergent relationships, and be inclusive of the imaginings, desires, and collaborative visions of all engaged. An intra-disci-plinary endeavor, artist, teachers, students, and museum educators aspire to "look beyond taken-for-granted rational, cognitive, curriculum contexts to attend to surprising configurations where bodies, things, affect, desire, matter, imagination, and pedagogy collide to form new assemblages and possibilities" (Gannon, 2016, p. 128).

One of these residencies has had a profound impact on the way I have come to think about the potential for STEAM curriculum and pedagogy to include ways schools and their inhabitants learn and "become with" (Mannion, 2019, p. 13) the material and discursive entanglements of their "more-than-human" (Panelli, 2010) and "not only human" (Whatmore, 2006) neighborhoods and worlds. Propelling this particular residency into action, the artist, returning from the year before to again participate in the project, arrived and exclaimed, "Wow! This neighborhood has re-ally changed!" And he was right, it had. Over the past year, the neigh-borhood had become immersed in a massive neighborhood revitalization project, motivated by city planners' proclaimed goals of countering post-2008 recession disinvestment, de-isolating and improving the quality of life for the residents of the neighborhood's long-standing and decaying public housing project, increasing the density of storm and floodplain resilient housing near transportation hubs, restoring brownfields to us-able condition, and reducing the occurrence of real and perceived crime in the community. Over the past year our middle school team, consist-ing of mostly nonresidents, had spent early mornings and late afternoons commuting from numerous towns scattered around the outskirts of the city. On these journeys, we were rerouted almost daily as we maneuvered around crane and bulldozer-blocked streets, orange cones, and cratered roads upheaved with open sewers and pipelines on our way to work. While we could see the changes occurring, as the residency planning progressed, it became clear that we were not really "seeing" what was happening in our school community where a considerable number of our students and their families worked and/or lived. In order to take a closer look at these changes, the artist launched the project by inviting residency participants on a walk-about.

Touring the neighborhood, as artists, educators, students, *and* as visi-tors and residents, we traipsed around demolition sites, peered over bar-rier fences, climbed over flooded ditches, and chatted with people we met along the way. Almost immediately students exploded with anxious, and at times, frenzied questions and exclamations: Why did they tear this down? Do you remember going to...? Where did the...go? Where will they go? Cool! Gross! As we wandered, zigzagged and at times puddle-jumped across local thoroughfares, what seemed to emerge was a critical, posthumanist, STEAM-based enactment of "curriculum-in-the-making"[2] (Schultz & Baricovich, 2010).

As we found ourselves entangled with mounds of brick and steel, mud, old churches, rats disturbed from their subterranean abodes, flows of redevelopment capital, and a coveted and eroding coastline, our not-only-human "becoming" almost immediately expanded and shifted our sense of who and what constituted our collective "we." Thrusting ourselves outward into the world, it became clear that the residency, our school community, and all that entailed, was intricately intertwined with the neighborhood in previously unimagined ways. Of course, the neighborhood had never really been "out there," but instead, might be more accurately described as "the terrain...of the present, material, somatic, affective, and historical stuff of our world" (Snaza & Weaver, 2015, p. 2). Indeed, the neighborhood was alive.

Against this backdrop, this chapter is an experimental engagement with critical, posthumanist curriculum theorizing as a thinking apparatus for reimagining an expanded, trauma informed "curriculum-in-the-making" (Schultz & Baricovitch, 2010). Theorizing in this way calls for an attentiveness to situated knowledges that allow us to recognize "condensations of response-ability" (Barad, 2014, p. 172), but also, importantly, it opens us up to multiple worldings and the potential for an affirmative politics of relationality. To begin, I briefly discuss displacement in the context of urban renewal as a form of unofficial trauma in order to contextualize fragments of the inhuman/human/not-only human assemblages at work in the lives of young people living and learning in re and de-vitalizing communities. I then offer Braidotti's (2018) notion of the "critical posthumanities" as a lens through which to reconceptualize enactments of "curriculum-in-the-making" in re/devitalized neighborhoods. Emphasizing the need for multifaceted theories, I argue for transdisciplinary practices that might contribute to critical, posthumanist reimaginings of STEAM and SEL curriculum that attend to the unpredictable leakiness of disciplinary boundaries, nurture the development of a critical consciousness amongst students and educators, enhance school community members' understandings of collective response-ability, and offer students creative, affirmative openings for a reimagined future. Lastly, I articulate an abbreviated Baradian "remembering" (2015, p. 406) of this middle-school, artist residency and its enactment of, and potential for, a critical posthumanist understanding of trauma informed curriculum and pedagogy.

UNOFFICIAL TRAUMA AND TRAUMA-INFORMED
CURRICULUM

Increasingly, educators in the United States are attempting to envision trauma informed curriculum and pedagogy as they grapple with seemingly unprecedented numbers of students experiencing traumatic events. Most often, these conceptions of childhood trauma are considered in "the context of 'rupture' or crisis moments" such as school shootings, natural disasters, or widely experienced local or national events (Mayor, 2019, p. 199). Additionally, most therapeutic approaches to trauma are focused on the individual and their symptom management, failing to consider the collective impact of "structural and systemic forces, such as exploitation, marginalization and cultural imperialism that lead to trauma" (Young, 1990, as cited in Escueta & Butterwick, 2012, pp. 325–326).

In recent years, social emotional learning (SEL) models have become dominant in mainstream public education settings in the United States. According to the Collaborative for Academic, Social, and Emotional Learning (CASEL), these models advocate a standards based approach to social emotional learning attached to core competencies which focus on "how children and adults learn to understand and manage emotions, set goals, show empathy for others, establish positive relationships, and make responsible decisions" (CASEL, 2020). These models,[3] which are frequently scripted, one-size-fits-all and prepackaged curriculum, most often fail to attend to the complex, cultural communities within which children learn and miss opportunities to be flexible in response to students' lived experiences and unique local contexts (Bailey, Stickle, Brion-Meisels, & Jones, 2019, p. 53). Additionally, while proponents argue SEL curriculum is trauma informed, most models focus trauma interventions exclusively on adverse childhood events.

Understanding trauma in these ways misses the "unofficial traumatization" (Alford, 2016, p. 47) that accumulates in our children's worlds via complex intra-actions amongst preexisting vulnerabilities, chronic conditions, and acute events. The distinction is important. While an acute event is most often easily identified and conveniently situated in a particular place and time, unofficial trauma, as described by Erikson, might be described as "a chronic disaster...that gathers force slowly and insidiously, creeping around one's defenses rather than smashing through them" (Erikson, 1994, p. 21, as cited in Alford 2016, p. 47). Due to these subtle and enmeshing traits, the impact of unofficial trauma poses significant challenges for educators.

These increased challenges are also, in part, due to effects of unofficial traumatizations that appear to be increasing exponentially, as ongoing geopolitical and civil aggressions and their military–industrial enactments, climate change, superstorms, biomedical disasters, and the complex intra-activities of advanced political economies contribute to increasingly unpredictable and unstable communities, neighborhoods, and lives. This instability manifests as a conglomeration of effects that become entwined with diverse, multi-scalar forces, material and discursive entanglements, and their differentially impactful effects. One such effect has been the emergence of a new "logics of expulsion," characterized by a drastic increase "in the number of people, enterprises, and places expelled from the core social and economic orders of our time" (Sassen, 2014, p. 1). In contemporary, K–12 public school communities in the northeastern United States, these expulsions are often recognized as displacements, a term used by social geographers to describe "enforced mobility in a variety of contexts and at different spatial scales" (Brickell et al., as cited in Elliott-Cooper, Hubbard & Lees, 2019, p. 1), including urban revitalization projects (Fullilove, 2016). Of great significance for educators seeking trauma informed practices, these effects are often mapped upon sites of urban renewal and/or gentrification projects and their entanglements with forced evictions, the multitudinous impacts of advanced capitalism, global flows of displaced peoples fleeing violence and economic insecurity, and/or the extreme effects of climate change.

When we consider displacement in these ways, the unofficial trauma occurring amidst neighborhood revitalization projects become open to reconceptualization as an articulation of the ways humans, nonhumans, places, spaces, and things become entangled in ways that trouble mainstream notions of trauma informed curriculum and pedagogy. Instead, an engagement with posthumanist thought becomes necessary, enabling us to rework our understandings of "curriculum-in-the-making" in ways that consider "more than human" (Whatmore, 2006) entanglement *and* affirmative politics as critical, posthuman tools for remaking our/selves and our historical Others in the context of unofficial trauma. In contemporary, neoliberal societies, where neighborhoods host collisions of archaic infrastructures, superstorms, floodplains, brownfields, grandma's house, immigration policy, neoliberal capital flows, and far-away drug wars, unanticipated tensions and alliances exist alongside historical sedimentations as they collaborate to acknowledge and reconfigure not only vulnerability and precarity, but the potential for affirmative politics and positive change as well.

THE CRITICAL, POSTHUMANITIES AS A LENS FOR THEORIZING CURRICULUM-IN-THE-MAKING

This discussion now turns to some ways Braidotti's (2018) particular theorization of the "critical posthumanities" might be employed to extend Schultz and Baricovich's (2010) notion of "curriculum-in-the-making" in ways that are attentive to the unofficial traumatizations occurring in contemporary public schools in the United States. I will begin by briefly summarizing Braidotti's characterization of the critical posthumanities as an "emergent field of thought," (Braidotti, 2018, p. 31) and I will then explore three of its most significant elements, emphasizing what distinguishes her work from some other, feminist, monist-oriented renderings of posthumanism.

For Braidotti, the critical posthumanities is a field composed of transdisciplinary knowledge that expands the traditional humanities via a recognition of a world that is vital, complex, and more than human. She elaborates, "We recognize that growing computational systems, security terrors, new biomedical forms and drastic ecological damage, amongst other factors, impel us to recognize the wider forms and constituents of the condition that is no longer nameable simply as humanity" (Braidotti & Fuller, 2019, p. 4). These conditions, she argues, call for transdisciplinary bodies of thought that are capable of registering the accelerationist tendencies of contemporary advances in science and technologies while continuing to attend to the intensification of social and economic inequalities on both local and global scales (Braidotti, 2018, p. 32). Crucially, this transdisciplinarity is not only concerned with the nonhuman or more than human subject of some, contemporary posthuman thought. Rather, she argues, fields of study concerned with human rights, mobility, migration, trauma, memory, and reconciliation to name but a few play a crucial role in "crossbreeding" previously distinct studies to help us better understand "the inhumane aspects of our historical condition" (Braidotti, 2018, p. 40) which have always been a part of being human.

Thus, one key element in Braidotti's conceptualization of critical posthumanist thought is the notion of transdisciplinarity. For her, transdisciplinarity rejects theoretical enclosures that create insides and outsides, and instead, promotes forging relations among theories "that are able and willing to open up" (Braidotti, 2018, p. 44). Importantly, this "opening up" allows for thinking spaces that are invested in "more than critical inquiries" as well as those that engage in critical inquiry of the "more than human" (Ulmer, 2017, p. 833). This gesture is important, since, for many, as Latour (2004) has argued, humanist renderings of the critique have "run out of steam." While this assertion only holds true for some branches of posthumanist thought, by opening up the theoretical landscape to allow for collaborations across previously distinct disciplinary enclaves, fresh renditions of static concepts become possible. For example, postcolonial engagements with cultural geography might engage with feminist, new materialist offerings around the agency of weather, opening up new knowledges to help us differently understand collisions and collaborations amongst fossil fuel companies, superstorms, nearly extinct nonhuman species, urban planning, and the lived experiences of diverse populations living in flood-plain communities.

Unlike some recent iterations of the posthuman in contemporary theo-ry, Braidotti's posthumanism does not reject less recent post-foundational theorizations that were particularly attentive to the asymmetry of human locations. Rather, she cautions, deployments of "new" art/science/social science transdisciplinarity that gesture toward a new successor regime with all that entails (surveilled borders, critiques of other, less "anti-human" the-oretical frames) threaten to reinstate humanist ideals in regard to the na-ture and function of knowledge via appeals to disciplinary purity. From this location, she argues for a rendering of posthuman knowledge "that con-stitutes a trans-disciplinary field of scholarship that is more than the sum of its parts" (Braidotti, 2019, p. 32), opening up posthumanist knowledge projects to affirmative, yet still grounded, ontological and epistemological politics of becoming.

This intradisciplinary "opening up" of theories offers a promising new approach to curriculum theorizing around unofficial trauma in schools. Rather than thinking about SEL or STEAM initiatives as distinct, curricu-lar and pedagogical endeavors, the unpredictable leakiness of disciplin-ary boundaries in schools offers new possibilities, as disparately concocted theorizings and their accompanying practices morph around re/devital-ized neighborhoods into opportunities for engagements with "curriculum-in-the-making." Local histories, residents' stories, decaying buildings and storm ravaged waterfronts converge with principles of engineering, stud-ies of superstorms, and individual and collective experiences of loss and displacement, as artistic renderings of possible and impossible designs are imagined and calculated amidst visions for a different and more equitable future. Notably, Braidotti's critical posthumanities take into account the vulnerabilities and agencies of humans and nonhumans alike.

This tendency toward openness brings me to a second, interrelated as-pect of Braidotti's critical, posthumanist cartography. For Braidotti, critical approaches to the posthumanities are informed by Spinozist theories of monism. This ontological perspective emphasizes the singleness of things and concepts, such as the universe, and thus reject the dualisms, such as the self and the Other, which contour Enlightenment informed, human-ist thought. Her theorizings remain materially grounded, however, in that they attach to relationalities amongst humans, more-than-humans and their worlds in ways that are nonlinear, but still situated and attentive to both "a feminist politics of location" (Rich as cited in Braidotti, 2019, p. 33) and situated knowledges (Harding, 1986; Haraway, 1988, as cited in Braidotti, 2019, p. 33). For Braidotti, these resilient feminist concepts constitute the original conceptual apparatuses of both embodied and embedded knowl-edge (p. 34). Of great significance to any curriculum theorizing around schools (which are always drenched with inequities), Braidotti's critical posthumanism grounds politics in ways that "account[s] for one's locations in terms both of space (geopolitical or ecological dimension) and time (historical memory or genealogical dimension)" (Braidotti, 2013, p. 46). Importantly, understanding knowledge in this way acknowledges that all knowing is multiple, partial, and selective.

This insistence on retaining a politics of location is of great significance for enactments of curriculum and pedagogy in schools that strive to be informed by understandings of unofficial trauma. Challenging the limitations of traditional SEL curricula and most mainstream STEAM models, a critical posthumanist approach informed by a politics of location allows curriculum participants to investigate the non-neutrality of science alongside ways disciplinary practices play out in real lives in real places. Coupled with the "opening up" of transdisciplinary thought, posthumanist theorizing that remains attentive to the ontological and epistemological complexities of difference in schools, invites a conglomeration of disparate theories to help school communities make sense of their worlds. Thus, theories informed by critical race, postcolonial, and feminist, new materialist lenses can collide, overlap, collaborate with and bounce off concepts from physics, biology, finance, and geology, all while entangling themselves with practices offered by cartographers, artists, scientists and oral historians.

The last element of Braidotti's critical posthumanism of significance here is her insistence that locational accountability be coupled with a creativity that is rooted in the affirmative potential of imagining ourselves and others anew (Braidotti, 2013, p. 46). Thus, despite her concern with the cruelties and "slow violence" inflicted on vulnerable communities by complex, contemporary global forces, she does not characterize her critical cartographies as negative, but rather argues that "they assist us in the process of learning to think differently about ourselves, in response to the complexity of our times" (Braidotti, 2018, p. 34). This approach is particularly impactful when working with young people living in traumatized communities, since it provides a tool for not only investigating what is, but it also offers us the possibility of reimagining what might be.

A CRITICAL, POSTHUMANIST RE-MEMBERING OF TRAUMA INFORMED CURRICULUM-IN-THE-MAKING

In this final section, I entangle Braidotti's notion of the critical, posthumanities with snippets from the artist-residency introduced in the prologue, as I work to articulate a form of critical, posthumanist curriculum theorizing via a Baradian re-membering. For Barad, re-membering is not attached to the memory of a rational, humanist subject who can consciously and accurately recollect events and impressions from the past, but instead involves the "entanglement of disparate parts" (Barad, 2015, p. 406). Resonant of Braidotti's call for transdisciplinary thinking that is more than the sum of its parts, for Barad, re-membered parts are not thought of as separate elements, but instead are conceived in relation to the division of parts and wholes. To illustrate, she describes writing as a form of "re-membering" in this way:

> [Writing] is a patchwork. Made of disparate parts. Or so it may seem. But why should we understand parts as individually constructed building blocks or disconnected pieces of one or another forms of original wholeness? After all, to be a part is not to be absolutely apart but to be constituted and threaded through with the entanglements of part-ing. (p. 406)

In these ways, she challenges the notion of "disparate parts" by instead arguing that parts are *connected* through the enactment of part-ing or cutting in an act of "cutting together/apart" (p. 406).

From this perspective, then, what follows is an active engagement with this notion of re-membering via a cutting together/apart of the neighborhood, an artist residency, an urban renewal project, and some experimental, posthumanist, curriculum theorizing. As such, it will re-member and re-imagine slices of dystemporally situated histories of intra-neighborhood communities, material/discursive engagements with superstorms, a waterfront, and student reimaginings of a redesigned, utopic neighborhood. Immersed in a human/not-only-human network, in these ways, re-membering involves "tracing entanglements" (p. 407) and exploring human and nonhuman networks via different ontological cuts.

The neighborhood re-membered

A diner/coffee shop/restaurant kind of place: black and white checkered floors, you know, like the old days....

As students formed groups to plan their designs for a new revitalization plan, they brainstormed places they had decided were most important for the well-being of the community. One unexpected characteristic of their work discussions was how many of the community members' memories they had absorbed via the informal interviews and conversations gathered on their walk-about. One group felt it important to create "diner/coffee shop/restaurant kind of place," designed to reflect the décor and "mood" of the old days. It would be a place where everyone would be welcome, and people could hang out on their days off.

Superstorms

Water is so pervasive. It gets in everywhere, it flows in, and you sort of treat it as something that does flow, that sometimes people don't appreciate that that flow can have such force [except] when you see one of the major floods [. . .] when it literally tears down a bridge.

In the past, people had houses with solid floors and if it flooded you swept it out, but now of course we have got your electrics and carpets, and you put your wooden floors in. Why do you do it when you know you are going to be flooded? (Whatmore, 2016, p. 43).

Teachers talking about the arrival of new immigrants after the hurricane: They are expecting hundreds of new students to enroll over the next several weeks due to the mass evacuation of Puerto Rico. Where will these students even live? They have no winter clothes. I can't fit one more student in my classroom.

Thoughts on the nonhuman

So if the nonhuman is neither neatly bounded, substantially (and morally) independent, and over there, nor insubstantial, dissolute, and in here, then what is it, what thing is nonhuman? And does it matter? The questions are intimately related, for we are talking about things that matter, or about how things matter (Hinchcliffe, Kearnes, Degan, & Whatmore, 2005, p. 644).

"The apartments stunk even worse after Sandy. And there was mold, a lot of mold. It was really gross." (Re-membered student comment)

Revitalization project details: The redevelopment of our current public housing complex is an extensive, multiphase project directed toward the revitalization of the neighborhood. Some sections of the neighborhood lie within the floodplain, and Superstorm Sandy's "call for action" included updated, new storm-resilient housing and local infrastructure near the waterfront. Along with a growing demand for private development in the waterfront area, our community has rallied to support this project.

Newspaper heading: **Rats, flooding complaints at construction site**
Human, nonhuman, not-only-human becoming
"Social-material processes that are characteristically massy, indivisible, unseen, fluid, and noxious have, problematically, remained hidden-in-plain-sight within multidisciplinary research with children and young people. For example, juxtaposing qualitative and autoethnographic data, we highlight children's vivid, troubling narratives of swarming rats, smearing excrement, and percolating subsurface flows of water, toxins, and racialized affects. In so doing, we develop a wider argument that key theorizations of matter, nature, and nonhuman copresences have often struggled to articulate the indivisibility of social-material processes from contemporary social-political-economic geographies" (Horton & Kraftl, 2018, p. 926).

"Joe has moved like three times since they tore his building down" (Student comment)

"Posthumanist approaches require us to pay attention to the more-than-human contexts within which young people come to take themselves up in the world, and to the affordances and capacities of worldly things and affective flows to shape young people's desires and ways of being in the world" (Gannon, 2016, p. 129).

People need a place they can go to feel safe and feel good about themselves

The 7th grade students regularly do community service at the homeless shelter and food pantry in the community. In doing research around homelessness, they noted that while shelters never had enough beds, many homeless people did not want to stay in shelters anyway. What homeless individuals most often talked about needing showers, laundry, and a safe place to keep their stuff. As a result, they designed a drop-in center with a check-in app where individuals could reserve laundry facilities, showers, lockers, and even parking spaces if they lived in their cars.

Teachers design a new unit

T1: I think our water unit should start with an inquiry into Flint, Michigan. They can study it from all sorts of angles, and they read "Flush" right around then too.

T2: Yes! And *then* they can design their run-off garden. It will mean something different for them.

CONCLUDING THOUGHTS

Unofficial traumatizations in school communities seem to be creating hotspots of precarity, vulnerability, and differential becomings in a world increasingly driven by the desires of postindustrial capitalism. The trauma inflicted upon neighborhoods is insidious, working at multiscalar levels that impact the well-being of our students in significant ways. In order to find other ways of being and becoming, we have to connect, even as we are "enmeshed in partial and flawed translations across difference" (Haraway, 2016, p. 10). Indeed, Haraway (2016) chides, "Becoming with, not becoming, is how we stay with the trouble" (p. 12). She elaborates, "We require each other in unexpected collaborations and combinations, in hot compost piles. We become with each other or not at all. That kind of material semiotics I always situated, someplace and not noplace, entangled and worldly"

(p. 4). In this brief chapter, I offered some experimental curriculum theorizing as a form of "curriculum in the making" in a not-just-human world. Importantly, I argued for an approach to understanding trauma informed curriculum and pedagogy that is transdisciplinary, situated, and open to multiple and different worldings, thereby creating space for a collective politics that is informed by intradisciplinary knowledge practices and affirmative ethics. Participating in and articulating these alternative becomings is not an easy task, but to do otherwise seems less than cowardly, and almost certainly complicit. It is the work of our times.

NOTES

1. STEAM, an acronym for Science, Technology, Engineering, Arts and Math is a movement coined and promoted by the Rhode Island School of Design in an effort to "transform research policy to place Art + Design at the center of STEM" by emphasizing "the symbiosis between the arts and sciences, reinforcing the ongoing value of the arts and humanities," and thus "better prepar[ing] future generations to compete in the 21st-century innovation economy" (RISD, n.d.)

2. Building upon Ellsworth's notion of "learning-in-the-making" which critiques "dead" knowledge and the "traffick[ing]" of curriculum as a commodity (2005, p. 1), Schultz and Baricovich (2010) notion of "curriculum in the making" that encourages participants "to critically assess social, political, and economic structures to see beyond surface causes; seek out and address areas of injustice" and "leverage participants' interest to engage in real world problem solving" (p. 49).

3. While an in depth investigation of SEL curriculum is beyond the scope of this discussion, it is important to note that while advocates of SEL curricula argue that dominant critiques are most appropriately directed toward implementation, staunch critics point out that the SEL movement has largely been dominated by White researchers creating programs designed to teach Black and Brown students in urban districts how "to persevere and regulate their behavior" (Starr, 2019, p. 70). More than a fad, SEL goals and practices have been linked to the post-World War II life adjustment curricula and its associated inequities.

REFERENCES

Alford C. F. (2016). *Trauma, culture and PTSD*. New York, NY: Springer Nature.

Bailey, R., Stickle, L., Brion-Meisels, G., & Jones, S. M. (2019). Re-imagining social-emotional learning: Findings from a strategy-based approach: To bring the benefits of SEL to more students, programs need to be flexible enough to adapt to local needs. *Phi Delta Kappan, 100*(5), 53.

Barad, K. (2014). Diffracting diffraction: Cutting together-apart. *Parallax, 20*(3), 168–187. https://doi.org/10.1080/13534645.2014.927623

Barad, K. (2015). Transmaterialities: Trans*/matter/realities and queer political imaginings. *GLQ: A Journal of Lesbian and Gay Studies, 21*(2/3), 387–422. https://doi.org/10.1215/10642684-2843239

Braidotti, R. (2013). *The posthuman.* Cambridge, England: Polity Press.

Braidotti, R. (2018). A theoretical framework for the critical posthumanities. *Theory, Culture & Society, 36*(6) 31–61. https://doi.org/10.1177/0263276418771486

Braidotti, R., & Fuller, M. (2019). The posthumanities in an era of unexpected consequences. *Theory, Culture & Society, 36*(6), 3–29. https://doi.org/10.1177/0263276419860567

CASEL. (2020). *What is CASEL?* Retrieved from https://casel.org/what-is-sel/

Elliott-Cooper, A., Hubbard, P., & Lees, L. (2019). Moving beyond Marcuse: Gentrification, displacement and the violence of un-homing. *Progress in Human Geography, 44*(3), 1–18. https://doi.org/10.1177/0309132519830511

Ellsworth, E. (2005). *Places of learning.* London, England: Routledge.

Escueta, M., & Butterwick, S. (2012). The power of popular education and visual arts for trauma survivors' critical consciousness and collective action. *International Journal of Lifelong Education, 31*(3), 325–340. https://doi.org/10.1080/02601370.2012.683613

Fullilove, M. T. (2016). *How tearing up city neighborhoods hurts America, and what we can do about it: Root shock.* New York, NY: New Village Press.

Gannon S. (2016). 'Local girl befriends vicious bear': Unleashing educational aspiration through a pedagogy of material-semiotic entanglement. In C. A.Taylor & C. Hughes (Eds.), *Posthuman research practices in education* (pp. 128–148). London, England: Palgrave Macmillan.

Haraway, D. (2016). *Staying with the trouble: Making kin in the Chthulucene.* Durham, NC: Duke University Press.

Harding, S. (1986). *The science question in feminism.* Ithaca, NY: Cornell University Press.

Hinchcliffe, S., Kearnes, M. B., Degenó, M., & Whatmore, S. (2005). Urban wild things: a cosmopolitical experiment. *Environment and Planning D: Society and Space, 23*(5), 643–658. http://doi.org/10.1068/d351t

Horton, J., & Kraftl, P. (2017). Rats, assorted shit and 'racist groundwater': Towards extra-sectional understandings of childhoods and social-material processes. *Environment and Planning D: Society and Space, 36*(5), 926–948. https://doi.org/10.1177/0263775817747278

Latour, B. (2004). Why has critique run out of steam? From matters of fact to matters of concern. *Critical Inquiry, 30*(2), 225–248. https://doi.org/10.1086/421123

Mannion, G. (2019). Re-assembling environmental and sustainability education: Orientations from New Materialism. *Environmental Education Studies.* Advance online publication. http://doi.org/10.1080/13504622.2018.1536926

Mayor, C. (2018). Whitewashing trauma: Applying neoliberalism, governmentality, and whiteness theory to trauma training for teachers. *Whiteness and Education, 3*(2), 198–216. http://doi.org/10.1080/23793406.2019.1573643

Panelli, R. (2009). More-than-human social geographies: posthuman and other pos- sibilities. *Progress in Human Geography, 34*(1), 1–9. http://doi.org/10.1177/ 0309132509105007

RISD. (n.d.). *RISD: Academics: Public engagement.* Retrieved from https://www.risd .edu/academics/public-engagement/#support-for-steam

Sassen, S. (2014). *Expulsions: Brutality and complexity in the global economy.* Cambridge, MA: Belknap Press of Harvard University.

Schultz, B. E., & Baricovich, J. E. (2010). Curriculum in the making: Theory, prac- tice, and social action curriculum projects. *Journal of Curriculum Theorizing, 26*(2), 46–61.

Snaza, N., & Weaver, J. A. (2015). Introduction: Education and the posthuman turn. In N. Snaza & J. A. Weaver (Eds.), *Posthumanism and educational research* (pp. 2–11). New York, NY: Routledge.

Starr, J. P. (2019, March 21). Can we keep SEL on course? *Phi Delta Kappan, 100*(8), 70–71.

Ulmer, J. (2017). Posthumanism as research methodology: Inquiry in the Anthropo- cene. *International Journal of Qualitative Studies in Education, 30*(9), 832–848. https://doi.org/10.1080/09518398.2017.1336806

Whatmore, S. (2006). Materialist returns: practicing cultural geography in and for a more-than-human world. *Cultural Geographies, 13*(4), 600–609. https://doi. org/10.1191/1474474006cgj377oa

SECTION IV

LIVED EXPERIENCES
WITH POLITICAL TRAUMA SURVIVORS

CHAPTER 12

REFLECTION

Recently Arrived—Still Under-Served: Language Learning and Teaching in the Shadows

Michelle Angelo-Rocha
University of South Florida

Lisa Armstrong
University of South Florida

Ann Marie Mobley
University of South Florida

Dionne Davis
University of South Florida

As of 2020, there were nearly 5 million students enrolled in public schools in the United States who were designated as learners of the English language (National Center for Education Statistics, 2020). According to a report released by the Office of Academic Achievement on limited English

Making a Spectacle, pages 127–139

proficient (LEP) students (also referred to as English language learners, ELLs), 70% were enrolled in dual language and/or bilingual programs in Florida. These students did not make progress during the previous school year and did not pass the reading, language arts, and mathematics standardized testing (Department of Education, 2018, p.123). English learners' academic underachievement is rooted in improper educational policies and practices.

This chapter is our collaborative reflection on the points of concern raised above. Drawing from literature and our empirical experiences, we report on the difficulties that multilingual emergent students and families face in ELL programs at K–12 urban public schools in the southwest area of Florida and how we are implicated. In this self-examination, we share some of our struggles, ensuring that children and families are supported in overcoming barriers associated with the formal education system, such as its reliance on a dominant language (English), restrictions, and bureaucracy associated with one's immigration status and exclusionary sociocultural norms and values. Our goal is to contribute to the conversation and offer diverse perspectives in terms of racial and ethnic populations, learning spaces, ages, and our own positionalities and struggles to attend to the needs of the groups of students who are under-served. Educators who share their curricular practices and reflections, as we do below, can contribute to the debate on how to advance the bilingual and dual-language educational programs in the United States to attend the needs of ELL students properly.

BACKGROUND AND POSITIONALITY OF THE AUTHORS

Our positionalities are fundamental to our analysis and self-reflection. Lisa, Ann Marie, and Dionne are African American women who have experience as teachers, mentors, and school administrators in K–12 public schools and in multilingual emergent programs in Florida. Michelle, a Brazilian *mestiça* from a low-income background, immigrated to the United States as an adult and is gaining proficiency in English. As doctoral students with domestic and international status, we have collectively volunteered or worked as teachers, teacher assistants, substitute teachers, and administrators helping emergent multilingual K–12 students and adult refugees of diverse ethnicities to learn English while maintaining their primary or preferred language(s).

During the course of working in our respective positions, we have witnessed the frustrations of students and families attempting to overcome language barriers within educational systems in order to secure better educational and socioeconomic opportunities. We decided to meet and exchange our personal classroom experiences. During our conversation, we concluded that the four of us face similar frustrations about how educational programs, curriculum, and policies attend the needs of ELL students. In the excerpts from our conversations shared below, in order to protect those who face greater risks, we have refrained from identifying which of us is being quoted.

THEORETICAL FRAMEWORK

This reflection is inspired by the method *currere* developed by the curriculum theorist Pinar (1975/1994), where he encourages teachers and school leaders to self-reflect on their past and present experiences as students and educators; in light of that, these student-educators can use self-introspection and awareness to envision and create better futures for their students. Through self-reflection, any educator can motivate themselves to innovate thoughtful contributions, embolden more debates, and implement strategies and policy reforms that benefit students. *Currere* involves analyzing experiences. Such analysis can help us avoid previous mistakes and reduce the distance between ourselves, students, and students' families. Our collaborative self-reflection is a consciousness-raising effort to identify actions and interactions in which individualism and other cultural, linguistic, and socioeconomic values operate to the detriment of those we aim to serve.

We use critical race theory (CRT) lenses to analyze the educational experiences which have short and long-term resonance in the lives of students and families who are fluent and literate in one or more languages other than English, including ourselves. This involves examining how CRT can be used as an instrument to decolonize Western knowledge and challenge practices of racism in the curricula, educational programs, discourses, and pedagogical practices (Yosso, 2002). Inspired by Crenshaw (1989, 1991), we use the concept of intersectionality to analyze how racism, ethnicity, classism, linguicism, and other expressions of power affect relational dynamics and practices in educational settings. Through CRT, we challenge racial-ethnic inequality in schools and help to create approaches that make students with emerging multilingualism feel recognized and respected.

OUR EMPIRICAL EXPERIENCES
WITH ELL STUDENTS AND FAMILIES

Since the 2016 onset of President Trump's administration, the Southern Poverty Law Center (2019) reveals that cases of hate, racism, and xenophobia in schools have increased significantly. The report shows that school leaders failed to address the majority of these cases, and in 57% of the anti-immigration cases, no one was disciplined (p. 5). Both xenophobia and institutional racism are barriers to learning for ELL students already often the target of rejection. Many educators, however, may be unaware of the presence of such biases. In 2017, a Tucson Arizona district judge ruled that the ban on the ethnic studies program was not only backed by ethno-bias but also by racial animus (Muñoz, 2020). Ethnic biases in schools, especially with current anti-immigration political discourses and policies, are sources of political trauma. This political trauma, influenced by President Trump's anti-immigration rhetoric, contributes to ELL students' sense of shame over their identity, their physical features, their accent, their family, and their cultural background.

Compounding the obstacles that immigrant children and families already face, Pinar (2004) states that "teachers today are reduced to technicians, managing student productivity. The school is no longer a school, but a business" (p. 27). In most cases, teachers do not have the power, time, and autonomy to create original teaching designs and techniques that help students succeed based on students' individualities: cultures, intelligence mixes, learning styles, interests, and so on. Rather, strained under the demand for state-mandated assessments, teachers are left with little-to-no time to be responsive to students and parents. Administrations prioritize state-mandated performance over cultural sensitivity. Furthermore, thousands of educators today are unseen doing invisible work, often not being recognized for their heroic efforts (Amanti, 2019). Heroic or not, a sense of failure defeats many educators and school leaders.

Due to communication challenges and the unfortunate issue of aging out, ELL students are often transferred within the public-school system from standard classrooms to special education classrooms, which fail to address ELL learner needs. In some cases, administrations go so far as to move these students to different schools, an act that does little to address language barriers, chronic relocations, and inadequate housing, food, transportation, parental employment, and family support. This results in frequent student absences and isolation. In many cases, students have not had multilingual advisors or trained mentors to help them overcome their fears, traumas, and language difficulties; as a result, students felt motivated to drop-out of school. These continued systematic practices cause emotional distress among students and their families. During the course of our work, immigrant families often expressed that they did not feel welcomed in educational environments due to their ethnicity, their lack of English language proficiency, their immigration background, and their phenotype. Other similar cases report that immigrant learners and their families avoid schools due to the very real fear of deportation and the subsequent emotional stress and trauma of living with such fear causes (Capps, Castañeda, Chaundry, & Santos, 2007; Crawford, 2017; López, 2010). In some instances, multilingual emergent students experience a decline in motivation and self-confidence, declines often overlooked by their educators and school leaders. Additionally, language barriers, literacy, immigration status, and economic instability complicate the building of relationships between teachers and parents and so hinders parental participation in the educational process. This further threatens the inclusion and academic success of immigrant children. The research and our work demonstrate that the more under-served students are, the more excluded they become. This impacts not only their progress in school but how they socialize at home and in their community.

In an ethnographic study with low-income Latinx communities in Los Angeles, California, Monzó (2016) found that middle-school students internalized racism and oppression. Internalized oppression is when students unconsciously create negative perceptions of themselves associated with their ethnic-racial and cultural background. While writing this reflection, two of the authors shared similar examples of internalized oppression in the classroom of ELL middle-school students:

> I have students who do not speak English and could not succeed in a traditional school, so the school district ended up moving them to my school due to their lack of language proficiency, age, and resources to succeed. The majority of my ELL students ended up being retained in their previous school and aging out. Those same students refused to speak Spanish or their native language. They told me: "Teacher, I do not like to speak Spanish. I do not want anybody to know that I speak Spanish." I asked, Why? As a teacher, I am really trying to work on the self-image of my students, but several of them refuse their own cultural background. (Author 813)

> One day I was working as a substitute teacher in a middle school. A Mexican girl asked me where I am from, and I said: "I am from Brazil, and you?" Slowly she started to get excited and shared her story with me, and how her parents immigrated to the U.S. During our conversation, she paused and told me: "I think I am ugly, and I am embarrassed by my Mexican features [my hair and facial features]." She also told me that she was embarrassed about her culture and for speaking Spanish. She is tired of being a translator for her mother and siblings. Her dream was to be recognized as an American because being an American is beautiful, and nobody was going to make jokes or laugh at her. I had to stop everything that I was doing and have a conversation with her. I told her how beautiful she was, and she should be proud of her culture and her native language. She is bilingual, and being able to speak different languages is a unique opportunity. She knows different cultures, and she is from a diverse and beautiful country. She should be proud of herself and her family roots. (Author 711)

In fact, students shared with us their stories of being called by their own teachers, "One more lazy alien in America," and told, "You and your family should go back to your country. Here you are not trying enough. There you can speak your language and have your easy life" (Author 813).

Children and adults who internalize racism believe that they and their community are broken, ugly, inferior, unintelligent, failures, and that they do not deserve success. Monzó (2016) states that "schools, through their policies, practices, and curriculum, highlighted the importance of dominant Euro-American knowledge, values, and beliefs" (p. 161). Current educational practices force students from nondominant ethnicities and languages to assimilate into dominant American culture and ignore their cultural backgrounds, traditions, languages, ethnicities, and family values. This causes conflict between students and parents and also impacts how students value themselves, their relations, and their communities. Bronfenbrenner (1986) explains that students' experiences in schools impact child and parent relationships and the children's self-esteem, critical thinking, performance and development, and future decision-making. We often encountered during the course of our work middle and high school students ashamed of themselves and of their families due to their Latinx appearance and/or because they have a strong accent. These shared stories demonstrate in the classroom institutional racism and acts of microaggressions by both teachers and classmates.

Stereotypes and jokes, such as illegal and lazy immigrants, criminal Mexicans, whore Latinas, terrorist Muslims, are just a few choice insults ELL students hear and internalize. This greatly influences students' learning outcomes; students' sense of belonging; and students' physical, psychological, and emotional health (anxiety, panic attacks, pre, and post-immigration trauma, and depression). In 2019, Sangalang and colleagues conducted research with 3,268 Asian and Latin American migrants, and refugees in the United States. Findings show that discrimination, immigration status, state-based violence, and incurred pre- and post-immigration traumas caused long-term anxiety, psychological distress, and depression disorders for study participants (Sangalang et al., 2019). In our case study, several students preferred to remain silent in order to feel more like a "traditional" student. These same learners explained that they preferred to be "invisible" in the classroom for fear of being misunderstood, disciplined, and judged by their classmates, teachers, and school leaders. One of our team highlighted how ELL students can be ignored and fade into the background:

> Our ELL students are falling between the cracks. A lot of the time, they are quiet, so they do not have behavior issues. And guess what happens with students who do not have behavior issues? Nobody notices them. Do you know why? Because they are not very expressive, and they are quiet. As a teacher who does not have a lot of time or does not understand the struggles faced by ELL students, you end up overlooking them. Sometimes teachers look more to the ones with behavior issues or to the good students because they

are more visible. What happens to our students who are quiet? They end up falling between the cracks. By the time the teacher notices him/her, it is already late, and this student is already struggling or failing. Majority of the time they speak "good" English. Some of them can talk to you in English, but as a teacher from a different discipline, you have no idea what is going on with your ELL student. Several times they already left English as a Second Language (ESOL) courses, but they still do not have the reading, and they end up failing on their tests. When I have a student struggling with English, I always try to understand the culture and language of this student. I try to find ways to help this student, and I adapt the curriculum according to the student's reality. However, I would argue that not everybody does that. Lots of teachers are not going to ask, look, and see what the first language of this student is. Do you know why? Because it is easy to assume that this child does not know. (Author 847)

Acts of care and efforts to understand students' lives, cultural backgrounds, and their individual struggles are fundamental to the support of emergent multilingual students born in different countries with different cultures and ways of thinking. However, the American educational system is not prepared to appreciate the stories of ELL students or remove language barriers, embrace students' accents, and bolster their vocabularies; it is easier to ignore these students and fit them into boxes and labels than to understand influential factors of their educational processes and emotional and psychological development.

A SYSTEM THAT SETS (ENGLISH) LANGUAGE LEARNERS UP TO FAIL

A Latinx student in our study arrived recently in the United States with little proficiency in English but was still required to take a standardized assessment test in English without extra time or a translator. One of our team shared their observations:

> Our educational system set up immigrant children for failure. How can you expect this child to really perform in standardized testing if they are forced to take a test in a language that they cannot understand, without a translator, extra-time, or a dictionary? Sometimes they can use a dictionary, but in many cases, this same student can speak fluent Spanish because that is his/her first language at home, but they cannot read in Spanish because they did not learn how to write and read in their first language. Several times we also have students from other countries besides Latin America, and we do not know how to communicate with them, and we do not have professionals prepared to attend their needs. (Author 524)

Our colleague's report shows a lack of resources and trained professionals coupled with enforced standardized testing, and counterintuitive educational policies fail the students and undervalue teachers' work. This was a common concern across our team's conversations about policies and policy impact on the lives of immigrant students in both the short and long term. State assessments are used to predict negative future outcomes, such as decreased chances of college acceptance, low economic status, incarceration, and early pregnancy. A lack of adequate educational provisions ensures a majority of multilingual emergent students will fail exams and therefore fail to graduate. Low assessment scores affect future opportunities, such as college, scholarship, work, and so on.

Standardization of education in the United States is biased and promotes negative impacts on most student experiences; it also restricts and undervalues teachers' abilities to innovate and explore powerful methods, means, and modes for instruction and personalization of learning. According to Kim and Wiehe-Beck (2016), standardization of English language arts, literacy, and mathematics affect the learning process of K–12 students and their behavior in the classroom. ELL programs can ignore the individual needs of students and suppress parts of student's identities, influencing how they communicate and how they feel about their native language. Cortez, an ELL student in California, was diagnosed in kindergarten with expressive language disorder due to difficulties in English reading and writing (Srikrishnan, 2019). For many years, Cortez's single father, who was also an English learner, did not know that his daughter was labeled from K through 12th grade as a student with learning disabilities (Srikrishnan, 2019). Theoretically, Cortez graduated high school ready to apply for her dream job in technical training. However, instead of receiving a high school diploma, Cortez received a certificate of lesser qualification, meaning she was not seen as a capable student (Srikrishnan, 2019). As a result, Cortez was not allowed to apply for her technical training. Not only did this impact Cortez's emotions, but it also undermined her personal purpose and self-confidence.

Per Muñoz (2020), schools in non-White, low-income communities with high numbers of Black and Latinx students, intentionally prepare students for low-skilled jobs. Very often, these schools employ English-only instructors and lack multilingual professionals who understand students' cultural backgrounds. These schools lack enough resources to motivate the engagement of students in creative and critical thinking. Excessive policing and restrictions cause fear and repression in students. This is a strategy to make students assimilate English and American culture and encourage them to forget or be ashamed of their ethnic roots, or suffer limited access and opportunities. McLaren (2009, 2012) calls this action a *culture killing* rooted in a Eurocentric curriculum that engineers the invisibility, the silence, and the alienation of people of color.

Concerned about how language, race, and identity influence emergent multilingual learners, Crump (2014) proposed a theoretical framework known as critical language and race theory (LangCrit) as a means to understand how "race, racism, and racialization intersect with issues of language, belonging, and identity" (pp. 207–208). Through LangCrit lenses, we can see how power relations and social exclusion happen in educational settings via language and how acts of racism and White nativism are reflected through language. Enforcing English in schools where a significant number of students are English learners is a form of oppression through which White norms are imposed by teaching ELL children to forget and/or reject their own language and cultural background. As described in aforementioned stories, the more the public school system values English-only, the more K–12 students will feel embarrassed about who they are. Matsuda (1991) writes:

> Your accent carries the story of who you are—who first held you and talked to you when you were a child, where you have lived, your age, the schools you attended, the languages you know, your ethnicity, whom you admire, your loyalties, your profession, your class position: traces of your life and identity are woven into your pronunciation, your phrasing, your choice of words. Your self is inseparable from your accent. Someone who tells you they don't like you the way you speak is quite telling you that they don't like you. (p. 1329)

Currently, the U.S. public education system focuses on White-centered public policies and curriculum as well as English-only courses and standardized tests where ELL students are forced to take in English despite language difficulties. Consequently, this system marginalizes and excludes ELL children and their families. More K–12 children are forced to assimilate and speak English only. This directly and indirectly causes English language learners to forget who they are, to forget the stories of their ancestors, to forget their traditions, and cumulatively forget their identities. This results in the sense of emotional, educational, and socioeconomic failure for both the students and their families.

LACK OF TEACHERS AND TRAINING

During our conversation, one of the team shared some of the difficulties faced daily by students, teachers, and school leaders:

> In my school, I only have one teacher fluent in Spanish to help all the Hispanic students of the entire school. I try my best to do what I can to help my students. I am glad we have phones that can help us to translate and communicate with each other. (Author 524)

Inadequate training and lack of bilingual educators who understand the importance of language and culture are just a few of the top issues faced by ELL learners. Statistics show that one out of 10 public school students in the United States is enrolled in ELL programs with poorly trained teachers (Sanchez, 2017).

Walker, Shafer, and Liam in 2004 conducted research with more than 400 teachers from kindergarten through 12th grade about their attitudes towards ELL students. The researcher's findings revealed that more than 68% of teachers were not interested in having ELL students in their classrooms. Approximately 24% of educators declared that it was the responsibility of ELL students to assimilate to the American education system and its culture, and 87% of the teachers did not receive any professional development training to help students from different ethnic and language backgrounds (Walker et al., 2004). Such malfeasant attitudes and practices are in direct opposition to ELL student success. Based on our own experiences in schools, a lack of support and vocational training are critical issues in the American education system. Pew Research Center (2019) projects that by 2050, one in five Americans will be non-English speaking. For this reason, the American government must invest in school reform and professional training if educators, school leaders, and instructional staff are to respond to this population effectively with sensitivity and respect.

In a 2017 podcast, Ruchi Agarwal-Rangnath stated that "our classroom walls, the expectations we set for our students, our body language, how we connect with families, what resources are available, what we choose to say or not say, all give students a clear message about how we feel about them, how we support them, and how we care about them" (Ferlazzo, 2017). Multicultural training is essential to help educators and school leaders become more conscious about how to appropriately and effectively work with ELL students and their families. Furthermore, a flexible curriculum and program will allow educators to more readily adapt to and respect the individualities of each student and the difficulties that they face. The fluid adaptability of educators is fundamental to the demanded assimilation of immigrant children. Such systemic changes can prevent microaggression, acts of xenophobia, and institutional racism, and these changes can potentially ripple across American society.

FINAL THOUGHTS

The stories discussed in this paper are examples of how education policies, English-language assessments, standardizing testing, and a lack of professional training, time, and inclination fails ELL students and sets them up for decreased choices and opportunities in life. The team believes that schools have the potential to be powerful partners within under-served communities that promote healing and recovery of these communities from sociopolitical and economic trauma. Embracing student diversities and challenges as educators is vital if these poorly served students are to see themselves as agents of social transformation not only for themselves and their communities but for the world (Freire, 1970). When ELL students feel recognized and welcomed, their self-esteem improves. Their motivation and engagement increase, and they are more likely to add their voices to the conversations. Teaching immigrant families to share their voices is paramount; the more socially excluded ELL children and families feel, the more likely they to remain marginalized, living in the shadows, feeling socially excluded, all the while suffering sociopolitical and economic traumas. These families often feel invisible, live in poverty, are exploited, and do not have access to basic life supports that counter and mitigate a cycle of poverty, exploitation, criminalization, and deportation.

McVee (2014) argues that empathy is a crucial tool to reduce stereotypes, racism, and microaggressions in schools. Through *currere*, teachers and leaders can help students and families thrive if education policies and practices work to deconstruct systemic value-driven biases and stereotypes, but this work must happen across student skin colors and privileges. Non-ELL students must be taught to think more deliberately about how they treat peers of different cultural backgrounds, and this must be supported with proper training for teachers and school leaders. But again, a dismantling of current institutionalized value-driven biases is required. The education system must also work to end the oppression of teachers and to recognize and value teachers' investments and genius.

Teachers need the flexibility not only to write their own curriculum but also to adjust it to accommodate specific learner individualities. Districts need to develop and implement more trauma-informed training and practices in order to build safer environments for students and families of diverse backgrounds. Students and families from diverse backgrounds are more apt to feel safe and accepted if their stories, struggles, and identities are welcomed and respected as part of the American story. Such acceptance will encourage a safer world in which these students and families may thrive. Policymakers need to rethink policies, pedagogy, curricula, standardization, and the corporatization of the American education system.

ACKNOWLEDGMENTS

The first author of this article expresses deep and abiding appreciation for the wonderful mentorship of Dr. Vonzell Agosto and the support of Trace

Taylor, founder of Community Leveraged Learning. We could not have done this project without your support.

REFERENCES

Amanti, C. (2019). The (invisible) work of dual language bilingual education teachers. *Bilingual Research Journal, 42*(4), 455–470.

Bronfenbrenner, U. (1986). Ecology of the family as a context for human development: Research perspectives. *Development Psychology, 22*(6), 723–742.

Capps, R., Castañeda, R. M., Chaundry, A., & Santos, R. (2007). *Paying the price: The impact of immigration raids on America's children.* Retrieved from https://www.urban.org/sites/default/files/publication/46811/411566-Paying-the-Price-The-Impact-of-Immigration-Raids-on-America-s-Children.PDF

Crawford, E. R. (2017). The ethnic of community and incorporating undocumented immigrant concerns into ethical school leadership. *Educational Administration Quarterly, 53*(2), 147–179.

Crenshaw, K. (1991). Mapping the margins: Intersectionality, identity, and violence against women of color. *Stanford Law Review, 43*(6), 1241–1300.

Crenshaw, K. (1989). Demarginalizing the intersection of race and sex: A black feminist critique of antidiscrimination doctrine, feminist theory, and antiracist politics. *University of Chicago Legal Forum, 140,* 139–167.

Crump, A. (2014). Introducing langcrit: critical language and race theory. *Critical Inquiry in Language Studies, 11*(3). 207–224.

Department of Education. (2018). *The biennial report to congress on the implementation of the title III state formula grant program – school years 2012–2014.* Retrieved from https://ncela.ed.gov/files/uploads/3/BiennialReportToCongress.pdf

Ferlazzo, L. (2017, September 23). Response: Approach race & implicit bias by "listening to students." *Education Week Teacher.* https://blogs.edweek.org/teachers/classroom_qa_with_larry_ferlazzo/2017/09/response_approach_race_implicit_bias_by_listening_to_students.html

Freire, P. (1970). *Pedagogy of the oppressed.* New York, NY: Continuum International.

Kim, J., & Wiehe-Beck, A. (2016). Understanding "the other" through art: fostering narrative imagination in elementary students. *International Journal of Education & the Arts, 17*(2).

López, M. P. (2010). *Persistent inequality: Contemporary realities in the education of undocumented Latina/o students.* New York, NY: Routledge.

Matsuda, M. (1991). Voices of America: Accent, antidiscrimination law, and a jurisprudence for the last reconstruction. *The Yale Law Journal, 100,* 1329–1407.

McLaren, P. (2009). Being, becoming and breaking-free: Peter McLaren and the pedagogy of liberation. *Teoría de la Educación, Educación y Cultura en la Sociedad de la Información, 10,* 256–281.

McLaren, P. (2012). Objection sustained: Revolutionary pedagogical practice as an occupying force. *Policy Futures in Education, 10*(4), 487–495.

McVee, M. (2014). "Some are way left, like this guy, Gloria Lanson-Billings": Resistance, conflict, and perspective taking in teachers: Discussion of multicultural education. *American Psychological Association, 20*(4), 536–551.

Monzó, L. (2016). "They don't know anything!" Latinx immigrant students appropriating the oppressors' voice. *Anthropology & Education Quarterly, 47*(2), 148–166.

Muñoz, J. (2020). Assault on Mexican American collective memory, 2010–2015: Swimming with sharks. *Journal of Latinos in Education, 19*(1), 101–103.

National Center for Education Statistics. (2020). *The condition of education: English language learners in public schools.* Retrieved from https://nces.ed.gov/programs/coe/indicator_cgf.asp

Pew Research Center. (2019). *U.S. population projections: 2005–2050.* Retrieved from https://www.pewresearch.org/hispanic/2008/02/11/us-population-projections-2005-2050/

Pinar, W. F. (1994). The method of *currere. Counterpoints, 2,* 19–27. (Original work published in 1975)

Pinar, W. (2004). *What is curriculum theory?* Oxfordshire, England: Taylor & Francis.

Sanchez, C. (2017, February 23). English language learners: How your state is doing. *NPR.* Retrieved from https://www.npr.org/sections/ed/2017/02/23/512451228/5-million-english-language-learners-a-vast-pool-of-talent-at-risk

Sangalang, C, Becerra, D., Mitchel, F. M., Lechuga-Penã, S., Lopez, K., & Kim., I. (2019). Trauma, post-immigration stress, and mental health: A comparative analysis of refugees and immigrants in the United States. *Journal of Immigrant and Minority Health, 21*(5) 909–919.

Srikrishnan, M. (2019, February 5). Labeled disable at an early age, a former student looks back with regret. *Voice of San Diego.* Retrieved from https://www.voiceofsandiego.org/topics/education/labeled-disabled-at-an-early-age-a-former-student-looks-back-with-regret/

Southern Poverty Law Center. (2019). *Hate at school: Special report.* Retrieved from https://www.splcenter.org/sites/default/files/tt_2019_hate_at_school_report_final_0.pdf

Walker, A., Shafer, J., & Liam, M. (2004). "Not in my classroom": Teacher attitudes towards English language learners in the mainstream classroom. *National Association for Bilingual Education Journal of Research and Practice, 2*(1), 130–160.

Yosso, T. J. (2002). Toward a critical race curriculum. *Equity & Excellence in Education, 35*(2), 93–107.

CHAPTER 13

INTENTIONAL CAREGIVING THROUGH LOVE AND CARIÑO

Mixed Status Families Responding to Issues of ICE and Im/migration

Larisa Callaway-Cole
Oklahoma State University

ABSTRACT

This chapter will explore the child-rearing practices of multigenerational mixed-status Mexican-American families and the ways in which these families used *cariño*, or love and care, to resist oppressive politics, specifically in regard to im/migration and Immigration and Customs Enforcement (ICE). These family stories, collected through a *plática*-based methodology, offer perspectives into the ways in which families protect and care for their children, although often through very different modalities. The following themes characterize the findings: influences on mothering and caregiving, children's awareness of ICE and im/migration, the importance of togetherness and living life in resistance to current politics, and the dynamic nature of cariño. Examining the strengths of family child-rearing using a culturally relevant lens, like cariño, situates families as expert knowers and carers in the face of political trauma.

Making a Spectacle, pages 141–154
Copyright © 2021 by Information Age Publishing
All rights of reproduction in any form reserved.

Hateful and divisive discourse has become pervasive in the United States regarding im/migration, race, sexual orientation, religion, gender, and socioeconomic status. Further, contemporary alt-right politics have both contributed to and promoted this hatefulness through dialogue, policies, and actions aimed at marginalized populations, especially since the 2016 U.S. presidential election. While the politics of oppression are not new (Ali, 2017; Negrón-Gonzales, 2017; Shirazi, 2017), there has been a resurgence of targeted hate on children and families. When facing the concerns and fears of our sociopolitical climate, families are exposed to political trauma (Alford, 2016). Trauma specifically affects children and families who have faced migration, especially those who faced forced migration (Wiese, 2010). In understanding the process of acculturation, where families build connections between their home culture and the new one they have entered into, it can take a significant amount of time to heal throughout this prolonged exposure and processing of new culture (Wiese, 2010). Migration can invoke trauma even if not forced, but chosen, due to the multiplicity of sociocultural contexts that im/migrants live in and navigate through (de Haan, 2012). It cannot be overlooked that one of the most important things to support children through trauma is unconditional love (Pizzolongo & Hunter, 2011). Through this love and care, children's resilience may be built to sustain them in contexts of stress and uncertainty.

Focusing specifically on issues related to im/migration and Immigration and ICE in the United States, this research considered the ways in which two multigenerational mixed-status Mexican American families are adapting and coping with their sociopolitical realities. I sought to understand how families' love shaped their familial and community relationships and how those relationships shaped their loving caregiving. Further, I hoped to gain an understanding of resistance and transformation demonstrated in the Latinx community as families moved through the current challenges of our sociopolitical context. Documenting and highlighting the stories of marginalized families is imperative in a culture of silence and erasure. The stories told by co-collaborators in this study are situated in their truth, understanding, and lived experience. This chapter will focus on the stories of these expert caregivers' loving resistance in the face of political trauma.

ROOTS OF STORYING AND LOVE

Theoretically, this research is foremost situated in the power of story. Drawing from critical raced-gendered epistemologies (Delgado Bernal, 2002; Fierros & Delgado Bernal, 2016), including critical race theory (CRT) and Latino critical race theory (LatCrit), the power of story is addressed through the use of counter-narrative, stories entrenched in "naming one's own reality" and "voice" (Ladson-Billings & Tate, 1995, p. 56). The need for counter-narrative comes from the perpetuation of dominant discourse, about marginalized people and a one-dimensional perspective of who they are (Moss, 2015). Story, and storying, focuses on the telling and re/telling of stories, the living and reliving of those stories. Stories are fluid and constantly in motion as we interact with them. Stories are not fixed, historical accounts, but alive and part of our humanness (Phillips & Bunda, 2018). When shifting the focus of counter-stories from "matters of fact" to "matters of concern" (Latour, 2004), we begin to draw upon the complexities of meaning-making and contextually driven relationships. Doing so helps to complicate stories about people (Fujimoto, 2013), reinforcing a rich and diverse framework for multiple ways of knowing and being in this world.

Love is a powerful element in the face of oppression. Love is relational (Noddings, 2012), requiring significant contributions from all engaged in the relationship. Because love cannot be commodified or transposed, and therefore exists outside of the capitalistic and neoliberal frameworks of our society (Hinton, 2015; Lynch, 1989), it cannot be bought or undone. This is especially significant in the context of the love that exists among marginalized families and communities. Focusing on the relationships among Mexican-American families and their caregiving practices, I examined many cultural values and sites of value transmission that exist among Latinx families including *respeto, familismo, convivimiento, bien educado, dichos, conversaciones,* and *consejos.* Ultimately, these values add up to an all-encompassing value of cariño, or love and care, for their children.

A definition of love cannot be static (Lanas & Zembylas, 2015) because it is constantly in flux, working in countless ways to connect people. Engaging in loving relationships with those close to us helps to extend that love to strangers and develop community (hooks, 2001). To help understand how love challenges oppression, Freire (1970) offered:

> Because love is an act of courage, not of fear, love is a commitment to others. No matter where the oppressed are found, the act of love is a commitment to their cause—the cause of liberation. And this commitment, because it is loving, is dialogical. As an act of bravery, love cannot be sentimental; as an act of freedom, it must not serve as a pretext for manipulation. It must generate other acts of freedom; otherwise it is not love. Only by abolishing the situation of oppression is it possible to restore the love which that situation made impossible. If I do not love the world—if I do not love life—if I do not love people—I cannot enter into dialogue. (p. 78)

This dialogic process of interaction is central to critical theory and calls on us to act with love in undoing oppression. The bravery required takes strength and a commitment to action; with action, love is critical. In the face of political oppression, this dialogic process is crucial in families' survival and ability to thrive in raising their children. This dialogic process situates caregivers in a position of liberatory praxis through the education and child-rearing decisions they make on a daily basis to support their children's development within the family and the community.

Love also has the potential to unite and strengthen relationships as an act of resistance. hooks (2001) asserted that fear is used as a compliance strategy to ensure obedience. She noted that this fear promotes sameness and withdrawal from the unknown, and those different from ourselves. This strategy has been used in a variety of ways by our national governance through the murder of im/migrants (Chavez, 2018), and the separation of children from their parents at the U.S./Mexico border (Miroff, 2018). When we move against fear and instead choose love, hooks (2001) argued that this "choice to love is a choice to connect—to find ourselves in the other" (p. 93). This love does not necessarily rid us of our fears but helps one to live in love and to know they are not alone (hooks, 2001). When living through love, families find themselves in positions of strength and power. This love has the ability to shape their relationships within their families but also in the larger community.

OUR RELATIONAL WAY OF BEING

My relationships with migrant and mixed-status families began long before this research endeavor. Many years ago, I had the opportunity to design culturally relevant curriculum design for migrant preschoolers and their families. My early childhood teaching experience involved working with families who recently migrated to the United States. Most recently, I have been engaged with a nonprofit advancing the needs of our local indigenous community and teaching many first generation-going university students.

The family conversations I had between me and co-collaborators were situated in a plática methodology (Fierros & Delgado Bernal, 2016) and a loving-relational methodology (Laura, 2013, 2016). Employing a loving-relational methodology helped to focus both my theoretical perspectives with my personal and ontological concerns, focusing deeply on the preservation of my existing relationships with co-collaborators in this research. It was clear to me throughout my study that the relationships between myself and co-collaborators came first, and through these historical relationships and trusting contexts, the stories and conversations collected would enhance the intentionality of the research and subsequent findings.

A plática methodology focused on conversational, shared data collection. Together we were co-collaborating and co-researching, in dialogue about lived experiences and knowledge that were shared, theorized, and (re)constructed (Fierros & Delgado Bernal, 2016). Pláticas required me to be honest and willing to share my thoughts and ideas alongside those of my co-collaborators and deeply process all conversations and stories shared as data. Because of this, all conversations were valued equally in data collection and data analysis. Whether these were conversations over dinner or picking children up from school, or when a recorder sat between us, all conversations were perceived as fundamentally important to the research project. Often, in more Westernized semi-structured interviews, many researchers engage in pláticas to gain entrée with an interviewee in order to then answer their interview questions. A plática methodology, on the other hand, is not a warm-up to a Western way of orienting methodologically or method of collecting data. Instead, the plática discusses lived experience and recognizes this as an imperative part of the research conversation, not as extraneous.

Using a plática methodology was particularly important for situating this research because it is relational. Centering this entire project around relational trust and ways of knowing honors the relationships I have with the co-collaborators and my desire to engage in dialogic processes (Freire, 1970). A plática methodology also engages the preservation of storying and the development of stories over time through unstructured conversation. Lastly, and most importantly, a plática methodology honors cultural ways of knowing and communicating shared in these family households—they are platicando within their households already.

This research project occurred over the course of 5 months in the family homes of two Mexican American women who had studied with me prior at the university where I teach. Both families live in neighboring towns in an agricultural and urban county of Southern California. Both women are raising young children and are also trained in early childhood education. Throughout my time in their homes, I spoke with six family members. In the Díaz/Martinez family home, I spoke with Sarita,[1] her husband Cesar, and Sarita's mother Elena. In the Puentes family home, I spoke with Angela, her mother Miriam, and her uncle Ben. The families and I engaged both inside and outside their homes, with field notes being taken of outside activities like outings to school, church, or birthday parties. Conversations were recorded in the homes, later transcribed in the language they were spoken (English or Spanish), and then coded for emergent themes and relationships among stories.

Sarita and Angela were former students, and I had established strong relationships with them. These relationships were both characterized by depth and shared mutual trust. Sarita and I have known each other for 10 years now. She was my cooperating teacher when I was a student teacher in my undergraduate program. Having that shared history is quite special and helped our relationship grow more as she studied with me at the university while she completed her bachelor's degree. Her children had visited my office, and I had met her mother before I even invited her to engage in this work with me. I met Angela when she entered my university classroom. Not long after, initial conversations began at the White House about ending the Deferred Action for Childhood Arrivals (DACA) program. In class, we discussed this news, and I shared a poem written by a young child reinforcing my values around migration and the respect and care that should be given to all people, a value that translated to safe spaces in our classroom. After class, Angela told me she is undocumented and that my discussion helped her feel safe sharing with me. In later semesters, she shared more about her migration story and we became close. These relationships continued to grow throughout the research process and our engagement together. These are relationships that continue. There is no researcher/participant contrast. I valued their input on the project and its directions and still do. These are "my people" (Laura, 2013, p. 291), people who exist for me outside the space of our research and also within.

STORIES OF LOVE AND CARIÑO

These findings are drawn from a larger study about families' child-rearing practices in resistance to ICE and im/migration rhetoric, and experience in the United States, particularly Southern California. The presentation of these stories is rooted in my commitment to counter-story and positioning the voices of my co-collaborators as creators and constructors of knowledge. These counter-stories present a strengths-based and intersectional lens regarding lived experience and conceptualizing the layered and entangled relationships among family members, with me in co-collaboration, and within the broader scope of the community. Focusing on the ways in which families intentionally parented with love at the center of their resistance, the following themes emerged: influences on mothering and caregiving, children's awareness of ICE and im/migration, the importance of togetherness and living life in resistance to current politics, and the dynamic nature of cariño.

Influences on Mothering and Caregiving

Both Sarita and Angela's family histories are characterized by the sacrifices made by their mothers and their initial migrations to California from Mexico. Sarita's mother, Elena, migrated to California before she was born. Angela made this migration herself as an adolescent. Both women described the strength of their mothers in relation to who they are today.

In the Puentes household, Angela faced the experience of her mom needing to leave their Mexican state of Hidalgo to go to other Mexican states in search of work. Later, when Angela was 6 years old, Angela's mother Miriam migrated to California alone in order to work and support herself and her family living in Mexico:

> My mom decided, you know what, I need money, my kids need clothes, they need food, and they need a nice future. I remember waking up one day and she wasn't there anymore. Because she had actually left, [and] she couldn't say goodbye. I just remember my aunt telling me, "Oh, your mom says that she loves you and she'll be in touch with you," but I had no idea where she had gone. When they say *el otro lado*, I was like, "*el otro lado*, what does that even mean?" I didn't even know there was another world besides where I actually lived.

Miriam's move changed Angela's relationship with her mother because her uncle and grandma cared for her in Mexico for the next several years. She faced challenges reuniting with her mother when she later migrated to California as a teenager. Later Angela acknowledged the sacrifices her mother made in retrospect, something which was easier for her to do once she was a mother herself:

> She always felt guilty, "It's my fault I left you. I should have been there." But now that I'm a mom, I [realize that I] was stupid. I never should have made her feel bad. She did what she had to do. She sacrificed time to be with us so that she could provide a better future. I wouldn't be here [without her]. I wouldn't have a degree, and I'm the only one in our family to have a degree. [I wouldn't] be bilingual. [I wouldn't be able] to actually work here if it wasn't for everything that she did. It puts things in perspective.

Sarita described her sister Mariana's experiences as a young girl, which were different from Sarita's experiences, particularly because they are 13 years apart and because Mariana made the migration from Mexico to California as a young child with their mother Elena. Sarita highlighted the experiences that characterized Mariana's early childhood:

> [My sister, Mariana] was born in Mexico but she was raised here. My mom was working in the fields and I wasn't born yet. She had nobody to watch my sister, so she left her living with my aunt and uncle here in Oxnard. That's where my sister has a lot of resentment against my mom. My mom says she had to [leave her with our aunt and uncle] because she didn't want to wake her up and take her to the babysitter. It was better to just leave her with [our] aunt and uncle and they would just take her to school with the other children. It was easier for my mom. But my uncle had a different punishment style and would punish them really bad and hit them with the belt. That's what Mariana remembers the most. My mom said, "It wasn't because I didn't love you. It's because I had to work to provide for you." She left her for a year or two with

my aunt and uncle then went and got her. My mom and sister lived together when she was older and could take the bus by herself.

Mariana's experiences highlight the challenges faced by the separation of a child from their caregiver. While Elena worked to provide for her family, she had to make sacrifices, which ultimately affected her relationships with her children. While some experiences were negative, Sarita noted that she draws much of her strength from her mother, who she described as being very independent. She highlighted cultural clashes between her and her husband when it comes to marital obligations and roles, especially surrounding household responsibilities. Sarita acknowledged Elena's life, and what she learned from being raised by a single mom:

> With my mom, she's never had a husband until now, and I was raised like that. I saw my mom always being independent and working, and not relying on anyone to pay bills. That's how I was raised. It's like, I have to pay my bills. I'll take the car, the bus, or walk, but I'm going to get there.

These stories of strength, perseverance, and love are demonstrated through caregiving and the sacrifices made by Sarita and Angela's mothers and the impact of these experiences on the caregiving practices and values of both women. Among all family members, there are multiple layers of complexity in their stories of raising children, especially through migrations. These influential relationships with their own mothers directly influence the ways that they show love to their own children.

Children's Awareness of ICE and Im/migration

Together we discussed the level of awareness children generally have in regard to what they hear going on regarding ICE and im/migration in their communities. Both Miriam and Ben argued that children do know what is going on, whether it impacts them directly or not. They said that children are seeing these events unfold on the news, on television, and through smartphone use. Miriam and Ben discussed the fact that children see videos on the internet, like issues regarding the migrant families on the border. Angela argued that she did not think Miguel knew or understood much about im/migration and deportation issues, but her mother Miriam insisted that he did gesturing toward the couch across the room where Miguel was sitting. It seemed implied that if children hear us discussing these topics, then we are making it known to them. However, Angela noted her desire to protect Miguel, for him to not have to understand these issues and not have to worry. She also discussed the concerns of children who are more aware of their family's status due to possible experiences or knowledges of detention and deportation. For example, Sarita recalled her son, Frankie's experiences since Trump's election and his worries:

> When Trump came in and said, "We're going to deport everybody," I think because of [Frankie's] experience, it upset him. He doesn't remember a lot, but he does remember his father got deported. He would come home and cry and say, "My friend so-and-so is scared that they're going to take the mom or the dad, and some kid says they're going to take both of their parents." And he would cry for them because he already went through it. I think as a child, he was really scared. He was scared for his friends and his family.

Frankie's concern for his friends and family exists in spaces unknown, our lack of knowledge of what could happen, or what will happen. This lack of knowing, and wondering consumes Angela too, as she wonders about what will happen for herself as she awaits information about an adjustment of status and the desire to protect Miguel from holding the burden of knowing:

> But one thing that I do worry about is when I have to go out and do my interview for my residency. If I leave and they say, "You have to stay longer." Because maybe Trump will decide you have to do the process outside of the U.S. What's going to happen to [Miguel]? Am I going to have to leave him here? I don't want to leave my kid. My mom did that for me, and it sucked. And I don't want to do that to him. It's that kind of fear. But I don't think [Miguel] understands right now. But I never really talk to him about it. I'm pretty sure if I did, he would still be kind of like, "Well, what does that mean?" I think I want to protect him from that right now. I don't think I would want to bring it up.

Children's awareness in both Sarita's and Angela's family homes are very different. These differences have to do with the experiences each family has had with migration and status and the ways in which they discuss these issues with their children.

Being Together and Living Life

Angela discussed the importance of having family close together. She hoped that her mom, Miriam, would be moving back to Ventura to live with her and Miguel soon:

> I think once [my mom] moves back it will be better for her because she'll feel that at least if anything happens, at least we're together. But I think just staying together [is a form of resistance] and [being] how we've always been, you know? Because it's always been the "what if?" type of situation [regarding

legal status]. So, we don't focus much on it so it doesn't get to us. Because otherwise we would be afraid to even go to the store.

Angela's sentiments about not living in fear, lest it consume your daily life, is reflective of her desire to be resistant by continuing to live her life in the way she always has.

Sarita was very engaged around the topic of spending time with her children. She was adamant about the importance of giving children your time and being together as a family. Sarita expressed,

I try to spend more time with them because anything can happen. It was like that, too, with my step-dad because he recently got his green card. I want [the children] to have memories and cherish the time that they spend with [their grandparents], or more with my husband now. Sarita and her family are resistant to the current threat of deportation policies by ensuring that the time her family has together is well spent. Sarita ensures that they are close and together and that she does things with the children, building and sustaining their relationships through meaningful interactions.

Dynamic Nature of Cariño

Love and cariño are embodied in family values that are part of daily life in both households. It is important to note that love is dynamic. It evolves and shifts. It does not always look the same way for each family, or even the same way that a family member cares for each child.

When it comes to sociopolitical context, Angela noted her desire to protect Miguel, for him to not have to understand these issues and not have to worry:

I don't think [Miguel] understands. But I don't even think I want him to understand especially with everything going on. All the bullying and stereotyping of people. It's not something I want him to be aware of.

For Sarita and her family, transparency is key in helping their children understand their family circumstances. Sarita tells her children the reasons that it is important they keep the door closed and locked at home so that their dad is protected if ICE were to come to the door. The children, including the 5- and 6-year-olds, are very aware of Trump's feelings toward Mexicans, and how that sentiment extends to their father. Sarita recalled the discussions she has had with the children about what they would do if Cesar was deported:

I [told the children], "Yes. We're going to be sad. Daddy won't be here, but we're going to see how we can manage." And we've talked about it. Like I said, I've told him, "I would not go with my children [to Mexico] at this moment because this is all they know. They know the United States, California, Oxnard. This is all they know. And I would not take them to a new place." He says he agrees with that because he knows that they are going to be okay with me. But I do know that I [would find ways for the children to see their dad and be with him].

MEANING MAKING

It can be argued that stories contribute to our humanity, to our humanness (Phillips & Bunda, 2018). Stories have a way of exposing our entangled ways of knowing and being, the knowledges and insights of a person or family. These stories are passed down, from generation to generation, sustaining our cultures. (Re)turning to story allows us to build connections among one another and think deeply about shared human experiences, for example, the experience of raising young children. Within this project, the stories of these families are presented through the voices of co-collaborators. The gaze with which I viewed these families was one of strength, engagement, and love and looked *with* the families at the present circumstances of our sociopolitical context. Their humanity must be valued (Jaramillo, 2012), especially in the face of surviving and caring for their children in the face of political trauma. These stories of raising families further support the shared connections of humanness and the realities of lived experience.

The importance of stories presents itself throughout this study but is particularly amplified through the voices of co-collaborators and through their (re)telling of various aspects of their lives and stories of their communities. For example, during my first plátcia with Angela, she discussed her family members who passed away in Mexico soon after her arrival in the United States. This (re)telling of her story was heart-wrenching, with tears flowing down her cheeks. I later cried listening to the recordings while transcribing, feeling her pain. That afternoon before I left Angela's house, I asked her if she was okay and if it was okay to talk about those details of her life. She said yes, and that talking about them made her feel better, that she does not have an opportunity to talk about it much. This alludes to the power of story, the possibility to listen, and (re)listen, the opportunity for each time you tell a story for it to bring you closer to yourself (Cisneros, 2015).

Understanding the dynamic interpretations of love and cariño allows us to focus on the ways that families raise their children in response to their contexts, both individually and collectively. For example, Sarita pays careful attention to her son Frankie because of the trauma he faced when his father was deported. Frankie struggled psychologically, lost his speech, and became emotionally unregulated. Sarita had to find resources herself to support him and keep him safe. Because of this, she is firmer with him sometimes, and it comes from a place of love, like when she makes him sit down to do his homework right away after getting home. Angela shared so much love for her new niece as if she were her own child. She is so proud of the man her brother has become and thrilled that he has a family of his own, an extension of her own.

Love is not the same for each family because every family's context is going to be embedded with different values or interpretations of those values. Sarita shares important information with her children to show care, to protect, and to educate them. This honors the dialogic process that is loving relationality (Freire, 1970). By sharing information about their family's mixed status, she helps the children become informed advocates within their own household, allowing them to take action to protect their family and also advocate for other children they find themselves in relation with at school. Angela keeps things from Miguel in hopes of not having to burden him with adult worries. While Angela's approach is not dialogic with Miguel, it is with her trusted family and friends. She discusses with them ways to protect Miguel from growing up too quickly as she faced in her own childhood. This dialogic process also honors action on behalf of her son. Both approaches to caring for their children through challenging sociopolitical contexts honor the ways in which they love their families.

As the similarities, differences, and complexities of these stories show, it is crucial that early educators take the time to get to know their families and engage them in meaningful relationships. Sarita was particularly engaged around this topic, noting the importance of early educators being very aware of their communities and their families, then using this knowledge to support them. She gave the example of helping a family member in her classroom know about ways in which she could access financial resources such as the Supplemental Nutrition Assistance Program (SNAP) or CalWorks. She also discussed support for knowing information about how parents could attend college, how they could access childcare services, and most important to Sarita, what types of services were available for mental health, should families need help for their children or themselves. This desire to be in community and share knowledge with others particularly honors connection making and living in community with others to support loving relations (hooks, 2001).

Utilizing love as a framework for examining family strengths and approaches to child-rearing offers a unique perspective to interpret love as a cultural way of knowing and being and acknowledges the ways in which the culture and spirit of love guide child families in raising their children. Through the development of counter-stories, we can more deeply understand the complexity of caregiving and loving and honor the many ways there are to raise children. Examining the strengths in family child-rearing using a culturally relevant lens has the potential to contribute to a growing body of literature that situates families as expert knowers and carers.

NOTE

1. All collaborator names have been changed to protect their identities.

REFERENCES

Alford, C. F. (2016). Trauma is political. In *Trauma, Culture, and PTSD*. New York, NY: Palgrave Macmillan.

Ali, A. I. (2017). Trumpal fears, anthropological possibilities, and Muslim futures. *Anthropology and Education Quarterly*, *48*(4), 386–392. https://doi.org/10.1111/aeq.12219

Chavez, N. (2018, May 30). She came to the U.S. for a better life. Shortly after her arrival, she was killed. *CNN*. Retrieved from https://www.cnn.com/2018/05/27/us/texas-border-patrol-shooting-victim/index.html

Cisneros, S. (2015). *A house of my own*. New York, NY: Knopf.

de Haan, M. (2012). The reconstruction of parenting after migration: A perspective from cultural translation. *Human Development*, *54*(6), 376–399. https://doi.org/10.1159/000334119

Delgado Bernal, D. (2002). Critical race theory, Latino critical theory, and critical race-gendered epistemologies: Recognizing students of color as holders and creators of knowledge. *Qualitative Inquiry*, *8*(1), 105–127. https://doi.org/10.1177/107780040200800107

Fierros, C. O., & Delgado Bernal, D. (2016). Vamos a platicar: The contours of pláticas as Chicana/Latina feminist methodology. *Chicana/Latina Studies*, *15*(2), 98–121. Retrieved from https://thisbridgecalledcyberspace.net/FILES/3943.pdf

Freire, P. (1970). *Pedagogy of the oppressed*. New York, NY: Seabury Press.

Fujimoto, M. O. (2013). Resisting the dominant narrative: The role of stories in Latina educational success. *Journal of the Association of Mexican American Educators*, *7*(1), 28–47. Retrieved from https://journals.coehd.utsa.edu/index.php/AMAE/article/view/127

Hinton, K. A. (2015). Should we use a capital framework to understand culture? Applying cultural capital to communities of color. *Equity and Excellence in Education*, *48*(2), 299–319. https://doi.org/10.1080/10665684.2015.1025616

hooks, b. (2001). *All about love: New visions*. New York, NY: HarperCollins.

Jaramillo, N. E. (2012). *Immigration and the challenge of education: A social drama analysis in South Central Los Angeles*. New York, NY: Palgrave Macmillan.

Ladson-Billings, G., & Tate, W. F., IV. (1995). Toward a critical race theory of education. *Teachers College Record*, *97*(1), 47–68. https://doi.org/10.1080/10282580701850413

Lanas, M., & Zembylas, M. (2015). Towards a transformational political concept of love in critical education. *Studies in Philosophy and Education, 34*(1), 31–44. https://doi.org/10.1007/s11217-014-9424-5

Latour, B. (2004). Why has critique run out of steam? From matters of fact to matters of concern. *Critical Inquiry, 30*(2), 225–248. https://doi.org/10.1086/421123

Laura, C. T. (2013). Intimate inquiry: Love as "data" in qualitative research. *Cultural Studies–CriticalMethodologies, 13*(4), 289–292. https://doi.org/10.1177/153270 8613487875

Laura, C. T. (2016). Intimate inquiry: A love-based approach to qualitative research. *Critical Questions in Education, 7*(3), 215–231. Retrieved from https://eric .ed.gov/?id=EJ1114637

Lynch, K. (1989). Solidary labour: Its nature and marginalisation. *The Sociological Review, 37*(1), 1–14. https://doi.org/10.1111/j.1467-954X.1989.tb00018.x

Miroff, N. (2018, May 29). Trump's 'zero tolerance' at the border is causing child shelters to fill up fast. *The Washington Post.* Retrieved from https://www.washingtonpost .com/world/national-security/trumps-zero-tolerance-at-the-border-is-causing -child-shelters-to-fill-up-fast/2018/05/29/7aab0ae4-636b-11e8-a69c-b944de 66d9e7_story.html?noredirect=on&utm_term=.96ad16ba54d1

Moss, P. (2015). Time for more storytelling. *European Early Childhood Education Research Journal, 23*(1), 1–4. https://doi.org/10.1080/1350293X.2014.991092

Negrón-Gonzales, G. (2017). Political possibilities: Lessons from the undocumented youth movement for resistance to the Trump administration. *Anthropology and Education Quarterly, 48*(4), 420–426. https://doi.org/10.1111/aeq.12223

Noddings, N. (2012). The language of care ethics. *Knowledge Quest, 40*(4), 52–56.

Phillips, L. G., & Bunda, T. (2018). *Researching through, with and as storying.* London, England: Routledge.

Pizzolongo, P., & Hunter, A. (2011). I am safe and secure. *Young Children, 66*(1), 67–69. Retrieved from http://www.the-registry.org/Portals/0/Documents/ Credentials/Leadership/Documents/PromotingResilience_Pizzolongo0311 .pdf

Shirazi, R. (2017). How much of this is new? Thoughts on how we got here, solidarity, and research in the current moment. *Anthropology and Education Quarterly, 48*(4), 354–361. https://doi.org/10.1111/aeq.12222

Wiese, E. B. P. (2010). Culture and migration: Psychological trauma in children and adolescents. *Traumatology, 16*(4), 142–152. https://doi.org/10.1177/15347656 10388304

CHAPTER 14

REFLECTION

A Testimonio of Political Trauma: Coyote Meets His Match

Paul Perez-Jimenez
University of Texas Rio Grande Valley

ABSTRACT

As a testimony recounting a spectacle that includes internalized oppression, this *testimonio* (testimony) details the subalterns' attempt to recover their agency from dehumanizing aggression. Considering that politics is an act of power and that power can easily become aggression therefore oppression means that anyone with or in power must show extreme care. These extremes tend towards a balance. This testimonio attempts to take back some of that power as equity. But, more importantly, it highlights internalized gender oppression. The male Latinx narrator details an aggression experienced by a Latinx couple at a bridge crossing and is made aware of further oppression seen from the Latinx female point of view. While we start the third decade of the 21st century in which oppression has been recognized and rejected, internalized oppression hides its offensive tendencies behind a power struggle within the Latinx community and gender equity. The testimonio concludes that oppression can only be overcome through empathy and love.

Making a Spectacle, pages 155–163

The most striking moment of brutality that I experienced as a member of the Latinx minority involved a situation of internalized oppression that was tinged by misogyny. Padilla (2001) describes the cruelty as a "distress pattern," originating externally and manifested in two forms: "First, upon members of our own group—particularly upon those over whom we have some degree of power or control...Second, upon ourselves through all manner of self-invalidation, self-doubt, isolation, fear, feelings of powerlessness and despair" (p. 62). Moreover, this double whammy configuration constitutes aggression or political trauma (Zembylas, 2008).

In my classroom, I ask students to associate keywords to understand their meaning such as context with background and politics with power. Considering that politics is an act of power and that power easily can become aggression and oppression means that anyone with or in power must show extreme care (Cross, Overall, Low, & McNulty, 2019). These extremes tend towards a balance. This testimonio attempts to take back some of that power as equity. While we start the third decade of the 21st century in which oppression has been recognized and rejected, internalized oppression hides its offensive tendencies behind a power struggle within the Latinx community that has received little attention (Bonilla-Silva, 2015; Padilla, 2001; Pyke, 2007).

Brown-on-Brown oppression is everywhere, in our offices, school, and classrooms. In my 98% Latinx classroom, I have witnessed students berate other students as inferiors, and I must often point it out as unacceptable. What is worse is what Adams, Bell, and Griffin (1997) term, "internalized domination: when members of the agent group [such as Latinx boys or men] accept their group's socially superior status as normal and deserved" (p. 76). Freire (2014) calls "domination the pathology of love" whose cure includes dialogue with the world (p. 89). I can further attest to a firsthand example of this internalized oppression and offer my version of equity as a dialogue with the world through this testimonio.

TESTIMONIO

John Beverley (2008) defines testimonio as a subaltern "narrative told in the first person by a narrator who is also the real protagonist or witness of the events she or he recounts and produced as text by an interlocutor" who is not of the same "subaltern condition" (p. 571). Underscored as an auto-ethnographic lived experience and "reflection involving how it happened, is happening, or may happen," attempts to "integrate emotional, spiritual, and moral parts of [ourselves] with the intellectual and analytical in order to hold on to the personal connection to" and make sense of traumatic oppression (Pensoneau-Conway, Adams, & Bolen, 2017, p. vii; Perez-Jimenez, 2019, p. 3). As the interlocutor, and in contrast to Beverley's definition, this testimonio is my attempt to "more than empathic liberal guilt or political correctness, [this] testimonio seeks to elicit alliance" and in solidarity with my partner, elicit identity and political agency (Beverley, 2008, p. 581). I concur with Reyes and Curry Rodríguez's (2012) version of testimonio "to bring to light a wrong, a point of view, or an urgent call for action" (p. 525).

However, I cannot stress this enough, the aggression was experienced by two and, therefore, different, and I cannot compare my version to my partner's. In solidarity, I can reflect, write, and vocalize the indignation that ironically brought and bound us together. Therefore, the backdrop for this testimonio is a lived love story as the silver lining forged by oppressive circumstances. And, instead of delving into the festering hate of the oppression and losing the freedom to be human, we chose compassion, empathy, and love.

COYOTE

While I recognize the oppression derived from a situation in which I made a real "spectacle" of myself, "the feelings of powerlessness and despair" defined me actively and passively. It pushed me to self-define as mistrusting and fearing authority, and I was defined by it (Perez-Jimenez, 2019). As part of that identity, the title mentions coyote, which works as an allusion on several levels. As to who the coyote is, I leave it up to the reader to decide, but offer a different question: Can every character in this testimonio be the coyote?

As a child of the 1970s and 1980s before online access to unlimited entertainment, Saturdays were reserved for cartoons such as Bugs Bunny, Yosemite Sam, and my favorite, Wile E. Coyote, who excelled at getting into trouble under the most ingenious circumstances. His contriving plans should have worked; however, they were always matched and thwarted by the pragmatic Roadrunner. Wile E. Coyote and the Roadrunner serve as examples of the yin and yang that foreshadow part of this testimonio.

Continuing the motif of the coyote as preying is only a hop skip away from the wolf as the ultimate male power-wielding aggressor that I do not identify with; however, I must mention it in light of the aggression in this testimonio. Yet, in the Latinx community, the coyote has another meaning. The Public Broadcast System's (PBS) *Frontline World* in conjunction with *The New York Times* investigated "the rapidly expanding business of smuggling humans across the U.S. Mexican border" and the "human smugglers, or coyotes, to get illegal migrants into the United States" (Vree, n.d.). Therefore, coyote, as a smuggler who must also setup meticulous plans to accomplish his trafficking task, serves to further the allusion in this testimonio.

PRELUDE TO LOVE

Like most, I prefer the stability of a plan; however, life experiences rarely follow predictions, and sometimes we find that occurrences go beyond anything we could have imagined, let alone predicted. And, they mold our character. This is my testimonio of political trauma that impacted my character and lifelong relationship. It began when I dropped out of college in my sophomore year, seeking to experience the real world. Somewhere along the way, I started that experience working for a customs broker, and in time, it eventually led to working as an expatriate specializing in supply line logistics in manufacturing in Mexico making a good living.

Expats working in Mexico had it good in the late 1980s and 1990s. And, I worked as a purchasing or materials manager for several Fortune 500 companies such as AT&T, GM, TRW, Ametek Aerospace, enjoying the benefits of working as an American out of the country. I was in my early 30s when, again, I returned home. I had just ended a 2-year assignment in Monterrey, Mexico, which had given me a taste for the jet setting crowd in places like Chicago, Los Angeles, Kuala Lumpur, Mexico City, and Singapore. I felt powerful and in control. Too much of a good thing can become tedious, bad; after 2 years, I got tired of that life. And, if anyone ever claims that men do not have a biological clock, they are much mistaken, turning 30 for me triggered that alarm. This life-changing instinct urged me to seek a life-long partner. I knew it was time for me to marry and settle down. I started by returning home to the safe and familiar of home in South Texas.

My plan was rather simple, find a job close to home and find a lifelong partner. My career and experience landed me a job in one of the many twin-plant manufacturers along the border. Eventually, I became aware of and loathed the oppression indirectly inflicted on the locals, and ultimately it bade me change careers (that is a different story). Yet, at that time, somehow, my colleagues understood my readiness to settle down, and I was set up on the only blind date that I ever had with a coworker. However, she worked on the third shift, which started at 11:00 p.m. and ran through 7:00 a.m. As one of 10 Americans in that plant, I worked from 8 a.m. to 5 p.m., so we agreed she would stay an hour later, and I would come in an hour earlier. I have never been early to anything in my life and predict that I will even be late to my own funeral. I was late. She was not happy, but I was eager to make it up. I asked her to a posada Christmas party. However, not before she let me know her feelings. I recall shaking her hand and feeling a grip that sent me to the verge of complaining. She greeted me, saying, "So you're the reason why I have forgone getting home to sleep." And, it sounded so accusatory and derogatory that I turned red with shame. Later, I was to find out that blushing had been my best option along with apologizing and attempting to make it up, and I was eager to try the latter.

We went to the party, and I attempted to show off my new car. Much like a strutting bird showing off what I had. I know I was ostentatious, but I was trying to impress. I recall during dinner, my date asked if I had a girlfriend, and I had just broken up with my third girlfriend from Monterrey, Mexico, and I had pictures of her. I made the mistake of showing the image, which my date simply tore up in front of me and valiantly claimed that I would no longer need it. Although not sure of what that meant, it, along with several margaritas, gave me the courage, and I upped the ante by continuing the party at a nightclub. The border was different back then, and what was known as the red-light district teemed with American tourists eager to spend dollars to party. Three margaritas, two hours of dancing, made one happy go, lucky man. So, I did what anyone in my situation would do—I asked her to be my girlfriend. However, since she did not speak English, I fumbled my Spanish and asked her to be my lover instead. It caused such a turmoil that I had to vouch I was not married, which meant I again had to make it up to her; we decided to go out for breakfast at three in the morning.

THE AGGRESSION

I wanted to further show off by having breakfast at the International House of Pancakes (IHOP) on the American side of the border, which was my second mistake. She quickly pointed out that she could not cross over, for she did not have a passport. I was accustomed to crossing over every day and had become desensitized to any consequence at the customs checkpoint. I told her it was not a problem; I did it all the time. She was to simply reply "Yes" to the question asked, which was usually "Are you a U.S. citizen?" We practiced the word, making sure she did not pronounce it "jez" instead. When we got to the customs checkpoint, the officer asked me if I was a U.S. citizen, and I said yes, and he turned his attention to her, asking, "And you, young lady, what country are you from?" Her voice was confident, and she pronounced "yes" correctly just as we had practiced, but her eyes relayed a doubt that knew we were in trouble. We were led to the custom's offices at four in the morning, and she was placed in an office while I was interrogated out front by a customs officer. The gentleman, I stress the word with sarcasm, for he was far from one, looked at me and cynically declared, "That little piece of ass better have been worth it." I was flabbergasted and attempted to explain I was just trying to show off to my girlfriend and had drunk a bit too much tequila. I tried to explain. The response was sobering, "You better call someone to pick you up because we have impounded your car for attempting to introduce an illegal alien as contraband." I attempted further protest in the last effort to exert a semblance of agency and was blatantly threatened with a cavity search.

Further indignation was reserved for my companion who was categorized as something other than me, as an illegal alien and contraband. But the ultimate indignation identified her as a "little piece of ass," she was branded a sex object. In hindsight, the officer could not have been more abusive, and rather than humanely explaining the circumstances, he was degrading and seemed to take pleasure in humiliating. And, he was a fellow Latino, which made it worse since he appeared to take liberty in demeaning my new girlfriend. Rather than treating us with dignity, we were branded as scum and treated as such. He was in a place of power, and we were experiencing a moment of internalized oppression and domination (Adams et al., 1997, p. 76). However, as an American citizen, I was allowed to stay. My Mexican girlfriend was not even spoken to directly; she was simply one to send back without any explanation. And, even though she was not sure of what was going on or what was said, she held her poise, never lost her composure, and seemed determined not to relinquish her dignity.

At four in the morning outside of the customs offices in Hidalgo, Texas, I called my father but got my mother, and both came to pick up their 30-year-old son after a gullible attempt to smuggle someone into the United States. I felt like a giddy teenager.

YIN AND YANG—COYOTE AND ROADRUNNER LOVE

I often remember the giddy feeling I experienced back then and attempt to explain it to my wife who brushes it off, proving that we are remarkably opposites. She is fearless; I am not. I am patient; she is not. She is street smart; I am book smart. On the day that we announced our engagement, her mother asked me why? "She cannot cook." "I know," I told her. "I can," insinuating that I was not looking for a maid or an incubator for my offspring but an equal partner. My wife and I have discussed this subject on more than one occasion, and we both concur that we sought qualities in a partner that contrast and complement. She loves horror movies, I jump at every scene and prefer science fiction, which she abhors. I am incredibly ticklish, and she is not. She is frugal while money burns a hole in my pocket. I have always known that my potential is infinite, but I can easily get sidetracked. I need someone that does not pull punches to stay on track and motivates me to do the same. Although I am positive, my imagination tends towards pie in the sky. She is down to earth and pragmatic. I am romantic at heart and want to be eulogized while she claims funerals are a waste of flowers and money. In other words, if our friends were pressed to label one of us as a fierce coyote, after they stopped laughing, would all point to my wife.

She has, on several occasions, told me about a story that sends shivers down my spine while she nonchalantly brushes it away. A friend of hers asked her if she knew a good painter since she needed one of her rental houses painted. My wife simply said, "Why? We can do it and save a lot of money." So, they started. The house they were to paint was old and smelly. The backroom had a distinct black soot stain that started halfway up the wall as if a candle had been placed too close to the wall. There may have been some sort of altar set there at some point. My wife set newspapers on the floor of that room while her friend picked up breakfast. My wife placed an open gallon of paint on the paper, which was strategically placed in the middle of that room. She realized that the brushes were in a different room, and she went to get them. When she returned, the newspaper had been crumpled into a ball, and the paint had been taken out of the can and dumped on the floor. It was not poured because the can was clean along the edges. Clearly, something sinister was in that room. I would have had a heart attack and run out screaming like a banshee. Intrigued and curious, she picked up as much of the paint as possible, redistributed the newspaper, and cautiously began to paint. Anyone that does not know her would think that she continued as if nothing happened or that maybe she did not recognize the implications, but on the contrary, she was very much aware. She recognizes fear but can refrain from internalizing it—that is, control and courage. These qualities are some of the main reasons why I asked her to marry me.

BACK TO THE AGGRESSION

Returning to the giddy moment outside the customs offices, as I stood with my father on my left and my mother on my right chastising me for doing something so stupid, I held up my hand in an attempt to explain and point out the young lady that was being released through a side door back to Mexico. My words to my mother have ever endured, and regardless of the dire situation, I happily said, "Mother see that girl over there, I will be marrying her." I think my mother may have inferred some doubt, and my father smiled. He did point out that we could not just have her go back on her own, primarily since *peceras* (buses) did not run at four in the morning and that we should make sure she got back home safe. So, while my father drove and my mother drove shotgun, my newfound girlfriend and I sat quietly in the back seat like two love-smitten teenagers.

POST AGGRESSION

Several days after the incident, during our traditional Christmas party at home, my brother's in-law surprised me with a gag gift—a pair of tighty whities on which the Spanish words *Coyote del Año* (Smuggler of the Year) were written with a black sharpie, referring to another one of my ingenious failed plans.

Although she could easily have chalked up the blind date as a total failure and rejected me as a total nincompoop; she did not. And nine months later, we got married. In hindsight, her poise under pressure in that customs office sealed our fate. Although that customs officer exemplified internal oppression in treating fellow Latinx with disdain, it also occasioned the chance to shine. The trauma, oppression, and insult flung at us by that customs officer never caused her to lose composure. He may have held power over us, but to this day, I have never met anyone else that can remain calm under pressure in that manner.

Soon after, she and I picked up the impounded car and began a life together. Even though she is 13 years my junior, she continues to be my equal life-long partner. Returning to when I met her, she says that my blushing, apologizing, admitting I had done wrong showed compassion and attracted her to me. Most men, according to her, would have stood their ground, and much like the rude customs officer usurp power to say, "So, what of it." They claim control and must manifest it with aggression. And, with this comment, she stresses the difference in the gendered experience of aggression. While I have no doubt, the aggression influenced me as fearful, it also may have impacted my wife as fearless; reactions that accentuate our binary tendency. This underscores that although I declare solidarity, I can never be a true feminist, for I will never know the female experience of that aggression. Where I saw uneducated, barbaric rudeness, she felt controlling domination. And although I cannot directly liberate her from the internalized oppression, I, therefore, focus on the compassion that has freed us from the negative aspects of the aggression. In a final note, this manuscript molds my stance on freedom by emphasizing the act of that love, as Paulo Freire (2014) explained, "Because love is an act of courage, not of fear, love is a commitment to others. No matter where the oppressed are found, the act of love is the commitment to their cause—the cause of liberation" (p. 89). I am convinced the consummate free person is magnanimous and, "losing compassion forfeits the right to freedom" (Perez-Jimenez, 2019, p. 28). Those choosing to live without compassion are bound to justify their choice by antagonizing, and if they hold any authority, it includes wielding it as political trauma.

REFERENCES

Adams, M., Bell, L. A., & Griffin, P. (1997). *Teaching for diversity and social justice: A sourcebook.* Hove, England: Psychology Press.

Beverley, J. (2008). Testimonio, subalternity, and narrative authority. In S. Castro-Klaren (Ed.), *A companion to Latin American literature and culture* (1st ed., pp. 571–583). Malden, MA: Blackwell.

Bonilla-Silva, E. (2015). The structure of racism in color-blind, "post-racial" America. *American Behavioral Scientist, 59*(11), 1358–1376. https://doi.org/10.1177/0002764215586826

Cross, E. J., Overall, N. C., Low, R. S. T., & McNulty, J. K. (2019). An interdependence account of sexism and power: Men's hostile sexism, biased perceptions of low power, and relationship aggression. *Journal of Personality and Social Psychology, 117*(2), 338–363. https://doi.org/10.1037/pspi0000167

Freire, P. (2014), *Pedagogy of the oppressed: 30th anniversary edition.* London, England: Bloomsbury.

Padilla, L. M. (2001). But you're not a dirty Mexican: Internalized oppression, Latinos, & law. *Texas Hispanic Journal of Law and Policy, 59,* 61–113. https://academic.udayton.edu/race/01race/latinos01.htm

Pensoneau-Conway, S. L., Adams, T. E., & Bolen, D. M. (2017). Doing autoethnography. *Doing Autoethnography,* 1–5. https://doi.org/10.1007/978-94-6351-158-2_1

Perez-Jimenez, P. (2019). A critical bricoleur assumes positive intent; Pablito's Problem (Doctoral dissertation). Retrieved from ProQuest Dissertations and Theses Global. (27544028)

Pyke K. D. (2007). Defying the taboo on the study of internalized racial oppression. In E. Elliott, J. Payne, P. Ploesch (Eds.), *Global migration, social change, and cultural transformation* (pp. 101–119). New York, NY: Palgrave Macmillan.

Reyes, K. B., & Curry Rodríguez, J. E. (2012). Testimonio: Origins, terms, and resources. *Equity & Excellence in Education, 45*(3), 525–538.

Vree, M. (n.d.). *The coyote's trail.* Retrieved from https://www.pbs.org/frontlineworld/stories/mexico704/history/coyote.html

Zembylas, M. (2008). The politics of trauma in education. In *The politics of trauma in education* (pp. 35–52). New York, NY: Palgrave Macmillan.

CHAPTER 15

PATRICK STAYS SILENT

East African Refugee Transition in American Education

Michaela Inks
The University of South Florida

ABSTRACT

This chapter examines education policies including the Consent Decree of 1990, No Child Left Behind, and Every Student Succeeds Act in order to critique the models and norms of education they have established in Florida. The goals of these policies were to ensure linguistically diverse students' rights to education in public schools. However, in the context of an increasingly diverse student body, budget cuts due to administrative prioritizations, and the introduction of new educational policies, does the Consent Decree of 1990 maintain its standards of free and equal education for all students? In my research with refugee students from the Democratic Republic of the Congo (DRC), I have found current policies to have negative effects (e.g., mental and social) for Black refugee students with diverse linguistic, cultural, and historical backgrounds. I conduct classroom observation, interviews, employ anthropological and educational theories, and review policies to highlight barriers to graduation among Black refugee students in underfunded schools.

Making a Spectacle, pages 165–177
Copyright © 2021 by Information Age Publishing
All rights of reproduction in any form reserved.

* * *

They lack so much. They lack the background knowledge. A lot of these kids never went to school. Not only the kids from the Congo but my Honduran kids coming in have a level three education, third grade. They are missing so much. They just don't have the basic concepts. They don't have the basic structure in their own language. They don't even have the academic language in their own language to be able to transfer to English. So they lack the skills, the concepts in their own language. It makes it easier if they know the planets and the universe and the constellations. If they know that in their language they can just transfer the knowledge. They don't have that. The biggest thing is the gap in what they know in content compared to our students. (Kline, personal communication, 2019)

My colleagues and I were invited to the local high school to help tutor Swahili speaking students at a local high school because many of them were said to be "lacking" in English and in subject knowledge such as science, math, and language arts. These students are characterized by their age (14–17) and their African refugee status. The purpose of tutoring was to help students complete their schoolwork and practice their English. All the students participated in silent behaviors such as not participating in classrooms, ignoring teacher questions, removing themselves from socializing situations. Mrs. Kline, their teacher who invited us to come tutor, said she was especially concerned for Patrick who could spend the entire school day with his hood up and head down on his desk.

The "lack" that Mrs. Kline refers to is characteristic of students with limited or interrupted formal education (SLIFE) (DeCapua, 2016; Montero, Newmaster, & Ledger, 2014; Potochnick, 2018). SLIFEs have had at least two years of interrupted formal education or no formal education at all. Formal education is described as standardized institutions where students are expected to participate in a set curriculum for long periods a day. A SLIFE will have a difficult time keeping up with the expectations of the curriculum because they are unfamiliar with the institution and testing measurements. In the case of the Congolese, this is likely a result of their inability to attend public institutions due to reasons of safety, political instability, war, poverty, and limited availability of classroom space. Kondo, a junior, told me he and his sister could not go to school in the refugee camp because "they were killing students." Another student shared that she feared speaking because her accent would "make me sound dumb and get people to bully me."

Educational policy and public schools in Florida remain unprepared to receive these students despite a well-established history of refugee reception. The Consent Decree of 1990 will be a major focus of critique. Other educational policies, such as No Child Left Behind and Every Student Succeeds Act, will also be used as examples of policies that facilitate an unequitable learning environment. A critical review on the politicization of education policy will reveal changes that need to be made to decrease drop-out rates of Black refugee students. Students, such as these from the DRC, are subjected to a politicized education and punished for resettlement in Florida public schools. In the context of an increasingly diverse student body, budget cuts due to administrative prioritization, and the introduction of new educational policy, the Consent Decree of 1990, and policies like it, reduces the quality of free and equal education for linguistically diverse students. I conducted 6 months of observation of refugee students from the DRC. I also completed 18 interviews from teachers, students, parents, and community leaders to investigate policies that maintain a high drop-out rate in the urban Florida high school context.

ENGLISH LEARNER STANDARDIZED LANGUAGE

English speakers of other languages (ESOL) is used in the United States to describe programs implemented in public schools that provide accommodations, specialized curriculum, and teachers whose goal it is to increase student English proficiency enough so that students can attend schools without these accommodations. An ESOL teacher can teach one or two ESOL classes a day but can also teach classes for the English proficient student body. This term is provided from U.S. and state policy such as the Consent Decree of 1990 and is used commonly in practice.

English as a second language (ESL), English language learner (ELL), English learner (EL), ESOL, and culturally and linguistically diverse (CLD) are terms used to describe students who are in the ESOL program but can also include students located out of the program. ESL and ELL are most commonly used in practice to refer to students who are in the ESOL program, while CLD can be used more broadly to discuss students in schools who have learned or are learning more than one language (Herrera, Morales Cabral, & Murry, 2013). Most of the terms refer to student education in terms of English proficiency and therefore are limited to describing students within institutions that use English as the primary source of educational language. In order to support the argument of this chapter, which critiques the prioritization of English proficiency in free and equal education, I will use CLD to refer to students within the Congolese cohort and other students participating in the ESOL program. The major critique with this use of language is that it presupposes knowledges are easily transferable from one language to another (Cummins, 1999). When a student is "lacking" in English proficiency the goal of Florida schools is to increase proficiency and place other subjects out of the students' focus, while still attending those courses.

DIVERSE STUDENT BACKGROUNDS IN FLORIDA

The proportion of the U.S. student body made up of students in the ESOL program is increasing (over 10% of total students nationwide) despite policies that limit migration into the United States (WIDA, 2016). Since Florida schools are the fourth largest (with 288,000 students described as ELLs) in CLD student proportion, it is important to highlight research done on its diverse student body (ELL Information Center, 2016). The national rate of graduation for ELs is 63%, and in the state of Florida, the rate of graduation for ELs is 55% (Sanchez, 2017). Hillsborough's School Strategy Plan (Eakins et al., 2017) reveals that only 17% of migrant students were making gains in English language as of 2017. In addition, this particular county's Black student population are graduating at a rate of 79%, which is 6% less than the national average (Eakins et al., 2017). Florida has had a long history of refugee student entry into public schools. This section will focus on three groups: Cubans, Haitians, and Congolese to make comparisons with public school experiences in Florida.

MARIEL BOATLIFT OF 1980

The Mariel Boatlift from Cuba occurred over the course of several months in 1980 and introduced 11,000 Cuban students to South Florida (Garcia, 1996; Silva, 1985b). Schools had major issues integrating students into the established system of education due to their sudden arrival, linguistic, and cultural differences (Silva, 1985a). The structure of schooling between Cuba and the United States reflected their communist and capitalist attitudes, respectively. Students were being confronted with a new language, history, and classroom teaching method. Those that could not assimilate to the changes were forced to leave schools. Older students especially fell "into the cracks" and replaced their institutionalized education with low-income jobs (Garcia, 1996; Silva, 1985). This was the third wave of Cuban refugee arrivals from Fidel Castro's regime. The reception of this group was incredibly mixed in the United States, even among Cubans who had fled to South Florida during prior waves.

The media descriptions of the Mariel Boatlift refugees were described much differently and led to a more hostile environment for these new arrivals (Garcia, 1996). The media revealed that Castro had initiated his temporary policy of allowing Cubans to leave freely in order to smuggle criminals out of Cuba. Castro released political prisoners so they would leave on boats, not violent criminals. The Cubans that arrived via the Mariel Boatlift were of a lower socioeconomic status who could not afford travel during previous waves. The combination of race, criminalization, and resource liability crept its way into the overloaded school systems of South Florida, causing many students to lose out on accessing a free and equitable education.

HAITIAN MIGRANT STUDENTS

The media perception of Haitians greatly impacted their arrival to South Florida in the 1980s and 1990s. After the 1990 census, a conservative estimate of 150,000 Haitians were counted in Florida, only 7% of which were reported to have arrived prior to the 1970s (Stepick & Swartz, 1998). Many structural issues such as poverty, food instability, and political unrest were listed as reasons Haitians fled. Their reception was largely negative and coincided with the U.S. political declaration of Haitians as "economic refugees" thus creating the perception of choice and drain at the cost of taxpayers.

The Florida high school experience of Haitians in the 1990s comprised of first- and second-generation Haitians. They lived in a crisis of identity in which their Blackness was conflated with African Americans (Stepick & Swartz, 1998). Haitian high schoolers negotiated this identity crisis by "covering-up" their ethnicity or embracing it. Students would hide their Haitian backgrounds because they did not want to be harassed or beat up by other students. They instead behaved as an African American student was expected to by showing less interest in doing well in school and focusing on social aspects such as dressing fashionably. They would also hide their accents. Haitians that made their identity known were new arrivals. As a result of their visibility, they were isolated, harassed, and beat up by the other students, including Haitians "covering-up." They were also more likely to be interested in their American education than the students who hid their identity.

CONGOLESE REFUGEE STUDENTS

When the Congolese students heard my colleagues speak Swahili, they opened up and began conversing with us in both languages. We learned all the students were conversational in English and were excited to be a part of our tutoring program However, greeting Patrick was difficult. When I introduced myself in both languages, he barely spoke above a whisper. When we were given a space to tutor in the media center, he would watch for a long time before he began to participate. The media center was a difficult space to work with because there were many other students sitting at tables close by as well as classes being taught at the computer sections. The English alphabet lessons and the multiplication sheets became embarrassing to work on in front of other students. It took multiple weeks of trust and a private classroom to get Patrick to really engage with our lesson plans.

Refugees from the DRC were forcibly displaced by ethnic and gender-based violence that began with the Burundian wars, followed by the Rwandan Genocide, and then the First and Second Congo Wars (Baer et al., 2017). In the Congo, the violence was limited to the far eastern North and South Kivu region. These subsequent violent events took place in the Eastern portion of Central Africa forcing people to cross state boundaries between Burundi, Rwanda, Uganda, Kenya, and Tanzania in search of safety and stability. Two point four million Congolese remain displaced and nearly a half million sought asylum in neighboring countries (Cultural Orientation Resource Center, 2019). DRC refugees lived in refugee camps for 10–20 years. Education at the refugee camps was inconsistent or, in some cases, nonexistent. School days were split in half so primary education took place at a separate time from secondary education to account for limited space. Refugees from the DRC made up the largest proportion of incoming refugees to Florida in 2016 (Refugee Processing Center, 2016). The transition into Tampa high schools has been a difficult one for all the students to navigate.

In Tampa, preparation for Congolese refugees was limited due to major budget cuts to resettlement causing problems such as unstable work status, access to social services, housing instability, transportation, and transition into school (Holbrook, Baer, Mahoney, Obure, & Ackey, 2019; Roberta et al., 2017). Many students were placed into schools based on their supposed age despite the years of school they may have completed prior to their arrival. The experiences of bullying and harassment at school and work was created from anti-immigration sentiment. American teachers, students, coworkers, and case managers reacted negatively to major differences between the Congolese and themselves. The case workers saw the Congolese inability to maintain jobs as laziness. Neighbors in apartment complexes were reported to the police for staying outside the homes of the Congolese, banging on the door and shouting obscenities. Congolese were bullied heavily at schools for their conservative clothing, which runs counter to African American preferences for dress. They were also bullied for their hygiene, a result of limited access to services that could have provided basic hygiene supplies.

Issues such as food security, bullying, and high rates of dropout were common among Haitian and Congolese students (Holbrook et al., 2019; Roberta et al., 2017; Stepick & Swartz, 1998). All three groups shared similar experiences on the impact of age on arrival and the likelihood of graduating school. The perception of these populations by the greater public played out in their treatment in the public school system as well. A hostile school environment is cited as a major barrier to completing school (Hos, 2016; Jeng, Lim, & Hoot, 2015; Riley, 2015).

THE CONSENT DECREE AND
OTHER EDUCATIONAL POLICIES

It's called a consent decree and it says that the students are entitled, though they have a second language, to the same classes as the native-born students. They can use dictionaries in their native language to assist them. They can have shorter assignments. They can have extra time if needed for classroom tests and for homework and projects and the state testing. They can have modified subjects so if they can't actually do an essay for an English class they can come up with an alternative assignment. Those are the accommodations. (Mrs. Kline, personal communication, 2019)

The Consent Decree of 1990 was a response to the needs of Cuban refugees' mass arrival to Florida during the Mariel Boatlift of 1970 (Silva, 1985). The Consent Decree of 1990 was drafted from a lawsuit between the League of United Latin American Citizens (LULAC) and the Florida Department of Education. LULAC argued that the Florida school system was not allowing speakers of other languages to participate in a free and equal education thus violating human rights law.

The decree reorganized schools to effectively teach this group of Spanish speaking students. The Consent Decree of 1990 presupposes that the gaps are based only on linguistic differences but does not include cultural and historical backgrounds of diverse students (LULAC vs. FDOE, 1990; Valenzuela, Prieto, & Hamilton, 2007). Other subjects such as math, science, history, and literature are taught in English and are pushed to the side. Despite this, CLD students are still placed in these subject courses, many times with English proficient students, and expected to complete the work and pass the tests. There is conflict in the expectation that the ESOL program has for its new arrivals, thus causing months or years of curriculum to remain unlearned.

In U.S. high schools, CLD students are tested prior to entry for their knowledge in English and academic knowledge they are supposed to have attained based on their age. Students are expected to complete the ESOL program within 3 to 5 years, but some may take longer. In this study (Cummins, 1999), research shows that an average of 5 to 7 years is needed for CLD students to become proficient in English used in curriculum. The students remain until they show proficiency in English by getting a passing score on a standardized test, or more recently if they can show improvement in their authentic assessment of English language proficiency (USDOE, 2016). English has long been politicized as the language of communication in the United States (Sayers, 1996; Valenzuela et al., 2007). In schools, teachers' perceptions on students who do not speak English influence their expectation of their students' performance (Riley, 2015). English is used as an indicator of assimilation or wanting to live in America, and those who have not learned it are perceived as undeserving of the benefits of living in America. Policies reflect this harmful ideology when most classes and tests are supplied only in English despite the subject (Bondy, 2016; Sayers, 1996; Valenzuela et al., 2007).

Furthermore, No Child Left Behind was enacted during the second Bush administration and sought to erase the gap between affluent, White, middle class families and vulnerable students who could be classified as minority, poor in underfunded schools (Valenzuela et al., 2007). The law standardized teaching methods and implemented more consistent testing in order to monitor school progress. Progress was rewarded with more funding for students and teachers. This incentive-based performance measure exacerbates the issues at poor, underfunded, urban schools because there are larger structural issues that cause students to perform poorly that this law did not seek to correct.

The more recent Every Student Succeeds Act, considered those outside influences when grading performance by schools. For ESOL programs, this meant that funding could increase if alternative requirements were met outside of test scores "covering such areas as school climate, chronic absenteeism, suspension/expulsion rates, and college and career readiness" (Learning Policy Institute, 2015). Despite this policy's attempt to mitigate test fatigue, no major changes were noted among the high school teachers regarding standardized curriculum.

DISCUSSION AND ANALYSIS

The school that I attended for tutoring had 120 students who spoke 24 languages in its ESOL program. Assignment instructions were sometimes offered in Spanish, Portuguese, Arabic, and Swahili. Most assignments, forms, school resources and other important information gathering tools were available only in English and Spanish. The ESOL teachers that I had met during my time there spoke at most three languages: English, Spanish, and Portuguese.

> Normally the para goes into the classrooms to help them. They are supposed to sit there with the instruction and translate for the Spanish kids. I only have a Spanish para. We realized that we can't do that because I go to the classrooms and help when they need it. When the teachers specifically say "I need you for a test to translate or I need you today because I'm introducing a new unit" we'll go in. But we can't touch the 120 students in all their classes. (Kline, personal communication, 2019)

The Consent Decree of 1990 accommodations and resources are only available if funding can be provided, and funding can only be provided if progress is shown. This creates a feedback loop where ESOL programs with diverse students need more resources but also need to prove that they've earned those resources. Since the program is run without, students are not able to pass at a satisfactory rate and the school budgeting for the ESOL program becomes less. This is then combined with policies such as NCLB and ESSA that relies on standardized tests and teacher effectiveness based on the rate at which their students pass that test, in order to gain funding for the entire school. The CLD student test scores are included in those final evaluations based on standardized test scores despite their status as an atypical student.

Information gathered from interviews and participant observation revealed some perceptions that teachers have of their Congolese students: "They don't realize 'hey you know we have a different population' and they are more reluctant to modify." Like 'I can't give them a dictionary no one else gets a dictionary.' I hear that a lot" (Kline interview, personal communication, 2019). Everyday actions became a source of contention between the Congolese, other students, and teachers. One teacher was reported of accusing a student of cheating during a test because they were using a translation dictionary, one which does not offer definitions but supplies a direct translation of a word. The use of dictionaries and translation devices for tests in English is an accommodation allotted by the Consent Decree of 1990. I witnessed an instance where a teacher, who I was unfamiliar with, filled our classroom space with AXE spray after the Congolese students had left, in front of other students. These actions validate students who bully and harass based on language and hygiene.

The student drop-out rate was a major concern for the teachers. One of them informed us that the schools would encourage students to drop-out since they would not graduate "on time." I placed on time within quotations because students can remain in high school till the age of 21, and some of the students encouraged to drop out were as young as 15 years. The exact numbers of students who drop out in this county are not accurate because they only count students who have failed to complete high school before the age of 21 or were expelled (Eakins et al., 2017). Since 2015, Congolese refugees have been arriving in Tampa in much larger numbers. Only five high school aged students among this community have been recorded to complete a GED program or graduate from high school. With this information taken into consideration, I argue that these students do have time to graduate from Florida public high schools, but cannot generate test scores required to keep these schools minimally funded. CLD students standardized test scores count towards the school average which, then due to policies such as NCLB and ESSA, cuts funding and creates an environment where many students are neglected for students who are more likely to pass exams.

Congolese students have also shared perceptions that they have about some of their teachers. They felt that some teachers were mean to them and the work they gave was too difficult. This resulted in multiple instances where students refused to participate in class or complete their assignments. A lack of support from the teachers prevented students from participating in work that they could complete. Kondo, an older Congolese student, stopped attending our tutoring sessions entirely after the first week. He told me he knows he is not going to pass and would rather play soccer so he can become a professional player. Despite these negative experiences cited, the Congolese students remained hopeful that they would be able to graduate school and get a good job or enter college.

Tutoring revealed student backgrounds that were unknown to many of the teachers at the high school. Even my colleagues and I were confused when we began talking to a boy in Swahili, and he replied in perfect conversational English, "I'm Eritrean, I speak Tigrinya." Three of the students we tutored were from Haiti as well. This conflation of all Black migrant students facilitated friendships between them but also isolated them from the rest of the student body, which at this school was largely Latinx and Black Americans. Even the Congolese themselves are of diverse historical, ethnic, and educational backgrounds that can determine their social status in their community, their ability to succeed in school, and their transition to America.

We employed a think-pair-share teaching strategy (Herrera et al., 2013) during tutoring to get the students to share their knowledge and help each other. Patrick made a great leader in math. We built on math concepts he already knew in order, and he would turn around and lead the rest of the class in Swahili. Patrick lived in a refugee camp that allowed for him to leave and attend state schools. His familiarity with formal education systems was higher than many of his Congolese peers. However, the lack of support he felt from the teachers and other students prevented this revelation while he remained silent in other classes since his arrival over a year ago.

CONCLUSION

The public school experience for these students was gathered from interviews told by African refugee high schoolers, their parents, and refugee service employees. Teachers were gracious enough to share with me an oppressive view of their workplace because they are passionate about their students and wish to see changes occur. The arrival of refugees to Florida has gone through many stages and each group that comes brings obstacles to resettlement. While policies that create the Florida education system have created barriers for this group of students, they still argue for free and equitable education for all school-aged students that come to the United States.

The parents view their resettlement here as a unique opportunity for their children. "I want my kids to go to college. I am obligated to work for my kids and I work till my body hurts."

There are distinct changes that need to occur for African refugee students to graduate at higher rates. Educational evaluation must be thorough for each student upon arrival and include information such as years attended in previous schools and languages used in schools. Funding should be allocated and utilized to provide teachers or translators for schools that find themselves with a sizable cohort of other language speaking students. The schools should use those resources to provide as much material in languages commonly spoken in the homes of their students. Many of these students need peer mentors or tutors that can teach them ways to navigate the American education system. Volunteers can be found within the rest of the student body or in the community. Policies that punish schools for performing poorly year after year should reconsider the environment they create for their students and teachers and make drastic changes to allocating school funds. Migrant students that need additional accommodations should not be pushed out for fear of lower averages.

Patrick is still attending public high school; a different one with a largely White student population. This has not fixed the problems that occurred in the previous school. I am writing this chapter during the 2020 COVID-19 pandemic. Many of the newer refugee arrivals do not have internet or computers at home. The students cannot attend school online or contact their teachers. They are worried for their housing status, and they want to learn English so they can become independent and participate in schools. This pandemic shows the privilege of staying home and has unveiled to more of our society social injustices that were left unanswered.

REFERENCES

Baer, R. D., Mahoney, D., Holbrook, E., Inks, M., Obure, R., Bomboka, L., & Benton, K. (2017). *School harassment/bullying among Congolese refugees in the Tampa area—Part 1* (Presentation, Tampa Bay Refugee Task Force meeting, Tampa, FL, July 30, 2017).

Bondy, J. M. (2016). Negotiating domination and resistance: English language learners and Foucault's care of the self in the context of English-only education. *Race Ethnicity and Education, 19*(4), 763–783.

Cultural Orientation Resource Center. (2019). *About refugees.* Retrieved from http://www.culturalorientation.net/learning/about-refugees

Cummins, J. (1999). BICS and CALP: Clarifying the distinction. *Opinion Papers, 120,* 4–5.

DeCapua, A. (2016). Reaching students with limited or interrupted formal education through critically responsive teaching. *Language and Linguistics Compass,* *10*(5), 225–237.

Eakins, J., Gray, L. L., Hahn, S. A., Perez, K., Shamburger, T. P., Snively, M., & Stuart, C. (2017). *HCPS Strategic Plan: 2015–2020.* Retrieved from https://www.sdhc .k12.fl.us/docs/00/00/16/04/Updated_Strategic_Brochure_1_23_19.pdf

ELL Information Center. (2016). Retrieved from http://www.migrationpolicy.org/ programs/ell-information-center

Garcia, M. C. (1996). The Mariel Boatlift of 1980 origins and consequences. In *Havana USA : Cuban exiles and Cuban Americans in South Florida, 1959–1994* (pp. 46–80). Berkeley: University of California Press.

Herrera, S. G., Morales Cabral, R., & Murry, K. G. (2013). Special education issues in the assessment of CLD students. In *Assessment accommodations for classroom teachers of culturally and linguistically diverse students* (2nd ed., pp. 226–255). Boston, MA: Pearson Education.

Holbrook, E. A., Baer, R., Mahoney, D., Obure, R., & Ackey, F. (2019). Applying applied anthropology: A project with applied anthropologists, congolese refugees, and refugee service providers in West Central Florida. *Practicing Anthropology, 41*(1), 15–19.

Hos, R. (2016). Caring is not enough: Teachers' enactment of ethical care for adolescent students with limited or interrupted formal education (SLIFE) in a newcomer classroom. *Education and Urban Society, 48*(5), 479–503.

Jeng, S., Lim, J., & Hoot, J. L. (2015). Bullying in an increasingly diverse school population: A socio-ecological model analysis. *School Psychology International, 36*(3), 268–282.

Learning Policy Institute. (2015). *The Every Student Succeeds Act (ESSA).* Retrieved from https://learningpolicyinstitute.org/topic/essa

LULAC vs. FDOE. *Consent Decree.* Pub. L. No. Section 1003.56 (1990).

Montero, M. K., Newmaster, S., & Ledger, S. (2014). Exploring early reading instructional strategies to advance the print literacy development of adolescent SLIFE. *Journal of Adolescent & Adult Literacy, 58*(1), 59–69.

Potochnick, S. (2018). The academic adaptation of immigrant students with interrupted schooling. *American Educational Research Journal, 55*(4), 859–892.

Refugee Processing Center. (2016). *Admissions & arrivals — Refugee processing center.* Retrieved from http://www.wrapsnet.org/admissions-and-arrivals

Riley, T. (2015). "I know I'm generalizing but…": How teachers' perceptions influence ESL learner placement. *TESOL Quarterly, 49*(4), 659–680.

Roberta, D. B., Mahoney, D., Holbrook, E., Inks, M., Obure, R., Bomboka, L., & Benton, K. (2017). *Dietary issues and nutritional status among Congolese refugees in the Tampa area—preliminary report.* Tampa, FL: Prepared for the *Refugee Task Force of Tampa Bay* and the *Florida Department of Children and Families.*

Sanchez, C. (2017). English language learners: How your state is doing . *NPR Ed* . Retrieved from https://www.npr.org/sections/ed/2017/02/23/512451228/5-million-english-language-learners-a-vast-pool-of-talent-at-risk

Sayers, J. (1996). Accidental language policy: Creating an ESL/bilingual teacher endorsement program in Utah. *TESOL Quarterly, 30*(3), 611–615.

Silva, H. (1985). *The children of Mariel from shock to integration : Cuban refugee children in South Florida schools.* Washington, DC: Cuban American National Foundation.

Stepick, A., & Swartz, D. F. (1998). *Pride against prejudice : Haitians in the United States.* Needham Heights, MA: Allyn and Bacon.

USDOE. (2016). *Every Student Succeeds Act (ESSA).* Retrieved from https://www2. ed.gov/policy/elsec/leg/essa/index.html

Valenzuela, A., Prieto, L., & Hamilton, M. P. (2007). Introduction to the special issue: No Child Left Behind (NCLB) and minority youth: What the qualitative evidence suggests. *Anthropology & Education Quarterly, 38*(1), 1–8.

WIDA. (2016, October). *Formative portfolio assessment in the ESL classroom.* Session presented at WIDA 2016 National Conference. Philadelphia, PA.

CHAPTER 16

REFLECTION

Forced "Normalcy" as Political Trauma for Students With Disabilities

Caitlin Sweetapple
Shrub Oak International School

As a special education teacher, I strive for many things for my students. Being "normal" isn't one of them. I grapple with why society wants students with disabilities, or any students for that matter, to be just like everyone else. Why should teachers instruct students to mitigate certain behaviors just to make others who are accustomed to an ableist vision of "normalcy" more comfortable? Teaching "socialization" while not enforcing ableist "normalcy" is a particular challenge as I work with my students who have been classified as having autism spectrum disorders. Phetrasuwan, Miles, and Mesibov (2009) note, students with special needs often struggle with maintaining appropriate social boundaries and safety. One in three children who receive special education services are victims of some type of maltreatment (i.e., either neglect, physical abuse, or sexual abuse) compared to 1 in 10 nondisabled children who experience abuse (Davis, 2011). The children I work with and others like them often do not understand social boundaries

Making a Spectacle, pages 179–181

and safety in the same ways that their typically developing peers might, making them more vulnerable to these types of abuse in society.

These findings highlight the need for students with disabilities such as autism spectrum disorder, various developmental disabilities, and/or intellectual disabilities to learn applicable social skills in order to avoid being victims of abuse. However, as an educator who works with students with ASD and who strives toward celebrating difference, I have struggled to find a curriculum that represents socialization in a way that allows my students to be who they are and not try to embody the ableist, imaginary, "normal" child that society demands. Ostensibly, socialization curricula can assist students with disabilities in understanding their surroundings, relationships, and warning signs of abuse. Still, although there is a desperate need to teach students with disabilities social boundaries in order to protect them from abuse, many of the current curricula I have encountered emphasize assimilation into social society that does not recognize diversity, and especially not neurodiversity. I worry that these curricula are too rigid, too narrow; individual characteristics, family situations or social differences are not taken into consideration and one is left to assume that there is only one way of being social in the world, a neurotypical, ableist, imaginary, "normal" way of being.

When reading through the various social skills curricula, the ideological implications are negative and off-putting towards individuals with disabilities and teachers like me. Circles Curriculum created by James Stanfield Company, Inc. is not appropriate to teach students with disabilities how to interact socially. This is a curriculum that I have used as a special education teacher. I always felt uneasy about it but never took the time to understand why. I've come to realize that this curriculum tries to blend individuals with disabilities into society, rather than understanding their differences and adapting to them.

As a special education teacher, it pains me to witness my students stared at and ridiculed for their social differences. I dream of a time I can bring my students to the mall and not have them stared at for stimming, vocalizing, or asking strangers questions. Curriculums such as Circle Curriculum created by James Steinfeld Inc., "TeachTown: Exceptional Solutions for Exceptional Students" read as if the creators of these curriculums want to further assimilate individuals with disabilities into society, rather than society adapting to their differences. The recent neurodiversity movement has been put at the forefront by individuals with autism spectrum disorder and speaks to strength-based approaches rather than normalization (den Houting, 2019). But these curricula do not look at the strengths of individuals with disabilities; rather, they hinder students' personalities by attempting to have them fit into the social society that doesn't recognize their existence, much less value who they are.

The unspoken theory behind this curriculum is that everyone should act the same in social situations and have a set repertoire of behaviors when it comes to relationships with other people. This isn't realistic or respectful towards individuals who navigate the social world differently than neurotypical individuals. In fact, it puts the burden of change squarely on the shoulders of individuals who do not embody the ableist, imaginary norm, while society itself remains unchanged. I understand that change may not be easy for individuals who are uncomfortable interacting with students with disabilities, but I also understand that a student with a disability spends most of their school-aged years feeling uncomfortable and for that, neurotypical individuals must adapt.

It is alarming to me how many different ways special educators across the United States are teaching social skills to students with disabilities. There is a lot of interpretation to the educator, which highlights the need for standards when teaching social skills to students with disabilities. However, it is important that these standards respect students' differences and do not assimilate them. Individual needs of each student should be taken into consideration when teaching social skills. A social skills curriculum should be able to be practiced in real-life situations, celebrate individualized social differences, and be reachable for all types of students, not just students who fit into the majority. Students with disabilities should not be taught normativity, they should be taught diversely. We can keep our students safe while celebrating who they are. It is time for society to be comfortable with being uncomfortable.

We need to, as educators, focus on our student's strengths and celebrate their differences, otherwise, we run the risk of our students experiencing political trauma. We need to let our students be themselves while maintaining social safety, otherwise our student body will just be ordinary. By mitigating who they are we as educators are perpetuating forced normalcy and retraumatizing students psychologically.

REFERENCES

Davis, L. A. (2011, March 1). *Abuse of children with intellectual disabilities*. Retrieved from https://thearc.org/wp-content/uploads/forchapters/Child Abuse.pdf

den Houting, J. (2019). Neurodiversity: An insider's perspective. *Autism, 23*(2), 271–273.

Phetrasuwan, S., Miles, M. S., & Mesibov, G. B. (2009). Defining autism spectrum disorders. *Journal for Specialists in Pediatric Nursing, 14*(3), 206–209.

CHAPTER 17

REFLECTION

Parent Café Reflections

Matthew Bradley
University of Newcastle, NSW

Maura Sellars
University of Newcastle, NSW

Australia, over the past century, has promoted its humanitarian program in resettling refugees. Families from across the world were forced to escape as a result of war, political upheaval, and totalitarian regimes that have stripped away the rights of minorities to participate in the full experience of life. The public face of the Australian model has been undermined due to the complexities of implementation and the ineffective support provided. These cohorts of refugee and asylum seeker families were often resettled in areas that provided an economic advantage due to factors such as rental prices for both the government and the agencies charged with the administration of the program. This led to the establishment of closed communities, which have taken generations to establish a positive social and cultural identity in our broader society, as they were forced to create internal

Making a Spectacle, pages 183–189
Copyright © 2021 by Information Age Publishing
All rights of reproduction in any form reserved.

supports for themselves. These closed communities have attracted nega-tive attention from the media, increasing racism from wider society and a widening gap of values. This was due to the rejection of cultural behaviors that newly settled groups observed in the immediate community of resettle-ment. Much of these differences are the result of socioeconomic complexi-ties. This situation continues to the present day.

This was the context of the elementary school where I became principal in 2012. At the time, the school had a small population of newly arrived families of refugee backgrounds. The school was perceived by the wider community to be populated with the children of drug users and sex work-ers. Resources, work, housing, and welfare support were limited resources, and "new arrivals" were viewed as intruders who were taking resources away from those already in need. As an inner-city suburb, it was about to undergo gentrification, and over the next 4 years, the student numbers at the school tripled, with children of both aspirant locals and, at times, up to 46% newly arrived refugee families. The sudden influxes of large numbers of refugees placed stress on all systems within the school as I attempted to rapidly adjust policies, procedures, and pedagogies to ensure that all students had access to free, quality, and empowering education.

This autoethnographic reflection (Anderson, 2006) is focused on the parent café, which was an innovative strategy to reach out to my parent community. My coauthor, an academic from the university with which I am a research associate, has acted as a "critical friend" and helped shape these reflections to authentically illustrate the impact of the school's practices. This café was the catalyst in the building of trust within the refugee com-munity and was the initial most powerful mediator of the many difficulties that these populations endured as a result of political and bureaucratic re-straints that ensured these families remained "othered" (Foucault, 1991; Harwood, Muller, & Olssen, 2014; Perryman, Ball, Braun, & Maguire, 2017; Said, 1978). When working with families, I discovered support structures that were poorly timed and incomprehensive; ineffective information ses-sions, which were focused on their legal obligations and rights of residency; and the challenges to traditional family interactions and childcare prac-tices, which were unacceptable in their new homeland. Families were left essentially isolated and without the informed understandings necessary to participate actively as members of their new society.

The parent café was established with the support and seed funding from the NSW Department of Education. The purpose of the café was to create an environment and forum that would support newly arrived families at their point of need and assist in connecting them to their new community (Leithwood, Sun, & Pollock, 2017). Important when establishing this forum was the work that was completed as school staff in understanding the issues that faced these populations and the "typical" rollercoaster of resettlement patterns that featured as characteristics of this journey over time (Davidson, Murray, & Schweitzer, 2008; Deng & Marlowe, 2013; Watters, 2007). This professional work with the staff was designed to build empathy and understanding, to assist in suspending judgments, and to focus on the concerns and stories of participants. I found that this was particularly important in supporting staff in relation to vicarious trauma and their own well-being (Leithwood & Sun, 2017).

In order to establish a greater connection to this specific community, it was important to ensure that all participants could engage simultaneously. Participants came from approximately six major language groups and five major religious persuasions. I employed translators for all major groups and a coordinating community liaison officer. The team aimed to meet once a week at a time convenient, not to our school routines, but which suited the parent group. In the first weeks, we had only had a few people attend. These representatives only came from a sense of duty to some of the interpreters that had been employed. It was also understandable as some of the families resettled in our community had come directly from countries where their cultural, religious, and ethnic groups had been in conflict for generations.

Due to the levels of political and physical trauma, these families had been through; they were also distrustful of our intent as positional holders of authority (Saltsman, 2014). To assist in breaking down these barriers, as a principal, it was important to welcome our participants as I would into a family home, serving drinks and fussing a little. These actions were surprising and, at times, embarrassing for the parents as they challenged participant experiences and beliefs about schools and principals. This cognitive dissonance established the foundation of respect and a slower pace that was in stark contrast to the hurried appointments with government agencies typified by the neoliberal economies and efficiencies (Ball, 2013; Ball, 2016; Gary, 2016)

In these early days, it was important for participants to drive the agenda. There was significant time spent behind the scenes with advocacy to ensure results. Assisting families to find housing, blankets for warmth, the simple return of faulty goods, work experience that would lead to paid work, helping with the purchase of a car, and navigating schools for older children who were experiencing racism were all examples of café achievements. These successes, whilst they fell outside the remit of our school, were important in establishing trust and led, through word of mouth, to greater engagement and increased numbers of participants. With each success, additional members of the community came, quietly mentioning another family that needed assistance and asking if we could help them too. The success was that which encouraged families to move through their misgivings and suspicion. Families recognized that this group was nonexploitative in a political or economic sense.

As attendance rose and the café began to look more like a drop-in center, the group moved into a circle, and I began to share little narratives from my week or day. Often these were of my own parenting or children. These were simultaneously translated across all language groups. The slow storytelling due to the translation provided the opportunity for everyone to see the flickers of recognition and the self-effacing humor characteristic of Australia that also crossed cultural boundaries. Other families began to share stories from their week and demonstrate vulnerability to seek advice on how to manage different situations. This assisted in developing the narratives of shared experiences and highlighted our common values and aspirations for our children. This was powerful in connecting us across the group and produced belonging and social cohesion through the extension of the degrees of difference.

What was also becoming apparent through the sessions was the overwhelming theme of these communities being told no and what not to do, or what to do in simplistic terms without any of the reasoning or purpose behind the advice nor due attention to cultural sensitivity. This disempowered the participants' voices and opportunities for self-advocacy, leading to feelings of condescension, greater frustration, and distancing from the very supports that they were supposed to be accessing. I began to weave a counter approach utilizing the power of *yes* or *yes and*. Participants were empowered by the reasoning approaches used and their improved understandings of how to navigate systems (Anders & Lester, 2014; Lloyd, Kennan, Thompson, & Qayyum, 2013; McMichael, Gifford, & Correa-Velez, 2011). The school executive continued to engage in path smoothing to ensure successful mastery experiences. These experiences assisted to build self-efficacy and group self-assurance as they started reengaging with renewed confidence in the world around them. These experiences provided the participants with a sense of status as they were able to relay their success back into the group.

This café forum and the experiences that were associated with it assisted in reestablishing power dynamics within family units. This was often disrupted as children, due to their immersion experience in school, acquired English language skills and the confidence to navigate our shared world faster than their parents. It provided families with the confidence and techniques to engage in positive parenting and to understand how to assist their children to walk the edge between their two worlds. Our families gained a sense of belonging and acceptance in our community that reflected not only the dominant Australian culture but the shared values and experiences of our diverse, newly arrived, refugee families (White, de Quadros, & Kelman, 2017).

The provision of the open opportunities for dialogue and understanding meant that these families became more visible; the children began to be invited to play with their classmates and were permitted by their hitherto reluctant parents. Non-refugee families came to check what cultural aspects they needed to accommodate to make these new classmates welcome and comfortable, for example, small issues but a significant impact, such as providing halal at birthday parties. Special meetings began that were for mothers only to assist in providing community based cultural support driven by the wider parent community at large. As the school supported families financially to ensure their children had full and equitable access to all school experiences, they gave back by covering library books, volunteering in classrooms, and participating in fundraising events. One event that evidenced our community solidarity was when the school held a fundraiser; the event saw central African mothers braiding hair in a booth next to Afghani mothers drawing henna designs on hands. Through the initial interactions in the café, the school became known as a safe and welcoming space that continues. The local African Community Council approached the school to host Africa Day, which included representation from the high commission and performances throughout the day. The Tibetan community began to run language lessons from the school. The school hall was also used for diverse religious celebrations.

Our community found a place for all, supported the common aspirations for our children, but also for old dreams set aside due to the events which led to the trauma of the refugee experience. Two examples have stayed with me. A Sudanese man in his mid-50s decided to complete his law degree, which had been interrupted by war 30 years previously. An Afghani man navigated the system to allow him to complete a PhD that would reflect on the way Persian language structures influenced the status of women in that culture. These stories demonstrate the power of belonging and acceptance as a foundation of mitigating governmentality and continuing systemic indifference. Every student in the school benefited from our diversity. They were taught traditional African drumming, dances to celebrate Diwali, and integrated keywords across languages as they communicated in the playground. Their worlds became richer, and their worldview expanded, they developed real gratitude for their current opportunities and empathy for the experiences of others whilst accepting the students with refugee backgrounds and experiences as friends, classmates, and peers.

Government policies and the people who operationalize them do great harm and abuse their responsibilities by treating these newcomers with indifference. Many would agree that schools reflect society and the unforgiving system in which any school must operate. In this case, the parent café gave me the capacity and opportunity to treat these people humanely instead of treating them as faceless data to be lost in the statistics. Through their philosophies, insights, and actions, principals have the capacity to shape a school culture that humanizes the systems with which our most vulnerable communities are mandated to interact. Through initiatives such as the parent café implemented with patience, cultural sensitivity, and compassion, schools have the capacity to empower entire communities to live life more fully, through our interactions with families. The interactions of the parent café were acknowledged as moderating some of the emotional and political abuses to which the refugee families were subjected.

REFERENCES

Anders, A. D., & Lester, J. N. (2014). Navigating authoritarian power in the United States: Families with refugee status and allegorical representation. *Cultural Studies, Critical Methodologies, 15*(3), 169–179. https://doi.org/10.1177/15327 08614565453

Anderson, L. (2006). Analytic autoethnography. *Journal of Contemporary Ethnography, 35*(2), 373–395.

Ball, S. (2013). *Foucault and education: Disciplines and knowledge.* Retrieved from http://newcastle.eblib.com/patron/FullRecord.aspx?p=1189375

Ball, S. (2016). Neoliberal education: Confronting the slouching beast. *Policy Futures in Education, 14*(8), 1–4. https://doi.org/10.1177/1478210316664259

Davidson, J., Murray, B., & Schweitzer, R. (2008). Review of refugee mental health assessment: Best practices and recommendations. *Journal of Pacific Rim Psychology, 4*, 72–85.

Deng, S. A., & Marlowe, J. M. (2013). Refugee resettlement and parenting in a different context. *Journal of Immigrant & Refugee Studies, 11*(4), 416–430. https://doi.org/10.1080/15562948.2013.793441

Foucault, M. (1991). Governmentality. In B. Burchell, G. Gordon, & B. Miller (Eds.), *The Foucault effect: Studies in governmentality* (pp. 87–104). Chicago, IL: Chicago University Press.

Gary, K. (2016). Neoliberal education for work versus liberal education for leisure. *Studies in Philosophy and Education, 36*(1), 83–94. https://doi.org/10.1007/s11217-016-9545-0

Harwood, V., Muller, J., & Olssen, M. (2014). Foucault, power, and education. *British Journal of Sociology of Education, 35*(6), 933–945.

Leithwood, K., & Sun, J. (2017). Leadership effects on students' learning mediated by teacher emotion. In K. Leithwood, J. Sun, & A. Pollard (Eds.), *How school leaders contribute to student success the four paths framework* (pp. 137–152). Cham, Switzerland: Springer.

Leithwood, K., Sun, J., & Pollock, K. (Eds.). (2017). *How school leaders contribute to student success: The four path framework* (Vol. 23). Cham, Switzerland: Springer.

Lloyd, A., Kennan, M. A., Thompson, K. M., & Qayyum, A. (2013). Connecting with new information landscapes: Information literacy practices of refugees. *Journal of Documentation, 69*(1), 121–144. https://doi.org/10.1108/00220411 311295351

McMichael, C., Gifford, S. M., & Correa-Velez, I. (2011). Negotiating family, navigating resettlement: Family connectedness amongst resettled youth with refugee backgrounds living in Melbourne, Australia. *Journal of Youth Studies, 14*(2), 179–195. https://doi.org/10.1080/13676261.2010.506529

Perryman, J., Ball, S. J., Braun, A., & Maguire, M. (2017). Translating policy: Governmentality and the reflective teacher. *Journal of Education Policy, 32*(6), 745–756. https://doi.org/10.1080/02680939.2017.1309072

Said, E. (1978). Introduction. In *Orientalism* (8th ed.; pp. 1–28). New York, NY: Vintage Books.

Saltsman, A. (2014). Beyond the law: Power, discretion, and bureaucracy in the management of asylum space in Thailand. *Journal of Refugee Studies, 27*(3), 457–476. https://doi.org/10.1093/jrs/feu004

Watters, C. (2007). *Refugee children: Towards the next horizon* (1st ed.). New York, NY: Routledge.

White, J., de Quadros, A., & Kelman, D. (2017). Belonging and rejection: Racism, resistance and exclusion. *International Journal of Inclusive Education, 21*(11), 1081–1082. https://doi.org/10.1080/13603116.2017.1350315

SECTION V

POLITICAL AFTERMATH AND CREATING SPACE
FOR RECOVERY/HEALING

CHAPTER 18

NEUTRALITY AS LIGHTNING ROD

Contextualizing Teachers' Experiences in the 2016 Election Aftermath

Erin Dyke
Oklahoma State University

Jinan El Sabbagh
Oklahoma State University

Sarah Gordon
Arkansas Tech University

Jennifer Job
Independent Scholar

ABSTRACT

In the summer of 2017, we engaged in-depth interviews with four K–12 educators from various backgrounds, political perspectives, and U.S. Mid-South school communities about their experiences teaching in the turbulent im-

Making a Spectacle, pages 193–207
Copyright © 2021 by Information Age Publishing
All rights of reproduction in any form reserved.

mediate aftermath of the 2016 presidential election. Our analysis illuminates various gendered and racialized ways that teachers were disciplined into shutting down students' agitations and desires to make sense of the political traumas that affected them and their peers, intensified with the election of an openly White supremacist president. Using a metaphor of lightning as transformative learning that aims to redistribute power, our interviews suggest that despite such institutional discipline, teachers and students engaged certain strategies to undertake political study anyway. Yet, such sense-making within schools, as our interviews suggest, is always precarious and requires significant labor (affective and otherwise) to persist. Ultimately, we suggest the need to contextualize trauma/violence within a continuity of struggle against White supremacist, colonialist, and heteropatriarchal capitalism. Such a contextualization requires us to understand that schooling and its normative "neutrality" is institutionally complicit in enabling (rather than infiltrated by external) political traumas—climate collapse, rising wealth gaps, school shootings, police brutality, and so on—that we have long been differentially experiencing in the anthropocene.

For centuries, lightning rods have tamed the heavens, more or less unchanged. [. . .]
As legend has it, Franklin hopped on a horse in 1752 with key-adorned kite in hand,
determined to prove his conviction. The two pranced about under stormy skies until
the charged-filled atmosphere energized the key and confirmed his suspicions. More
than two-and-a-half centuries later, lighting rods persist—as decorative architectural
pieces, as vestiges of the past, and as mitigators of lightning's power.
—Robin Tricoles (2017, para. 1–3)

In the days preceding and following the election, the Southern Poverty Law Center (SPLC) collected survey data from more than 10,000 teachers across the nation to understand the impact of the 2016 presidential election on U.S. schools (Costello, 2016). Pointing to more than 2,500 educator-reported "specific incidents of bigotry and harassment that can be directly traced to election rhetoric... [including] assaults on students and teachers" (Costello, 2016, p. 4), the report argues the election caused increased violence "against immigrants, Muslims, girls, LGBT students, kids with disabilities, and anyone who was on the 'wrong' side of the election" (Costello, 2016, p. 6). They concluded that the election had an overwhelmingly negative effect on schools, with likely long-term consequences.

In an interview, Costello, SPLC report author, stated that teachers should tell students experiencing racist, xenophobic, homophobic, and misogynist rhetoric and abuse, "They are safe right now, that school is a safe place, that there are adults who care about them" (Sottile, 2017, para. 18). Three years later, the SPLC released an updated report based upon new national survey data that contradicted their earlier suggestions to educators, finding that, actually, "Most of the hate and bias incidents witnessed by educators were not addressed by school leaders" (SPLC, 2019, para. 12). This fact likely does not come as a surprise to many educators and students on the margins, who have historically experienced epistemic and physical violence formally or unofficially sanctioned by education institutions (Lomawaima & McCarty, 2006).

We engage an analytic metaphor of lightning as liberatory, unpredictable, rebellious learning (and, alternatively, neutrality as a lightning rod that aims to stifle such learning) to better understand the experiences of K–12 educators' experiences in the immediate, volatile aftermath of the 2016 presidential election. Arising out of a larger interview and survey study on the impacts of the election on Oklahoma teachers' experiences, we put four teachers' stories into conversation, engaging their differences and resonances to more deeply understand how normatively neutral and depoliticized conditions of schooling contributed/continue to contribute to the recent intensification of racist and gendered violence in schools.

Our analysis suggests the problems with presuming schools or classrooms are or can be "safe" spaces, where safety is understood distinct from the curriculum, or, relatedly, that schools are contained spaces where "danger" infiltrates from the outside (i.e., Trumpian campaign rhetoric). Rather, we must turn our attention to the institutional arrangements that expect and enforce neutrality, and question our investments in them. As we elaborate below, such arrangements enable, even foster, racist, gendered, and sexual violence in schools via the containment and repression of the meaningful study of power, politics, and difference.

NEUTRALITY AS LIGHTNING ROD

The education system has long had a vested interest in a depoliticized skills-based curriculum for most folks, where schools have been predominantly imagined as sites of reason, neutrality, and unbiased study. To maintain the fantastical imaginary of neutrality, schools are more often spaces that fore-close the "unruly, transformative learning" necessary or desirable for most people's daily life and survival (Patel, 2016, p. 400).

Learning from the way power operates in the physical world, we can begin to imagine why such unruly, transformative learning may be considered dangerous. Lightning occurs because the very air we breathe and the earth we stand on is always already charged, never neutral. We live in a dynamic electrical field where always-in-motion currents of energy are continuously produced through interactions between the negatively charged earth and the positively charged atmosphere (Rycroft, Israelsson, & Price, 2000). Lightning functions to keep the earth and atmosphere in a healthy and balanced relationship. Lightning, as with the aspirations of liberatory study, is a continuous transformative process that aims to redistribute power.

As the epigraph introduces, the power and unpredictability of lightning has always been a source of ire for the settler-state founders and their structures. Without Ben Franklin's invention of the lightning rod—a simple configuration of metal and grounding wire that harnesses and safely diverts lightning's power—so many things about our cityscapes would not be feasible due to the frequency of lightning strike-related fires. For example, modern school buildings (modern buildings in general) are required to have lightning rods so that, if (when) lightning strikes the structure, it cannot enter and spark the frame, the furniture, or the people. Instead, the power passes along the outside of the building through the grounding wire and into the earth, where it safcly dissipates (but does not disappear). Lightning rods are simple but effective tools for protecting structures and their interests.

The process of lightning illuminates neutrality as ideological. Take for example the ways some scholars have called for schools to become "safe" havens (cf. Burleigh, 2017; Derman-Sparks, LeeKeenan, & Nimmo, 2017). Kishimoto and Mwangi (2009) write, "safe space" is often a project that preserves institutional norms, or the marginalization of folks at the intersections of queer and trans, Black, people of color and/or indigenous, and girl/woman. They argue that "safety" is closely aligned with "conventional methods of teaching [that] prescribe a mess-free mechanical classroom environment." Instead we must "imagin[e] a transformative classroom that disrupts and blurs neat boundaries and opens up the classroom to become an extension of the world in which we live" (pp. 98–99).

Alternative to a narrative of schools as safe havens, Sondel, Baggett, and Dunn (2018) offer a more complicated notion of the role of schools and educators in these times. In their national survey study of teachers' responses to the impacts of the election on classrooms, the authors draw from the literature on collective trauma. They suggest that "a candidate whose campaign rhetoric was rooted in White supremacy was elected to the highest office in U.S. government by White voters from all backgrounds" was a "political trauma" (p. 176). They suggest we must contextualize such trauma within the historical experiences of students' marginalized in/by schools.

Our interviews, our own experiences, and scholarship on intersectionality affirm that schools are not and cannot be "safe havens" free of racism, sexism, gender violence, and xenophobia, for these are encoded in the very structure of schools (e.g., Ahmed, 2012; Kishimoto & Mwangi, 2009). They illuminate that meaningfully impacting the rise in White supremacist violence and fear in our schools and universities requires, as Kishimoto and Mwangi (2009) suggest, transformative modes of learning that can meaningfully engage politics, difference, and memory. Further, they illuminate that teachers experience the discipline of neutrality differently along the lines of race, class, language, gender/sexuality, ability, and more.

We story the experiences of four teachers in the aftermath of the 2016 presidential election. We interviewed each educator for approximately 1 hour and 30 minutes in February and March 2017. Our analysis is further contextualized by our study of an in-depth, anonymous survey of 25 educators with similar questions as part of a prior study (Dyke, Gordon, & Job, 2017). We chose to put into conversation these particular educators' not-uncommon stories[1] to illustrate the ways in which neutrality was wielded as a lightning rod in order to deter forms of learning that might meaningfully challenge—at the very least, help students make sense of—racial, class, gender, and other forms of violence in schools. Further, we chose these particular stories together to illuminate the ways in which institutions' discipline of neutrality (or, wielding of the lightning rod) is experienced unevenly across racial, gender, and ideological lines.

WINONA AND GLORIA: THE PRECARIOUS WORK OF CULTIVATING SPARKS

Winona, a White middle school language arts educator in a small town and from a working class background, reported that, in the lead-up to the election and just afterward, students demanded their teachers confess which political party they supported. Winona described her students as primarily anti-Trump in a school environment where it seemed that most of their teachers supported him. She described such disclosure as a tool used by students to identify allies and enemies:

> Before the election I noticed that tensions were very high in the classroom, and they were—my students were very quick to kind of pry into my personal life and try to see where my loyalties laid as far as who I was going to vote for. And, as a teacher, I felt an immense amount of pressure [from fellow teachers] to keep that information secret from my students. Now, there were other [Trump-supporting] teachers in the building that were not this way. They didn't feel that pressure, and they were very open about who they were going to vote for . . . So tensions were really high, and students were supporting this teacher and not supporting [that] teacher.

Winona's characterization of the environment of her school illuminates that teachers who held pro-Trump politics seemed to feel comfortable disclosing their views (the apparent status quo of her building) while Winona, a self-described social justice educator, felt pressure to remain silent from her colleagues and administration. She acknowledged that students' desire to locate their teachers' politics were rooted in the desire to understand, "Can I trust this person?" At the same time, Winona lamented the ways in which her students seemed to demand a simplistic answer, either Hillary or Trump:

> When students asked me, I would say, "Well, do you know what I stand for as a teacher?" And a lot of them know I stand for women's rights. I stand for equality. I stand for equity. That kind of thing. My strategy with that was to have them pretty much highlight, "All right, do you know who I am as a person?"

For Winona, the election was an opportunity to engage students in more substantive conversation about what they believed and why, and to challenge them to dig deeper and cultivate their own set of ethics in relation to those around them. These discussions with students were an extension of her social justice-minded pedagogy. For example, her curriculum interspersed her school's official, according to her, "old, dead White guy" curriculum, with texts that challenged notions of racial harmony or erasure (e.g., reading the White savior narrative of *To Kill a Mockingbird* alongside the complicated portrayal of White innocence in the anti-police brutality young adult novel, *All American Boys*). This practice was attacked by parents long before the election; some attempted to withdraw their children from her courses and had coordinated a social media campaign against her within a parent Facebook group. She reported feeling isolated from her colleagues, who she perceived as usually hostile to her own political values. She attributed her ability to practice social justice pedagogy to her students' high passing rate on state tests and (she stated, not unrelatedly) her principal's support when she received parental complaints.

Unlike Winona, Gloria described her school as having a progressive culture. Yet, she reported feeling similarly isolated and defensive of her social justice pedagogy to colleagues and administration. Gloria was[2] a social studies teacher and the only Black teacher in her school. She described her initial impression of the urban charter school as multicultural- and social justice-oriented. Soon after joining the school, however, she realized her administration's support of her social justice pedagogy was not substantive: "So, um, my thing that got me is like just because you put a charter school in a low-income area doesn't make you a social justice leader, and that's how it was labeled to me that [my principal] was that." This realization occurred soon after her principal took the school's teaching staff on what she described as a sensationalized "poverty tour" of a neighborhood where many of their students lived. She described exploiting her principal's efforts to appear in support of multicultural education: "He always tried to avoid [talking about social justice] so it made it easier for me to talk about oppressive things or talk about social justice because he wasn't going to say anything, [...] he also didn't want to tell the only Black female teacher that she can't teach social justice and race issues."

Gloria's pedagogy, in ways resonant with Winona's, attempted to cultivate students as critical thinkers who could understand in-tension historical narratives. For example, in teaching her students about the first Thanksgiving:

> Usually in the American public education textbooks you see that one perspective. You see the beautiful painting of the pilgrims and the Indians together. Whereas I took that lesson to teach perspectives, and we looked at the Wampanoag native account of what happened versus the American textbook account.

Extending this critical historical literacy, she demanded her students be able to articulate disagreement, tension, and participate in political debate. She described an unplanned moment in a 5th grade class where a White student made an anti-immigrant comment after the election. Her careful cultivation of students' discussion skills enabled her to support students to make sense of an emotionally charged moment:

> What I loved so much about this class is when I saw that I had to quickly regulate, I had to quickly like shift gears, and I allowed students to talk about how they felt about what was said. And so I was not profiling, like picking certain students. I just allowed the conversation to flow, and thankfully a lot of my Mexican students spoke up and that's what—usually in the classroom they don't typically speak up in that particular class, but this one they did. And they were very emotional, crying about their experiences and how their families have worked to be here or just sharing their background, and the class went silent. And I could really feel that empathy rising in my White students who don't have to worry about this or never thought about that perspective, but now they felt differently and were able to go home and, and talk to their parents or talk with their other friends about, "Hey, my friend is Mexican. My friend has someone that's undocumented, and this could actually affect them and I could lose my friend."

Gloria even describes how some of her White students really "latched on" to the social justice perspectives and thrived in these discussion spaces, yet were discouraged by their parents. Regarding one White student, Gloria said,

> She really was excited about learning about different issues and we talked about Terence Crutcher[3] and we looked at activism. She was very involved. Yet when she went home, she came back and said, "My dad keeps saying, 'Why do you always make us question everything? Why do you always want to ask these hard questions and get us to argue with each other?'" Like I'm not trying to get you to argue with each other. I just want to acknowledge that everyone has different perspectives.

Despite the purported progressive culture of her school, and her administration's tacit support of her pedagogy, Gloria felt isolated.

She felt her progressive White colleagues were largely disconnected from and dismissive of the daily realities she and her Black, Indigenous, Asian, and Latinx students faced:

> So I had to check myself so many times during [professional development] last year because I was just able to really reflect on what was being said around me. [...] So there were some times where [White colleagues] were joking about like Trump issues, and I'm like these are issues that actually I don't have the privilege to joke about.

Unlike Winona's experience where discussing the election was strongly discouraged by her administration, and "an unsaid rule that we don't discuss that in our classroom," Gloria was not necessarily discouraged by her administration from having those conversations. Yet, she reported that she did not see her White colleagues engaging in deeper questions or issues beyond mainstream White feminism:

> And although [addressing Trump's disdain for women is] important to me, too, I was also thinking about this wall being built. So like me, in my identity having to worry about—so it's like the intersectionality, like having to worry about these anti-feminist ideas that he has, but also having to worry about all these other things that affect my communities and affect my students.

She reported that her White colleagues did not take seriously the mental health impacts that the election was having on students. After 2 years there, Gloria left this school and moved on to another, tired of reminding her colleagues of her reality and that of the school's diverse student body.

Patel (2016) argues that learning often occurs as acts of marronage, subversion, and always in dialectical relationship with the structure of schooling. Evidenced by precarious administrative support and political and racial isolation among colleagues, Winona's and Gloria's efforts toward the difficult work of engaging memory, social violence, and difference around and beyond the election were only successful *in spite of* their school contexts. In each context, Gloria and Winona's schools dispersed attempts at lightning-as-learning via curricular norms that prioritized testing and academic performance data and through the minimization of students' social, racial, historical, and political experiences in and out of school as unrelated and incidental to the work of education. Through the additional, unpaid emotional labor of having to justify the various violations of their respective school norms, Winona and Gloria were disciplined into an expectation of neutrality.

MARIA AND ERIK: SPARKING RESISTANCE, RESISTING SPARKS

While Winona and Gloria aimed to cultivate sparks in their classrooms and were disciplined for it in various direct and indirect ways, the narratives of Maria and Erik illuminate the ways in which students' initiate sparks in resistance to the muting and containment of their real questions and worries about their worlds. They further illuminate the racialized and gendered ways such sparks are experienced as risky and in need of dispersal (or not) by the teacher.

Like Winona and Gloria, Maria felt institutional or other risks in communicating her political leanings to students when they demanded it, and these risks were primarily defined by her identification as a Mexican-American woman. Maria, who voted for Trump (with self-described conflicted feelings), taught in two middle school settings—one in a small town with primarily White students and White colleagues and the other an urban school with primarily Latinx students and White colleagues. At various points in the conversation, Maria spoke candidly that she was consistently trying to avoid being seen as "Other" by her White colleagues and students, and to be appreciated for her teaching skills:

> Well, [my White students] always wanted my opinion because I'm Mexican, and because Trump was talking about Mexicans being rapists and murderers, so they always wanted to know how I felt about that. And I never give what my political view is in class because I don't want somebody who likes my teaching style, or likes my approach to teaching, [to] then think, "Oh, well, then I'm gonna side with her that way." So I never say it.

Maria's White students often tokenized her and asked her to speak for all Mexicans, noting, "Because I'm Mexican . . . they wanted to know how I felt about that." Throughout her interview, Maria described her usual method of teaching as moving away from emotion and toward rationality, reason, and neutral engagement with the course material:

> As a person of color and a woman of color, we tow a weird line of how we are an advocate. I will share my stories, I will stand up [to] what's going on, but then I have to be careful of how I do it, because frequently we're considered too sensitive, that we're whining, that we're playing a race card, that we're a snowflake.

Throughout her interview, Maria expressed feelings of anxiety due to marginalization and tokenization because of her race, immigrant status, and status as an English language learner.

Her experience in a nearby urban primarily Latinx school was quite different. Describing her work with a group of students, she said they, as with Winona and our other participants, desired to know her political affiliations:

> And the first thing they wanted to know about me, before they've even settled down and talked to me about anything else, is who I voted for. And they were like, "'Cause Trump is gonna send me back, and I've never even lived there.'"

She felt comfortable disclosing and discussing her politics with students and their families in the community within spaces that were less official (non-classroom) or were perceived to be safer from White surveillance:

> If I go at [building relationships with students and families] from the avenue where I'm a Mexican woman, then they let me in. If I—as soon as I start speaking in Spanish, then they let me in. And so when they get to know me first, and then when it comes to the political, then it's like, "Oh, it's okay," you know. Some of them will forgive me. Some of them say, "Well, we forgive you. You voted wrong." Some of them will say, "You know what, I kind of never saw it from that perspective. I voted that way, too, and this was why."

Her conversations in community with students and families were not rigid or doctrinaire, and were rooted in a shared collective experience of being Latinx in Oklahoma. Interacting with White students and/or colleagues, Maria reported a sense of unease in discussing her political views or giving the impression that her classroom was not a neutral space. She felt being "political" would place her at risk of being seen as unprofessional. In her White school, she expressed concern that her occasional students of color would out her as biased and cause her to take on the kinds of additional labor that pushed Gloria out of her former school:

> I just want to be very careful because I don't want to be like a token, like a totem that [students of color] will automatically assume I'm going to agree. And so that's why I'm always really careful about being very, very neutral because I don't necessarily want to be an ally. I want them to see both sides. Because there's good in both and there's bad in both.[4]

Maria's struggle to be seen as professional in White spaces juxtaposed with the relative ease with which she discussed politics with her Latinx students and families illuminates that neutrality is disciplined through fear of consequences that are imposed differently and relatively. For Maria, her language, racial, and ethnic status, already positioned her as not neutral, and her efforts to be seen as neutral (professional, unbiased) resulted in classroom interactions where Maria felt she had to offer equal weight to "both sides" and deny solidarity or allyship to students of color. Maria's heightened sense of vulnerability was further informed by her contingent, non-tenurable work arrangement with each of her schools.

In the same small town district as Maria's primarily White school, Erik, a young early 30s White man and Trump supporter, worked at the high school as an English language learner teacher. He said that once Trump became a frontrunner, the election became a "hot button topic." Erik espoused a deep love for his students: "We're at the family level, you know, and I refer to us as a family, you know. When they leave every day, I tell them that, 'I love you and I hope you have a great day.'" And yet, by his own admission, they did not appear to return his affection:

> But I wouldn't say that we—whether they agree with me or disagree with me [in supporting Trump], it hasn't affected instruction or my relationship with the students or, you know. And I have been called racist a bazillion times, it comes with the nature of being a White male and working in that environment, you know. And again, it breaks my heart because I live for those kids, you know. And to have to defend to the principal why I'm not [racist].

Erik claimed to maintain neutrality through refraining from discussing electoral politics. Yet, quite different from the experiences of Winona and Gloria, Erik's attempts at engaging in more substantive political conversation were largely didactic, aiming to get students to the "right" answer and address what he perceived as his students' lack of understanding on the issues, including the issue of immigration, which continuously arose in the aftermath of the election:

> I have never disclosed specifically that, like, I was a Trump supporter. But I do have the conversation with them about things like, well, you know, I believe that there needs to be a formal process to people coming into our country, you know, and I try and facilitate those conversations by flipping it on them, you know. What if the United States was trying to go to Mexico, you know, and so what would that look like to you guys or how would that, you know, at what point can we just continue to let, you know, millions of people enter the country in a year, you know. What is that gonna look like for space, for food, for resources, you know?

From the authors' perspective, Erik appeared to feel comfortable discussing politics with his students, even under the threat that students may report him as racist to his administration.

In contrast to Gloria's Socratic method, Winona's attempts to engage her students to take their own ethical stances, or Maria's commitment to engaging her students to see "both sides," Erik attempted to lead his students to a particular "correct" viewpoint while appearing to diminish their own lived experiences of immigration. His own disclosure that his students accuse him of racism is at odds with his understanding that, "I think after a while they kinda get on the same page [as me]."

By Erik's own disclosure, his students called him racist "a bazillion times" because he is a "White male" and not because of his perspective that his Latinx students were the source of and solution to issues of racism in their school. Erik reported that, for the most part, the election did not cause much of a disturbance in his school. He said there were a few, "I guess you could say redneck backcountry, you know, Bible Belt Oklahomans who, you know, White males basically in the high school that said things they shouldn't have." He reported that these racist comments by "rednecks" were only a symptom of the deficiency of Latinx students. He stated, "I think they provoke three-fourths of the things that happen to them, you know, and so trying to get them to take a step back and look at that stereotype and, well, what can I do to make sure I don't fall into that stereotype."

Erik's students appear to resist his perception of them as deficient and incapable via humor. While Erik did not seem to recognize it as such, their witty pranks on him illuminate their own sophistication on such matters:

> So the day after [Trump] got elected, one of my students was gone. And, so, I was like, "Oh, where is this student today?" and they were like, "Oh, she got deported already 'cause Donald Trump got elected, you know." I didn't even think about it. Like, my hall pass is green and so one student left for the bathroom, when they came back the other kids wouldn't let him in until he showed them that green card, or his green card, aka my hall pass.

He reported their humor as a coping mechanism and their fear as valid. He simultaneously articulates his classroom as a "safe" space to joke and a place where such political processing is inappropriate:

> I want them to feel like that's a safe space for them to cope with [fear] by joking about it, but at the same time it's also not appropriate. So, it's been a struggle to find the balance between letting them feel safe and get that out now so that it doesn't repercuss somewhere else in the building...Their jokes are hidden everywhere, you know. We had vocab words, and they have to draw a little picture for their vocab words, and it was jumping over the wall or digging under the wall or, just so many—like, everywhere you look, it was like there was these little jokes. I spent a lot of class time addressing these issues.

Allowing his students to let off steam through humor was characterized as a means to control their trouble-making in other school spaces ("so that it doesn't re-percuss")—a "lightning rod" strategy to dissipate their power, channel it safely into the earth so that it did not disrupt the school. While Erik acknowledged and recognized the validity of their fear, for him, their jokes indicated a lack of in-depth understanding of the issues: "I think for most of them, fear and, or a lack of under[standing], like, 'I just don't know, I'm rolling with what my friends are doing but I really don't understand the actual political view or issues or agenda.'"

Unlike our other participants', Erik reported a sense of prerogative in educating his students on political issues. He even reported attempts to educate his students' parents on issues of immigration. He said their resistance to his attempts were evidence of their "bias" on the issue because they were immigrants themselves. Yet, even as he reported his students are his "family," he simultaneously reported fear of their collective power: "Well, I don't really, I never told the kids that I voted for Trump. Um, and to be honest, part of me still hasn't decided whether that was a good idea or not. [...] I don't know what would happen. They'd probably stage another coup, you know." This fear of yet another "coup" (e.g., reporting him as racist to administration) was quite different than that of Maria's or others', who often feared losing their positions. While Maria, Winona, and Gloria felt, in different ways, pressure from above via their administrations and colleagues to avoid deep engagement of controversial topics like race (lightning), Erik upheld school norms by imposing a self-serving form of objectivity (lightning rod) that universalized his own views and stabilized his/the school's authority.

CONCLUSION

We end with the understanding that, as the science of lightning suggests, lightning rods don't always work (Tricoles, 2017). Participants' teaching environments during and after the election were marked by students doing things in class and in relation to their teachers they reportedly never did in the past, including spontaneously erupting in political debates, demanding teachers' political affiliations, and increased palpable tensions that sometimes resulted in verbal and/or physical confrontations. Despite a school environment that ensured a superficial engagement with justice, Gloria created a space that demanded White students bear witness to the intensity of being an immigrant in America. And, Erik's students' trickster pranks pushed back against his stance on immigration reform that dismissed their own knowledge and experience. Our participants underscore Patel's (2016) assertion that "learning, as it turns out, involves unpredictability. Its consequences are often unruly in their unwillingness to be contained" (p. 399).

As we have illustrated, representing recently intensified racist, gendered, sexual, and White nationalist violence in schools as solely or even mainly the result of external forces (adult election rhetoric) can risk absolving schools of imbrication in such violence via attempting to "neutralize" and contain learning (among other ways). Most importantly, acknowledging this imbrication requires that we cultivate lightning in our classrooms and shift our analyses and actions toward our own institutions. Such a shift can help us to better identify and challenge the lightning-rod strategies institutions employ that limit transformative learning. Often such strategies are masked within the normatively neutral language of standards and performance data as the "real" work of learning. Yet, if we understand that lightning always-already sparks in classrooms (after all, lightning makes life possible), then institutions' lightning rod strategies are active (rather than passive or default) attempts to contain and repress our and our students' understandings about how power, politics, and difference operates to create our worlds.

Finally, our participants illuminate that such work requires strategies that mitigate the differential levels of risk in balking neutrality in their own classroom and institutional spaces. Taking cues from student-, teacher-, and community-led movements that have long been struggling against various sources of school violence (e.g., struggles for ethnic studies and against assimilation), we can strive to construct collective analyses and actions that can meaningfully broaden spaces that nurture (rather than disperse) transformative electrical energies within our institutions.

NOTES

1. See also Kohli (2018) and Carrillo (2010) for examples of studies that illuminate, especially, the risks, discipline, and hostility that teachers of color face in navigating expectations for neutrality and engaging critical, transformative pedagogies.
2. At the time of the interview, she was transitioning to a new school due to her frustrations with her work environment.
3. Terence Crutcher was a Black man murdered in Tulsa by police officer Betty Shelby in 2016 (CNN Wire, 2017, May 22).
4. Here, we recognize that this was stated in the context of an interview with a White person in a perceived position of authority. Even though one of the authors held no direct institutional authority over Maria, she was colleagues with those who did. Maria did not know the author well, at the time, and may have perceived there might be consequences to her responses (e.g., that she might be perceived as unprofessional and that this perception might circulate in some way). After this interview, Maria and one of the authors formed a friendship of support, offering further insight into understanding this response as guarded.

REFERENCES

Ahmed, S. (2012). *On being included: Racism and diversity in institutional life.* Durham, NC: Duke University Press.

Burleigh, C. (2017, March 27). The aftermath of Trump: A challenge for education leaders and a call for youth activism. *Berkeley Review of Education Blog*. Retrieved from http://www.berkeleyreviewofeducation.com/cfc2016-blog/the-aftermath-of-trump-a-challenge-for-education-leaders-and-a-call-for-youth-activism

Carrillo, J. (2010). Teaching that breaks your heart: Reflections on the soul wounds of a first-year Latina teacher. *Harvard Educational Review, 80*(1), 74–81.

CNN Wire. (2017, May 22). *Jury explains why they acquitted Tulsa police officer in fatal shooting of Terence Crutcher*. Retrieved from http://kfor.com/2017/05/22/jury-explains-why-they-acquitted-tulsa-police-officer-in-fatal-shooting-of-terence-crutcher/

Costello, M. (2016). The Trump effect: The impact of the 2016 presidential election on our nations' schools. *Southern Poverty Law Center*. Retrieved from https://www.splcenter.org/sites/default/files/the_trump_effect.pdf

Derman-Sparks, L., LeeKeenan, D., & Nimmo, J. (2017, March 27). Post election: What do we say to the children? *Berkeley Review of Education Blog*. Retrieved from http://www.berkeleyreviewofeducation.com/cfc2016-blog/post-election-what-do-we-say-to-the-children

Dyke, E., Gordon, S., & Job, J. (2017). Oklahoma is a moving train: On Trump and the (impossible) demand for 'neutral' classrooms in a red state. *Berkeley Review of Education, 7*(1), 85–93.

Kishimoto, K., & Mwangi, M. (2009). Critiquing the rhetoric of "safety" in feminist pedagogy: Women of color offering an account of ourselves. *Feminist Teacher, 19*(2), 87–102. https://doi.org/10.1353/ftr.0.0044

Kohli, R. (2018). Behind school doors: The impact of hostile racial climates on urban teachers of color. *Urban Education, 53*(3), 307–333.

Lomawaima, T., & McCarty, T. (2006). *To remain an Indian: Lessons in democracy from a century of Native American education.* New York, NY: Teachers College Press.

Patel, L. (2016). Pedagogies of resistance and survivance: Learning as marronage. *Equity and Excellence in Education, 49*(4), 397–401. https://doi.org/10.1080/10665684.2016.1227585

Rycroft, M. J., Israelsson, S., & Price, C. (2000). The global atmospheric electric circuit, solar activity and climate change. *Journal of Atmospheric and Solar-Terrestrial Physics, 62*(17), 1563–1576. https://doi.org/10.1016/S1364-6826(00)00112-7

Sondel, B., Baggett, H. C., & Dunn, A. H. (2018). "For millions of people, this is real trauma": A pedagogy of political trauma in the wake of the 2016 U.S. Presidential election. *Teaching and Teacher Education, 70*, 175–185. https://doi.org/10.1016/j.tate.2017.11.017

Sottile, A. (2017, January 13). How kids are handling the election of Donald Trump. *The Rolling Stone Magazine*. Retrieved from https://www.rollingstone.com/politics/politics-features/how-kids-are-handling-the-election-of-donald-trump-118658/

SPLC. (2019, May 2). *Hate at school*. Retrieved from https://www.splcenter.org/20190502/hate-school

Tricoles, R. (2017, August 31). The thunderstorm whisperers. *The Atlantic*. Retrieved from https://www.theatlantic.com/technology/archive/2017/08/the-thunderstorm-whisperers/538605

CHAPTER 19

MAKE AMERICA GREAT FOR ONCE (MAGFO)

Chantae D. Still
Universtiy of South Florida

We were saying my president is Black
Now we are talking about how 45 is orange.
It's my perception,
But his direction makes me believe he is the reincarnation of a 1885 Slave
    owner who claims
Christian principles and freedom while unwilling to relinquish the finan-
    cial gain that he profits off the backs of others, but still due to his
    wife he gets to continue his facade.
Hey... he likes some people who are foreign.

The IRS defines a non-citizen as an alien.
A foreign national who will need a naturalization process to qualify them
    worthy to be accepted
into this marginalizing nation.
What would have happened to those travelers or colonial ships,

If the first people known as the natives of this land, were able to keep this
same "You are an
alien" energy?

MAGA!!!
A slogan I receive like a whip across my back, a King beating baton slap, or
a threat of a
sundown town dragging by an Aryan brother because of that AGAIN.

A term that turns my mind to a past full of Mississippi burnings and current covert Jim Crow
thinking that I desire to interrupt.
Let's all learn from history's past as we try and revamp the future.
Can the first political republicans and the 1948 Dixiecrats please stand up?

What do you mean by again? It's the questions that I have got to know.
From 1619 beyond the 1700s My ancestors were kidnapped, taken
through a middle passage
where many died on a decrepit boat.
In 1830 Jackson signed treaties in the light and made ethnic cleansing
deals in the dark
encouraging "colonists to slit Indian throats."

In 1870s every state had the white knights of the KKK burning crosses and
in the 1950s Bracero
workers were being exploited while Rosa was fighting her way from the
back of the bus.
Just seven years ago Trayvon died while a clown vigilante tried to "Stand
his ground" against
some skittles, and still for those with brown skin the police guns take lives
before EMT can get
you to the hospital,
So, what part of AGAIN makes America great for us????

There are still laws making invisible walls,
Disproportionately impacting P.O.C.s from reaching the top.
Redlining, Disparate impact, economic inequalities have all got to stop.

People of color are like POW's playing heads or tails with a two-sided coin,
And yet people ignore the dominating oppressors but expect civilized
response for personal
amusement HOWEVER I AM NO SAMBO to be purchased & I WONT
subordinately entertain.

So I stand before you UNAPOLOGETICALLY BLACK,
Outside of Olivia Pope's I'm screaming F*** ALL WHITE HATS,
And this aint about PARTY because I am not into labels, and sometimes it
      needs to be shades
of purple instead of Red or Blue.
But you must admit, we need to make America great for ONCE,
Because when you say AGAIN, you're talking about times that were only
      great for those
Americans who look like YOU!

Author Chantae Still holding a "Make America Great for Once" hat with a
      shirt that reads, "I am not perfect, but I am Limited Edition."

CHAPTER 20

RENEGADE TEACHERS

Deconstructing Heteronormative Narratives in the Classroom

Mark Hickey
Oklahoma State University

Jinan El Sabbagh
Oklahoma State University

Megan Ruby
Oklahoma State University

The classroom is undoubtedly a space in which many identities, ideologies, and subjectivities are in constant intersection and interaction. Without conscious acknowledgment and reflection of these complexities at work within classrooms, teachers may unintentionally end up replicating harmful discourses modeled in the heteropatriarchal society from which they originate (Britzman, 2012; García & Slesaransky-Poe, 2010). The traditional schooling model in the United States has done little to accommodate the identities of students and teachers that do not adhere to the strict confines

Making a Spectacle, pages 213–221
Copyright © 2021 by Information Age Publishing
All rights of reproduction in any form reserved.

of a heteronormative identity. Living in one of the states whose anti-bullying and anti-discrimination verbiage in public schools excludes LGBTQ+ youth, it becomes more important than ever to be a renegade teacher that supports these marginalized students (Human Rights Watch, 2017). Acts of surveillance, censorship, punishment, and enforcement all work to maintain the order of heteronormativity against the recognition of its own fragility. In other words, heteronormativity itself is weakened when scrutinized and therefore needs institutions, like schools, to uphold heteronormativity and its attitudes and policies.

In this chapter, we draw upon our positionality as educators and queer/feminist scholars as well as the identities that inform the vantage points for our individual and group analysis. We have worked together for over a year as graduate students and educators in K–12 classrooms, advocating for students and ourselves. Our gender identities range from cisgender female to cisgender, non-binary female to cisgender, non-binary male. As teachers, we have worked in education for a combined 18 years of experience in largely populated school districts in the Midwest and East Coast. Throughout our work, over this past year, we have developed more refined theoretical approaches to analyzing moments in which heteronormativity works against the well-being of our students and ourselves. Our journeys have all been different, but similar threads of our experiences have converged to present obstacles that might be faced by educators when combatting heteronormative saturated American K–12 classrooms. Reflecting on the plight of queer students and teachers, as demonstrated in vignettes below, can be instructive for those of all identities teaching and learning together.

In the following vignettes, each of us, authors, explore how we counteracted the heteronormative constructs/narratives within our classrooms using our positions as teachers. Mark explores the weight and sense of paralysis that came after overhearing a student mocking a trans student aggressively, and the decisions educators made at that moment. Jinan transverses a political moment of a White man on trial accused by a White woman of sexual assault. Megan discusses the power within a name. Each one of these lived experiences disrupts the power structures of so-called "neutrality" and invites teachers and other educators to imagine a classroom beyond (many times damaging) heteronormative and gender constructs.

Through these vignettes, we aim to illuminate narratives and their resulting reflections that might be of benefit to educators and those who work in schools. By highlighting several instances where we had been witnesses to moments that temporarily disrupt the illusion of the heteronorm in our classrooms, we aim to expose how students and teachers have the opportunity to question the discourses that form the perceived neutrality of the classroom space (Lane, 2020). Out of these moments, come fragments that may serve as ideal prompts for advocacy and reflection for both students and teachers that promote introspection as a means for engaging with our own biases.

By our efforts, we intend to draw attention to the perceived neutrality of the classroom as an effect of the systems of power that sustain heteronormative culture at-large and begin to re-imagine the classroom space as a site for political and social re-imagination and re-invention. Through introspection, students and educators might begin to disentangle their complicated relationships with heteropatriarchal forces and histories of schooling, teaching, and learning to renegotiate their subjectivities (Turner, 2010).

CLASSROOM NEUTRALITY

The discussion on the classroom as a politically neutral space is rooted in assumptions of heteronormativity and White supremacy. Mason and Ngo's (2019) study continues the discourse that White supremacy and racism are still issues within schools and higher education institutions. They found that there was a backlash when colleges and universities discussed the role of White supremacy within their institutions, fearing that such discussion could "ruin the ideas of the American Dream" or that it contradicts the idea that hard work unfailingly leads to success in America (Mason & Ngo, 2019, p. 9). This notion that teachers/academics should only be "apolitical purveyors of absolute knowledge and truth" begs the question about who's truth is the truth to which the columnist was referring. The answer is not only in White supremacist structures but also in the heteronormative and gender constructs. As Lane (2020) states:

> Heteronormativity creates social conditions whereby the expectation of heterosexuality, acts upon the body and works in a concerted effort with stigma to maintain a general effect of keeping things in line. This normative dimension of existence is immersive and controlling; negative attitudes toward those who do not hold their place encourage re-alignment and heterosexuality is reinforced as the normal disposition. (p. 8)

When we live in a world that only shows heteronormative structures through the media, religious context, literature (often chosen by the teachers or administration), right wing politics, and other narratives, it can be challenging to see a world outside those constructs. It sets up the binary structures of power so if heteronormative is good then others are bad. When in reality, there are multiple lived experiences that make a binary impossible. Notably, queer theorists such as Hermann-Wilmarth and Bills (2010) suggests that binary categories of human identity (i.e., man, woman, Black, White) are less stable than to be assumed. Actually, people are more accurately portrayed as "border crossers" those who play with these unstable boundaries and resist rigid categorization. As educators, if we recognize this ideology, it may position us to encourage the students, community members, and other educators we work with to look past the socially and politically constructed borders that enforce normality (Berlant & Warner, 1998; Puwar, 2004) and into a world free from categorization based in a binary that we have become conditioned to accept.

The vignettes that follow will contend with the theoretical approaches above, drawing attention to the detrimental effects of the assumed neutrality heteronormative classroom. Generally viewed as classroom-based disruptions, the events in the vignettes below will be reframed as opportunities for reflection and analysis that can then be reconsidered as ideological disruptions that open up a space of temporal flexibility that is otherwise stifled by heteropatriarchal influence.

MARK'S VIGNETTE 1: PARALYSIS

Early in my teaching career, I spent a year teaching high school English in the Philadelphia area and surrounding suburbs in which several of my classes had students who identified as gender non-conforming, transgender, queer, or otherwise 2LGBTQ+. In one particular instance early in the year, I overheard a comment directed at a student named Jay (pseudonym) who identified as a trans man. It was intentionally malicious and meant to question the "validity" of his gender. Upon hearing the comment, a familiar sense of paralysis arose within me, a phenomenon that many queer and non-queer educators face when deciding to implicate themselves by intervening on behalf of queer, 2LGBTQ+, and other gender non-conforming students (DeJean, 2010; King, 2004). As a result of this familiar paralysis, I was unable to intervene immediately as I had intended.

Before I could fully process my feelings and fears after overhearing a student Collin (pseudonym) mock a trans student, a set of peers urged Collin to reflect on what he said and how it might have hurt the person being insulted. To my surprise, Collin did not respond defensively and instead began verbally processing with his peers to make sense of the impact of his comments. The situation, now diffused, ended with an apology from Collin to Jay (pseudonyms) and gratitude to the peer group for helping him understand how questioning the "validity" of Jay's gender was harmful to the individual and the classroom community.

I have experienced situations similar to the one above that resulted in more regrettable conclusions due to my inaction. Some of my moments of deepest shame from my early years of teaching are moments where I failed to properly defend students from demeaning acts directed at their perceived queerness out of fear for my own safety. I often blamed myself for my failure to intervene, not realizing as a queer educator that I am often caught in the "double binds" that queer bodies and minds are subject to when they inhabit non-queer spaces (Sedgwick, 1990, p. 70). I continue to examine and deconstruct my responses to these types of situations and work toward becoming a more responsive educator who employs meaningful introspection to improve my praxis.

JINAN'S VIGNETTE 2: CLASSROOMS AS POLITICAL "SAFE" SPACES

In my senior English class, students were more politically cognizant than ever before as they digested and discussed the incessant violence and hateful rhetoric of the Trump administration (Costello, 2016; SPLC, 2019). However, the Brett Kavanaugh hearing in the Fall of 2018 was the most emotionally charged, leading to positive shifts within the classroom. The conversation began on a Wednesday morning right before Christine Blasey Ford was scheduled to testify. Nearing the first break in instruction time, a White seventeen-year-old man Jamie (pseudonym), who had been increasingly vocal about seeking to understand the merits of Trump policies from the start of the semester, raised his hand and asked what I thought about the hearings. I knew at that moment, I had to be careful, but also, since I had established my classroom as a "nurturing and validating space within which to navigate the varying identities lived," I decided it better to allow this interpersonal dialogue (Garcia & Dutro, 2018, p. 381). The hearings had everyone (including my most apathetic senioritis-ridden students) interested. So, I asked, "Well, what are your thoughts?" He went on to regurgitate standard conservative talking points such as, "Why did she wait so long to bring this up"; "I don't trust her"; and, "If there were anything substantial, the FBI would have shared it" (see Severino, 2018; Chamberlain, 2018). Some of his fellow classmates immediately rushed to her defense, noting how Dr. Blasey-Ford had everything to lose and how we cannot comprehend nor judge how long it takes someone to work through such trauma. The exchanges continued and increased in volume as Jamie gained allies (all men), goading the women in the room who became increasingly frustrated and irate. As I refereed, I was glad to hear the bell signaling the end of this metaphoric boxing round. I was exhausted. I asked students to take a break (needing to re-calibrate as well). Reintroducing our mindfulness practice, I asked all to return to that moment of intensity, acknowledge it, and breathe through the discomfort, separating the feelings from the individuals that were voicing them. Their homework was to post on our Google classroom what they expect for future classroom discussions, which we edited and discussed that Friday. The idea being that the classroom would be a safe space for *all* participants, not just the loudest in the room. While not a healing moment, it brought to the forefront conversations of consent, rape culture, and the embedded heteropatriarchal bias in such conversations (Kamenetz, 2018; Moore & Reynolds, 2016).

MEGAN'S VIGNETTE 3: THE POWER OF A NAME

For the last decade, there has been a call for diversity and inclusion training (Ahmed, 2012; Ayers, Kumashiro, Meiners, Quinn, & Stovall, 2016; Puwar, 2004) in educational spaces. That training has also branched out to professional development for teachers on gender and sexuality (Linville, 2017; Quinn & Meiners, 2009) to help create a more inclusive school and classroom environment. As an elementary teacher, most of my career had been about challenging heteronormative ideas about gender in the sense of, "Girls can also help with moving things around the classroom" or "It's okay if boys have long hair." Later in my career, I took a mid-year junior high position teaching eighth grade science.

I had not darkened the doors of a middle school as a professional since my first internship in undergrad. I was surprised to find that many of my students had a need to feel wanted and included as much as the elementary students, although with the added burden of trying to discover who they are and who they wanted to be. For example, there was Danny (pseudonym), a trans nonbinary student who had started their transitioning during a development stage (i.e., early teenage years) that is difficult for most students. As a teacher, I have always had a policy of asking students what name they prefer at the beginning of the school year; that way, they feel comfortable when I call on them in class. Also, because adults set the tone of acceptance in the classroom (Slesaransky-Poe, 2013), with this being the middle of the year, I still felt that it was the responsible thing to do. So, I also mentioned that if anyone felt uncomfortable doing this in front of everyone that they could tell me in private.

Danny told me after class what pronouns they preferred, but I could see Danny was hesitant about something. I asked, "Are you okay" and "Would you mind if I use your chosen name and pronouns?" Danny hesitated for a moment then said, "My mother does not approve, and she has told the rest of the teachers to call me by my [dead name]. And since you are new, she will tell you to do that as well." My heart dropped as I thought about how much emotional support this student would need since their home life was not going to be accepting. Our eighth-grade team decided together that we would never use a student's dead name despite the parent's so-called well wishes. We resolved that if we talked to Danny's mom, we would do it under the guise that we were doing as she wished, although none of us ever followed through with her wishes. Being inclusive should not be a renegade act. Still, until all students like Danny feel comfortable to be themselves inside the hallowed halls of the education system, then a renegade teacher I will be.

DISCUSSION

In each of these cases, our encounters with heteronormativity in the classroom followed a general process. First, we recognized that the classroom's perceived neutrality was a zone of heteronormativity designed to sustain its existence and support its reproduction. Second, someone intervened regardless of social risk. Third, the intervention benefitted students and teachers who were not accommodated by the heteronormative design of the classroom. As renegade teachers, our specific actions followed a frame-work initiated by discomfort, rather than by its suppression or avoidance. Instead, we chose to use the discomfort as an impetus for challenging the source. Each of these vignettes was told through the perspective of a teach-er and involved students' reactions.

In both Mark and Megan's vignettes, the classroom community (whether the teachers or the students) strove to make the space inclusive for stu-dents who were trans. Similarly, Mark and Jinan's vignettes show how stu-dents rose to protest against the discriminatory and controversial topics that arose in class. In all these vignettes, the renegade teachers' roles stem from the initial recognition of the disparities of accommodation that per-sist in a heteronormative classroom space. The renegade teacher does not see themselves and their students as invaders of this space, but rather, as partners in creating a new space, redefined by its inhabitants and their collective identities (Puwar, 2004). The renegade teacher recognizes that teachers can be conditioned by society as well as their teacher preparation programs to seek out an apolitical space to maintain the appearance of neu-trality and the boundaries of comfort that enforce the zone of permission of what might be "acceptable" to talk about in classrooms. Renegade teach-ers realize these boundaries are constructed by heteropatriarchal political systems that have been embedded in the formation of common schools in the United States, and thus can be deconstructed through individual and community efforts within a classroom. They see discomfort as opportunities to create a consciousness of caring within a classroom community in which queer students are safe and validated. In all, vital members of the classroom community influence the ideological fabric of the classroom. The influence of the classroom community then belongs to those that inhabit it rather than the ideologies that shape it.

CONCLUSION

When viewed through the lens of queer theory, our experiences in these vignettes call educators to question, reflect, and engage in their own praxis to enable them to consider how taking an "apolitical" or "neutral" stance is not only harmful but inconsiderate to the students who live outside the predefined borders of the heteronormative classroom. This is and will be a renegade act. When one goes against the grain it is not an easy task, but taking the road of silence and status quo can be even more detrimental

(Puwar, 2004). Ignoring identities that fall outside the heteropatriarchal socially-imposed boundaries not only deleteriously affects students, but also the classroom space in which they are expected to learn. The classroom is the ideal space to (re)negotiate identities, political stances, and to develop "critical consciousness" (Freire, 2000) in the hopes of transforming a politically saturated society; one in which taking an apolitical stance would be tantamount to continuing the status quo that sustains oppression. As teachers and educators, we have a responsibility to be border-crossers (Hermann-Wilmarth & Bills, 2010) as therein lies the possibility to co-construct safer and more liberating spaces for our youth and ourselves. Accordingly, we believe we have a responsibility to stand in the gap for those students who are harmed by heteropatriarchal educational systems and schooling. To fulfill this responsibility, we keep carving out space that allows any student considered "deviant" a place to be who they are, despite any consequences from the administration, parents, or other educators.

REFERENCES

Ahmed, S. (2012). *On being included: Racism and diversity in institutional life.* Durham, NC: Duke University Press.

Ayers, W., Kumashiro, K., Meiners, E., Quinn, T., & Stovall, D. (2016). *Teaching toward democracy 2e: Educators as agents of change* (Vol. 5). New York, NY: Routledge.

Berlant, L., & Warner, M. (1998). Sex in public. *Critical Inquiry, 24*(2), 547–566.

Britzman, D. P. (2012). *Practice makes practice: A critical study of learning to teach.* Albany: State University of New York Press.

Chamberlain, S. (2018, September 24). *Kavanaugh denies sexual misconduct in Fox News exclusive: 'I know I'm telling the truth.'* Retrieved from https://www .foxnews.com/politics/kavanaugh-denies-sexual-misconduct-in-fox-news -exclusive-i-know-im-telling-the-truth

Costello, M. (2016, November 28). *The Trump effect: The impact of the 2016 presidential election on our nation's schools.* Retrieved September 22, 2020, from https://www.splcenter.org/20161128/trump-effect-impact-2016-presidential -election-our-nations-schools.

DeJean, W. (2010). Courageous conversations: Reflections on a queer life narrative model. *The Teacher Educator, 45*(4), 233–243. https://doi.org/10.1080/0887 8730.2010.508262

Freire, P. (2000). *Pedagogy of the oppressed.* New York, NY: Continuum.

Garcia, A., & Dutro, E. (2018, July). Electing to heal: Trauma, healing, and politics in classrooms. *English Education.* Retrieved from https://educatorinnovator .org/wp-content/uploads/2018/10/Electing_to_Heal.pdf

García, A. M., & Slesaransky-Poe, G. (2010). The heteronormative classroom: Questioning and liberating practices. *The Teacher Educator, 45*(4), 244–256. https://doi.org/10.1080/08878730.2010.508271

Hermann-Wilmarth, J. M., & Bills, P. (2010). Identity shifts: Queering teacher education research. *The Teacher Educator, 45*(4), 257–272. https://doi.org/10.10 80/08878730.2010.508324

Human Rights Campaign. (2017). *"Like walking through a hailstorm": Discrimination against LGBT youth in US schools.* Retrieved from https://www.hrw .org/report/2016/12/07/walking-through-hailstorm/discrimination -against-lgbt-youth-us-schools

Kamenetz, A. (2018, September, 21). *How to talk to young people about the Kavanaugh story.* Retrieved from https://www.npr.org/2018/09/21/650039170/ how-to-talk-to-young-people-about-the-kavanaugh-story

King, J. R. (2004). The (im)possibility of gay teachers for young children. *Theory into Practice, 43*(2), 122–127.

Lane, J. (2020). Using queer phenomenology to disrupt heteronormativity and deconstruct homosexuality. *Journal of Homosexuality,* https://doi.org/10.1080/0 0918369.2020.1733353

Linville, D. (2017). *Queering education: Pedagogy, curriculum, policy. Occasional Paper Series 37.* New York, NY: Bank Street College of Education.

Mason, A. M., & Ngo, B. (2019). Teacher education for cultural and linguistic diversity in the United States. *Oxford Research Encyclopedia of Education.* Retrieved from https://oxfordre.com/education/view/10.1093/acrefore/9780190264093 .001.0001/acrefore-9780190264093-e-297

Moore, A., & Reynolds, P. (2016). Feminist approaches to sexual consent: a critical assessment. *Making sense of sexual consent* (pp. 29–44). New York, NY: Routledge.

Puwar, N. (2004). *Space invaders: Race, gender, and bodies out of place.* New York, NY: Berg.

Quinn, T., & Meiners, E. R. (2009). *Flaunt it!: Queers organizing for public education and justice* (Vol. 340). New York, NY: Peter Lang.

Sedgwick, E. (1990). *Epistemology of the closet.* Berkeley: University of California Press.

Severino, C. (2018, September 4). *The Kavanaugh hearings: Spectacle, and civics lesson.* Retrieved from https://www.realclearpolitics.com/articles/2018/09/04/the _kavanaugh_hearings_spectacle_and_civics_lesson_137972.html

Slesaransky-Poe, G. (2013). Adults set the tone for welcoming all students. *Phi Delta Kappan, 94*(5), 40–44.

SPLC. (2019, May 2). *Hate at school.* Retrieved from https://www.splcenter.org/ 20190502/hate-school.

Turner, S. L. (2010). Undressing as normal: The impact of coming out in class. *The Teacher Educator, 45*(4), 287–300. https://doi.org/10.1080/08878730.2010 .508316

CHAPTER 21

REFLECTION

Sisyphus With a Smile:
On Finding Momentum Through
Political Trauma in Education

Nadia Khan-Roopnarine
Molloy College

I am an educator: brown, female, muslim, first-generation American, short.

I am a descendent of colonized peoples: from indentured Indian ancestors,
to parents who were born as bound British, then "given" Guyana, and moved
to achieve America.

I am a middle class kid from Long Island. But I'm also not.

My many identities have placed me in perpetual otherness throughout my
educational experiences as a K–12 student and beyond into college. Even
before I had the words to describe it, I always felt just on the outskirts of
my school communities. It was this perpetual othering (in addition to a
lifelong ambition formed in my bossy-big-sisterhood) that inspired me to
become a New York City public school teacher and a founding teacher of a
6–12 school in Brooklyn. Steeped in the revolutionary critical pedagogy of
Paulo Freire, I helped build, and continue to support and shape, a school

Making a Spectacle, pages 223–227
Copyright © 2021 by Information Age Publishing

that is dedicated to uplifting the voices and experiences of all members of its community. Lately though I have been restless, noticing and ruminating over things that in years past didn't feel so burdensome.

A colleague of mine has a mug that she often drinks out of; it comes to mind perhaps more than I might expect. On it, a crude drawing depicts a stick figure posing in what seems to be the wake of a boulder. From this artist's rendering, the relationship between the stick figure person and boulder is unclear. Above the picture is an accompanying Camus quote: "One must imagine Sisyphus happy." As an advanced placement English literature teacher, I am no stranger to the philosophies of Camus. My favorite unit to teach every year explores *The Stranger* within the context of existentialism and nihilism. As a class, my students and I spend the unit coming up with a group definition of existentialism and read quintessential existential texts such as *No Exit* and *The Metamorphosis*. I feel fairly confident with the intellectual content of existentialism.

The mug, however, has been drawing my attention for months now. Every time I am in a department meeting with my colleague, or passing her in the hallway engaging with students, if she has that mug, I am reluctantly fixated on the quote. I have turned the phrase around in my mind countless times and landed in a somewhat comfortable pessimism. I believe that Camus means that if one cannot imagine Sisyphus happy, then one is dooming him to ultimate despair. Sisyphus needs to be happy in our imaginings in order for him to believe he is fulfilling his purpose, in turn driving his hope, and giving his ineffectual task some sort of meaning. I have pitied Sisyphus: Although an evil King seemingly deserving of his eternal punishment, he cannot see the futility not only of his perpetual moving of the boulder, but of his own contentedness in doing so.

My colleague and I work at Spring Creek Community School, which was founded in 2012 using the teachings of Paulo Freire and the philosophies of bell hooks. We work to stay true to our founding mission and vision by positioning our school as a hub for the community, built to serve our families beyond the boundaries of our classroom walls. The very first day of school in our brand new building, the teachers toured our wide-eyed sixth graders through the facilities that would magnify their learning, foster their friendships, and house their heartbreaks for the next several years. I was optimistic. I took our building and my classroom as a major point of pride. I spent hours considering the perfect posters for the walls, the least restrictive seating arrangements, and the many ways I would create spaces for dialogue and inquiry. I think of myself as an actively anti-racist teacher, working to subvert the oppression of institutional racism in my school community. In the beginning, the work nourished my hope and my heart, as I considered the innumerable possibilities that lay ahead. I had a fairly ambitious sixth grade curriculum plan: We covered race, power, inequity, and activism, morality, philosophy, and mythology.

But now, 7 years later as a high-school teacher working with many of the same kids from those early teaching experiences, I find myself more and more sitting in places of despair. It was cathartic when our first senior class graduated in 2019, and I was overwhelmed with memories of those sixth grade students whom I had come to know and love over the years. This was the goal that motivated and sustained me through many difficult years. But in the wake of the graduation relief wave, and as my former students reach out for love and support they are not finding in their lives after high school, I feel immobilized. I am still struggling to find ways to meet the needs of my kids who are now young college students. This is my Sisyphisian boulder. I am thankful not to be in this struggle alone. As I stand at the bottom of the mountain, facing a boulder so large it obscures my vision, the moves I make to heave it to the top are supported by the pushing of my colleagues, our little institution bucking behind me, propelling us all forward and upward. But forward and upward to where, to what? I wonder, what might we find if and when we get to the top?

Sometimes I feel like I'm running really fast in the wrong direction. I told Taina that college was the answer. She could make it, I would make sure of it. She went.

Taina had no resources, no college community. Despite my best efforts, Best intentions, Taina is not living up to her inflated expectations. Did I do that?

Melissa only wanted to go away. To learn, escape, become who she was "meant to be." Our valedictorian. College dropout.
My
fault.

Here I am. Working toward equity while holding up the walls of institutional racism. Furiously equipping students with the tools to navigate oppression. While perpetuating our own.

Raj came back with a unique request: He wants to observe our classrooms. A math teacher? You? YES! Of course! What an honor you chose us.

Regular updates from my original
crew: Anita loves her school, hates
the kids. She was always too mature
for her peers. Jose had a hard time,
Didn't know he could ask questions.
Couldn't afford his text books. Zeena
found time for 20 hours a week, for
school, for taking care of her sister,
for helping her mom recover from
illness.

They can do it. Of course they
can.

Since our first graduating class, I find myself at a turning point. I recently engaged in a critical discourse analysis of my own advanced placement English literature syllabus. In the first four pages of the curriculum, 29 times I wrote what "students" would be expected to do, to demonstrate, to prepare for. But only once did I mention what the "teacher" would do, demonstrate, or provide, and that was a passing reference about scheduling individual conferencing. How could I not realize, not know, that I was devaluing student identities, experiences, and autonomy while perpetuating an "ideal" student in a way that could widen inequities? In my dismay, I returned to fundamental texts that helped shape my early pedagogy. I am reminded of a metaphor bell hooks (1994) uses in *Teaching to Transgress*:

> Then there are times when personal experience keeps us from reaching the mountaintop and so we let it go because the weight of it is too heavy. And sometimes the mountaintop is difficult to reach with all our resources, factual and confessional, so we are just there collectively grasping, feeling the limitations of knowledge, longing together, yearning for a way to reach that highest point. Even this yearning is a way to know. (p. 92)

I often feel like I can reach the top of the mountain, conquer it, and see it completely for what it is. I have many developed resources over the last few years as a classroom teacher, but I recognize that my knowledge and my experiences are limited. There is no way to know beyond my own limitations. But, as hooks reminds us, my desire to know or achieve is its own form of knowing. This knowledgeable yearning acknowledges our struggle, it recognizes our desires, and helps shape my hope for moving forward.

America is a snow-covered peak.
Generations of blizzards have hardened
the ice. Whiteness covering everything.

Underneath, a mountain. Regal. Strong.
Resilient. Powerful.

Once submerged under oceans
Stewed in a primordial sea. With
ancient magic teeming underneath.

It is raining.
There is
hail.

It only takes an avalanche to move the
snow.

One individual snowflake, although unique, lacks the force to start an avalanche. It is the collective effort of millions of snowflakes together that create the momentum required. A tumbling of snow from the top of a mountain, avalanches are incredibly powerful and can have a devastating impact in areas where they occur. Alone, a snowflake is meager, melting at the slightest whisper of breath, but piled together snow becomes a force of potential. It is upon this mass of snow that I as Sisyphus push forward, perpetually rolling my boulder up a snow-covered mountain. It is difficult to imagine a revisioning of an educational system when initiatives seem only to unmake and remake the issues built into it in the first place. I ask myself daily: What is the goal? Am I meant to support students through a system built to oppress them or to completely subvert the system? How does one go about toppling White supremacy when it is so deeply entrenched? And today, my only answer is to open pathways of dialogue with students, allow students to lead and let them tell us where they are, what they need, how to proceed.

I think of myself as Sisyphus, perpetually pushing my boulder and smiling to foster my own hopefulness and my own search for purpose, as my students and I struggle for equity. But my desperate need to smile as I climb is misguided. The students in front of me are not boulders needing to be pushed to the top of a seemingly insurmountable mountain. They have momentum of their own to guide me and show me the direction we need to go. With this realization, then, I am Sisyphus no longer, but finally, truly smiling.

REFERENCE

hooks, b. (1994). *Teaching to transgress: Education as the practice of freedom.* New York, NY: Routledge.

CHAPTER 22

"WE ARE STILL HERE"

(Not) Teaching Disruption, Interruption, Resistance, and the Creation of Change

Brian Gibbs
University of North Carolina at Chapel Hill

Kristin Papoi
University of North Carolina at Chapel Hill

The following query was posed by an applicant being interviewed while seeking admittance into a Master of Arts teaching program. "I've been wondering, as [a] student of color in predominantly White history classrooms and as an aspiring social studies teacher in a predominantly White field, how do we teach and learn history that is hard,[1] and sometimes quite ugly without traumatizing, or re-traumatizing, both students and ourselves?" The query served as a laser pointer to work we as organizers of the program have been recently asking. Specifically, how can teachers adopt a more critical approach (Parkhouse, 2017) to a pedagogy of political trauma (Sondel, Baggett, & Hadley-Dunn, 2018), which is trauma-informed while also being critical in approach and disposition.

Making a Spectacle, pages 229–247
Copyright © 2021 by Information Age Publishing
All rights of reproduction in any form reserved.

Before the 2016 presidential election and since President Trump took office, issues of tension and politically related violence have spiked in schools nationwide (Costello, 2016; Rogers et al., 2017; Sondel et al., 2018). Teachers have simultaneously indicated a purposeful avoidance of controversial issues, including topics of race, class, gender, LGBTQAI, and resistance (Costello, 2016; Rogers et al., 2017). With the rise of neoliberalism (Apple, 2006; Harvey, 2005), the political right has co-opted the discourse of resistance which has had the effect of rolling back gains made by minoritized groups, thus protecting dominant White ideology. Meanwhile, teaching about resistance and resistance groups in the social studies has become increasingly complicated as White supremacy has moved from the shadows of American society to an increasingly verbose, militant, and violent front and center. From the "march of the tiki torches" and the resulting violence in Charlottesville to the seemingly endless campus strife surrounding who and what groups should be permitted to speak, resistance and protest are increasingly employed by the right to reclaim ground lost since the end of the Civil War.

Framed by this sociopolitical context, succinctly and astutely, the aspiring teacher introduced above voiced the question we'd also been pondering: How can hard history be taught critically in a trauma-informed way? Emerging not from the hundreds of pages of data we collected in research studies, nor from the numerous, iterative drafts of this article, the inquiry rings true and bold. Emerging from the wonderings of an undergraduate student who intended to become a social studies teacher. This paper is an attempt at our response.

RESEARCH QUESTION

It is not enough to teach just critically. It is not enough to teach with a trauma-informed pedagogy. We must consider the question around which this paper is constructed: "How do teachers teach difficult knowledge critically using trauma-informed pedagogy (TIP)?" We seek to answer this inquiry through data that emerge from several research studies (Gibbs, 2018, 2019, 2020a, 2020b) in which teachers completely avoided or only narrowly taught complicated and violent history, citing fear of causing trauma or socio-emotional distress amongst their students as the reason. There were a few teachers who taught on and taught on thoughtfully. These are their stories.

History, when told authentically, is a horror story (Gibbs, 2019). A narrative of murder, death, rape, sexism, racism, homophobia, and violence emerges when history is examined critically. In the social studies literature, this has been referred to as teaching difficult knowledge or hard history (Costello, 2016; Levy & Sheppard, 2018; Zembylas, 2014). The content itself can be difficult, as in the case of this study having students examine military violence in war or racial violence. Still, the work is made even more challenging, depending on the geographic context in which the teaching is situated. As Levy and Sheppard (2018) argued, teaching the Holocaust is difficult, but in Poland or Germany, it is even more difficult. Furthermore, Zembylas (2014) reminds us that teaching this difficult history carries with it an emotional burden for both teachers and students that can leave emotional scars. We are interested in investigating how difficult knowledge can be taught critically, authentically, and with a trauma-informed pedagogy in spaces where the history deeply, and often quite personally, affects students.

METHODOLOGY

This paper draws from data collected in two multi-case studies of social studies teachers in the rural South, with each of the four teachers presented here representing a case (Yin, 1989, 2003). Due to the breadth of data collected, we decided to choose and tell powerful narratives that emerged from the data. In collaboration with the study participants, we selected particular stories that richly address aspects of the research question. Through these narratives, we contend that teachers' perspectives regarding the complexities of teaching difficult history in trauma-informed ways serve to elucidate areas of tension and in/congruence when undertaking this work.

Three types of data inform the bulk of the analysis: classroom observations, teacher interviews, and student focus group interviews, as described below.

Classroom Observations

We observed participants' instruction in four classrooms,[2] between two and nine times per classroom, during instructional units that included the teaching of war or lynching. We also recorded extensive field notes during these observations in the form of a running record (Wright-Maley, 2015).

Teacher Interviews

We conducted two semi-structured interviews with each of the four teacher participants. The first interview focused on the individual teacher's politics and ideology, views on teaching, descriptions of pedagogy, and their perspective on the time and place in which they were teaching. The second interview was driven by an elicitation technique where we asked participants to critique case studies depicting teachers teaching war and lynching using a variety of pedagogies and approaches (Barton, 2015; Creswell, 2008; Fraenkel & Wallen, 2006; Patton, 2002). Each semi-structured interview lasted between 90 and 120 minutes, and once transcribed, we conducted two rounds of deductive coding to reveal themes. In collaboration with study participants, we selected specific narratives that connected to dominant themes that emerged from our coding process. We wrote descriptive case memos, engaged member checks, and incorporated participant feedback into findings (Miles & Huberman, 1994). In addition to the formal interviews described above, we engaged in numerous informal conversations and interviews before or after observed lessons.

Focus Group Interview

We engaged a group of 18 students in one focus group interview[3] (Morgan, 2002) which lasted 45 minutes for the study focused on lynching. We asked students their views on whether and how lynching should be taught and whether or not the easily accessible photographs of lynching should be studied in high school classrooms. We engaged students with several prompts, then asked them to write about each and speak with a partner about what they wrote, before engaging them in a whole-class discussion. For the study focused on war, we interviewed four groups of students twice for 55 minutes per interview about their views on how war should be taught, the role of patriotism in schools, and media coverage of war.

THEORETICAL FRAMEWORK

The theoretical framework for this article is informed by disruptive and interruptive pedagogy—teaching that seeks to push students to analyze content more critically—and trauma-informed pedagogy—teaching which keeps students' background experiences and wounds in mind. Both frameworks are necessary because our data raise two complications: (a) How do you teach students authentic history about the military and racial violence when pushed not to by national and community pressure?; and (b) How do you do this without harming students who are intimately connected to this historical trauma?

Disruptive and Interruptive Pedagogy

To teach resistance and change, a disruptive or interruptive pedagogy is necessary (Achinstein & Ogawa; Mills, 1997). This disruptive and interruptive pedagogy asks questions not asked in the official curriculum (Apple, 2006), is more inclusive of content and pedagogical structures that appeal to and are more successful with students of color (Emdin, 2015; Ladson-Billings, 1994; Paris & Alim, 2018), and work to help students recognize and grow their agency (Gillen, 2014) and ability to make change (Vinson & Ross, 2015). A disruptive pedagogy is powerful because it occurs on the individual teacher and classroom level. It typically begins with the development of a strong classroom community, a strong student–teacher relationship, and a teacher who is asking students to *consider* alternative positions (Hess, 2009) and solutions, not *convincing* students of the rightness or wrongness of particular positions.

Disruptive or interruptive pedagogies are more broadly known as social justice teaching (North, 2009; Swalwell, 2013) or as critical pedagogy (Apple, 2006; Giroux, 1988; McLaren, 1998). Sleeter (2014) defines social justice teaching using pillars, which include: Situating families and communities in structural analysis, developing relationships with students, families, and communities; having high academic expectations of all students; and teaching an inclusive curriculum. Evans (2015) argues that social justice teaching demands the development of inquiry- and discussion-based pedagogies. These pedagogies are then focused on justice-oriented themes and questions to highlight power differences, issues of race and class, gender, and LGBTQAI that were not readily highlighted in the standard curriculum.

Critical pedagogy is an approach to teaching focused on systems of power and inequity, marginalized voices, and focused on resistance and efforts of change (Parkhouse, 2017). A critical theoretical frame purposefully challenges and seeks to interrupt the established system of reproduction (Apple, 2003, 2006; Giroux; 1988, 2011; McLaren, 1998), and calls for a developed praxis and *conscientização* (Freire, 1970), or critical awareness, which leads to inquiry, self-reflection, and social action. Critical pedagogy, then, is the engaged act of teaching with a critical theoretical lens (Shor, 1992, 1997), teaching against power and oppression and for liberation (Picower, 2011). Disruptive pedagogy is calling student awareness to critical issues and providing them a space to engage them and imagine if not attempt to implement solutions. The difficulty is finding the space or teachers believing they have the autonomy or agency to engage a disruptive pedagogy (Ross, 2016).

Trauma-Informed Pedagogy

Trauma-Informed Pedagogy (TIP) teaches difficult content with students' trauma in mind, using particular pedagogy and shaping particular curriculum not to have students avoid what could be triggering but instead fully engage it. Sondel et al. (2018) argue for a pedagogy of political trauma, offering support and guidance to children as they make their way through a time of heightened political threat in schools as women, people of color, Muslims, and those who identify as LGBTQAI come under increasing attack. TIP goes further by teaching with an awareness of the trauma students may bring with them to and experience in school. Poverty, racism, misogyny, and homophobia are just a few of the traumas students may have experienced before they arrive at school and the intersectionality of multiple types of trauma further compound the challenge that students may face.

Often, these wounds are exacerbated and perpetuated inside the classroom through curriculum and pedagogical trauma inflicted by teachers and instructional practice. TIP calls for engaging in restorative practices (Winn, 2018) that see and support the whole child, making classrooms not only safe but empowering spaces (Carello & Butler, 2015), that schools and classrooms are responsive to student needs (Overstreet & Chafouleas, 2016), the need to know your students, what they have experienced as well as the services your school offers (Venet, 2019). Race, gender, sexuality, and violence can and are often taught in ways that deepen, awaken, or inflict trauma anew. Too often, this causes teachers to avoid or "lightly" teach these topics out of fear of inflicting damage upon students. TIP (Gibbs & Papoi, 2020), teaches with a trauma-informed lens that educators teach with an awareness of the wounds students have and seek to thoughtfully and truthfully teach the history of violence.

WHAT WE LEARNED

Teachers feel an enormous pressure to conform, to teach the straight and narrow and avoid difficult topics (Gibbs, 2019). Most recently, teachers have been experiencing enormous social pressure to not teach critically (Gibbs, 2020). Teachers who have engaged their students in critical examinations of difficult topics have often approached it through a trauma-informed lens, seeking to understand their students and their wounds before engaging in the content. While this is an important and necessary approach, this push towards pedagogical disruption of making students see things differently or more clearly is not easy but is incredibly necessary. Although many narratives emerged from the data, we chose to focus on and tell four stories that we believe intersect and provide a thick description of the difficulties faced by classroom teachers as they attempt to teach more truthful historical accounts of history. Teachers face pressure and resistance from students, parents, and the broader community. Additionally, teachers must walk a difficult road as they attempt to teach authentically while keeping student socio-emotional health in mind.

Definitions and Words

Mr. James took part in a study examining the pedagogic and curricular choices teachers make on teaching about war to the children of soldiers during a time of war. The nine teacher participants indicated that their decisions about teaching about war were influenced by their perceptions of socio-emotional needs of their students, perceived community pressure to avoid controversial topics, the pressure to teach the district course of study, and the particular right-wing political passions inflamed by the backdrop of the 2016 presidential election occurring during the study. Mr. James described a "pulling back" from anything that might be labeled as controversial while Ms. Jackson, another participant, described a form of self-censorship where she avoided any pedagogical practices that might lead to students asking what she described as "complicated questions" that could lead to "the loss of my job." All nine participants reported a climate of fear that directly impacted their teaching practice and had impacted their students as well.

"Civil discourse...civil disobedience maybe...I think that's the next place to go. The students didn't know what to do." Mr. James teaches social studies in a rural county to a school that serves a high proportion of students whose parents are soldiers. He was describing his students' reactions to the protests instigated by the survivors of the school shooting at Marjorie Stoneman High School. Like many schools, the protest was school-sanctioned and supported by increased security and faculty participation. At Mr. James' school, the students could go outside to the football field, listen to the names being read, then stand in silence for 17 minutes. Teachers could go to the event if it was their preparation period or if their entire class chose to attend. Only three of Mr. James's students attended.

"It was a low point for me professionally. I was like, 'Don't you want to go?!' And they [the students] were like, 'No. We don't want to miss class, this is important.' And in my mind, I'm screaming, 'GO! GO! GO! Come on!!' And then, I have failed." He described speaking to other teachers about this and his disappointment that the students weren't interested in participating. "They were just like, why stir the pot? You know where we live. You know what we're living through. I just hung my head and was like yeah..." He understood. They were living in a time and a place of fear.

Ironically, Mr. James indicated that the students who stayed seemed interested in the topic. As he explained, "The students who stayed came in excited for the lecture...they were like 'We're still learning about civil disobedience right?' as they excitedly took out their notebooks. One student who is just so bright said, 'That Thoreau guy is awesome...I mean way to stand up for himself and for all of us.' She said this as students from other classes were marching out, leaving for the protest...and she was taking out her notebook to take notes on the lecture on civil disobedience."

Mr. James' students did not only seem to grasp the concept of civil disobedience, even within a controlled school setting but maintained that, in our current socio-political situation, civil discourse and civil disobedience are contested concepts. Scholar Wendy Kohli begins her essay *Teaching in the Danger Zone: Democracy and Difference* this way: "My assignment...is to say something about democratic education. I accept the assignment with enthusiasm...because of the importance it holds at this historic moment when the *rhetoric* of *democracy* is used by many for all sorts of *contradictory ends*" (Kohli, 2000). Mr. James described several of his students as "going from 0–100 in seconds," he snaps his fingers for emphasis. On controversial political issues (Hess, 2009; Hess & McAvoy, 2015), there's a reaction but no interest in engaging. Mr. James indicates that students respond almost immediately with, "You can't say that, you're supposed to stay neutral." There's little civic discourse, listening, or struggle.

While Mr. James argued that he had "pulled back too far" and failed to teach about "resistance," we have no evidence of how Mr. James taught prior to this study. We have no evidence that he engaged his agency nor that he taught for social justice. What we do know is that he felt pressure to teach less critically and to engage students in less examination of controversial topics in a discussion-based format that could lead to students raising difficult content and questions (Hess, 2009).

PROPAGANDA AND GEORGE ORWELL

Another teacher, Ms. Watson, indicated a similar experience, which caused her to "almost wither away from teaching anything." After the 2016 election, Ms. Watson said she felt a "sea change." As she said, "Things that were never said were beginning to be said, things that my students would never speak of...they began to. The president's words were coming out of their mouths. I was a bit afraid to teach about it, but I came up with a way to come at it more sideways, a propaganda unit." Wanting students to understand the uses of propaganda during times of war assigned her students to read *Animal Farm* by George Orwell. She felt that it would give students a lens to symbols and phrases and their subtle changes such as the transition from "Four legs good" to "Two legs better" from the text. Ms. Watson had students examine wartime propaganda from World War I and World War II to better understand how propaganda was illogical, and engaged students in Socratic Seminar (Adler, 1981; Roberts & Billings, 1998, 2011) focused on particular sections of the text. During one of Socratic Seminar, the confederate flag was raised as a symbol of oppression. In the county in which this teaching was taking place, confederate flags can be found everywhere from T-shirts to hats, to bumper stickers, to being displayed proudly in front yards. The issue heated up quickly and became reduced to a first amendment issue of "well we can; we have the right to display the flag." Ms. Watson was surprised by this. She had felt the students had gained an understanding of the uses of propaganda. Though she instinctively understood that some of her students would support the confederate flag, she had expected a more intellectual rather than emotional discussion.

The discussion was focused on the few pages where the animals have realized the pigs have changed the slogans on the barn door. The conversation began analytically enough:

> A male student said, "The rules on the barn are like the (U.S.) Constitution, right? They're written there to like set people free, no? It's a statement of their freedom." A female student responded quickly, "I think that's what it's *supposed* to be, but if you have to run off to find the goat to read it to you, and the goat can hardly read...I mean, come on, is it really?" Another female student added, "Yeah, why is it that people can't...well, the animals can't read? Why wouldn't that be like one of the first steps of the revolution after the farmer's gone?"

As the discussion ensued, students surfaced ideas identifying parts of the text they were unsure about, connecting *Animal Farm* to the content they were learning about war propaganda. The connections were generally thoughtful and useful, demonstrating that they understood the text and the content they were learning.

> The discussion shifted when a Black male student said, "I think the words on the barn are like the confederate flag. It meant one thing like back in the Civil War...it meant a country...but now it's like a symbol of power, of threat..." A White male student responded quickly on the first student's heels, "It's a historic symbol..." A White female student interjected, "*No*, it's not. I don't think the people flying it even know the history of it..." A White male student interjected, "You're stereotyping! *We're* all rednecks, uneducated, right?"

This student made it immediately personal by identifying himself with those who fly confederate flags. Ms. Watson intervened after the redneck comment and more directly facilitated the conversation moving it away from a seminar and the text and allowing students to speak about the confederate flag specifically. The conversation remained personal with several students all White and all male save one using the term "we" when talking about flying the confederate flag. Ms. Watson directly engaged the flag issue by asking when the confederate flag was created, for what purpose, when it began to be used again (after the Civil War), and what it was used for. The students didn't have all the answers, and Ms. Watson provided many. Ms. Watson couched her terms and her language, saying, "*Some* people use it as a symbol of White supremacy and oppression but *perhaps* not all." This equivocal stance seemed to empower the White critics and leave the Black students who were critiquing it a bit isolated.

At this juncture a Black male student asked, "I'm from New York... I've been here for like a year, I'm still not used to them [confederate flags]. I gotta be honest, they freak me out, they frighten me, and I think that's the point of them." All the Black students agreed, and several White students agreed as well. The White male students who had been dominating the conversation indicated as one student said, "I understand why you feel that way, but *we still have the right* [to fly the flag]." Three White students who had been vocal in the conversation indicated at the conversation's end that though "we can" fly the flag, "maybe we shouldn't" due to "a racist intent." Ms. Watson was proud of herself and the difficult conversation her students had. She felt she had planted the seeds for some deeper and perhaps more complicated conversations about this and similar topics. The students hadn't necessarily changed their minds but as Ms. Watson said, "that wasn't the point." The point, she argued, "was to have all students have a real conversation, listen to each other, and really talk to each other." Her plan had been to circle back around and get at what she had intended to, how the animals had attempted to resist the pigs. Ms. Watson was interested in engaging them in the counter-resistance after the initial revolution. She never did.

That evening, the phone calls began. Ms. Watson wouldn't share the specifics of the parent meetings that transpired other than sharing the words she used to describe them. These words included "wretched," "vengeful," "atrocious," and "life-altering." Recalling how a parent said, "You were trying to take away my child's right to resist... that's what the flag is. Resistance against White oppression and..." Ms. Watson stopped mid quote, took a deep breath, sighed, and stared at the floor. It seemed that the series of parents had not only challenged her pedagogy, they challenged her knowledge of content and her understanding of the past. As a result, she never returned to the conversation even when her students asked and purposely focused her pedagogy and curriculum away from anything controversial.

We Used to Teach About Resistance

The investigation into how war is taught to the children of soldiers involved nine teachers in three schools surrounding a large military base in the rural South. This study took place during and just after the 2016 presidential election as heightened tensions and polarization in schools was fomented by Trump's campaign rhetoric (Costello, 2016; Rogers et al., 2017; Sondel et al., 2018). Teaching about war near the military base has never been easy, but was made all the more difficult by the complicated politics, resentment, and anger of the 2016 presidential election. "Threading a needle" was a phrase used often to describe the decisions made weaving in and out of the pressures, responsibilities, and perceived and real socio-emotional difficulties that the teaching about war to the children of soldiers could present. The direct connection between students and the content made teaching resistance even more difficult.

Ms. Dixon, one of the nine teachers in the initial study described her current teaching as "towing the county line." She said it with a singsong voice that made its message no less devastating. Ms. Dixon was in her early 60s, a Navy veteran, and a teacher with 27 years of experience. She had grown afraid to teach resistance. "I had taught an experiential for years... I'd become famous for it or infamous maybe..." she told me. It was the World War I simulation that turns an ordinary classroom into the trenches of Europe. Desks are put together to form a narrow chasm, slides of combat are flashed on the front screen, often selections from Erich Remarque's *All Quiet on the Western Front* are read. Students are to "experience" just a bit about what it was like to be on the front. "The students walked in at the beginning of the year, talking about it. They used to get so excited." Students would early on begin to bring in helmets, shovels and other implements to make the experience "more real." "I didn't want them to experience war... but I wanted them to get a sense of the horror of it, the mindlessness, the damage was done. That way, I could teach about resistance, about the anti-war movement that began in Britain. After the trench, even though there was laughter, students understood that the war was scary and horrible."

The morning after she taught the lesson, just after she'd made the copies for the reading and inquiry into the anti-war movement, she was called into the principal's office. A grandmother had complained that the experience had been "too intense" for her grandchild and asked if it was in the "county course of study." The activity wasn't directly, and the principal informed Ms. Dixon she was not to teach that lesson again, and she never has. In fact, she's backed away from similar experiential pedagogy used in the past this year, fearing blowback from parents and the broader community. "I'm single. I will not be a burden on my [adult] children," she cited as a reason to teach differently this year. She, like several other teachers in the larger study, feared losing their jobs. When reminded of Hess's (2016) passionate argument about not sitting out this crucial time and teaching the election, her response was clear, precise, and succinct, "She doesn't teach here now does she?" When asked if she feels that her teaching is being watched or inspected more thoroughly than before, her answer was, "Not at all... no one ever comes."

District personnel rarely visited classrooms as well. Dixon was rarely observed and had signed her last three principal evaluation forms without any member of administration stepping inside her classroom. "They were all positive...why rattle the cage?" she replied when asked why she hadn't insisted on an evaluation. Even though no one was watching her overtly and with intent, though no one from the district offices had ever stepped foot in her classroom, she was resolute that she would never teach the lesson again and backed away from teaching resistance. A comfortable retirement, she confessed, was too valuable to her now that she was so close.

An Activist in Sheep's Clothing

Mr. Jones was the only teacher in the study who self-identified as an activist. "What kind of activist? The good kind," he said with a quick laugh and a wide grin. "I'm an all over the map leftist activist. Anti-nuke, anti-war, pro-Black Lives Matter, women, LGBTQAI..." and the list went on. What was interesting was that he only agreed to be interviewed away from his school, the only one of the nine. When pressed, he said, "Because I wouldn't give an honest interview" [if we were on campus]. He kept his activist life and his teaching life separate. While most teachers maintain some level of distance between these two selves, those who identify as activists (Catone, 2016) carry their activist work into the classroom. It most often impacts the pedagogy they use, the content they teach, the questions they ask, and often the types of schools they choose to teach in.

It was surprising that he identified as an activist after observing his instruction. While animated and a fast talker during interviews, he was reserved, intense, and taught as he described in a later interview, "straight down the line." That is, he taught the content standards the way the district wanted them taught, in the way the district wanted them taught with little variation. He lectured mostly, had students work in teams and groups occasionally, and had students complete individual assignments. He didn't organize his teaching around questions to be answered, problems to be solved, only content to know, and tasks to complete. The only times he shifted from this was the occasional question asked about content that raised the specter of race, class, gender, or resistance. This happened during his teaching of World War II when he was asked by the 442nd all Japanese Battalion who earned the most medals? It took several minutes of questioning and students mining textbooks and the Internet to determine that they were placed in harm's way more than any other unit. "Was that racist?" he asked, but left the question hanging and quickly moved on. He reported that he did not use discussion anymore and assumed a demeanor in his teaching that doesn't inspire discussion because, "I don't want the discussion to go sideways, to lead to something that I don't want to talk about in the class-room," something controversial.

In a later interview, he revealed, "I used to use a lot of discussion, So-cratic Seminar, problem-solving teamwork... I used to ask a lot of big ques-tions... then one day a student asked me during class, 'Mr. Jones, you're a liberal, right? I bet you're one of those activists, right? Isn't that un-Ameri-can?' He was smiling, so I wasn't sure if he was joking, but it rattled me." He said the student just sat back down, never asked a question like that of him again, even earning a good grade, but he never felt right about the inter-action. There was no overt threat, the student seemed to be asking out of interest rather than angst, but it left Mr. Jones uneasy. His state has no col-lective bargaining protections, and tenure was recently rescinded, making Mr. Jones feel quite exposed. A few weeks later, he started getting hang-up calls. At that time, his daughter had just been born, and it rattled him again. Mr. Jones decided to separate his activism from his teaching permanently. Mr. Jones argued that both education and activism were important, but chose to keep them separate, saying, "It's just safer that way." A lifelong member of the democratic party, he also re-registered as an independent saying, "It's public record, the kids are going to look, it's too tempting, es-pecially this year (election year)," and began taking his wife's car when he attended activist meetings. Mr. Jones believed the students were less likely to recognize her car and so less likely to recognize him on the way to and from these events. He regrets that he can't teach the way that he wants to, but Mr. Jones seems to have made his peace with the decision. "I do what I can," he says, "by raising particular questions at particular times, but that's all I'm comfortable doing now."

The teachers who want to be renegades all found themselves in a tight spot. Feeling direct or indirect pressure, being told, or feeling pressured, they chose a safer route. Their jobs, their families, their standing were all threatened. They conformed, they shrunk, they chose to wait. I'm curious about what will happen if the pressure recedes. Will they return to their former selves, or might they be forever changed?

DISCUSSION AND IMPLICATIONS

Returning to the original inquiry framing this paper—"How do teachers teach difficult history critically using a trauma-informed pedagogy (TIP)?"—our analysis suggests that a contextually-bound trauma-informed pedagogy is warranted. A disruptive pedagogy, one that challenges the typical thinking of students (which is often informed from sources outside of school), must be blended with a trauma-informed pedagogy that deeply understands the students' context and communities. A disruptive pedagogy is needed to raise the critical consciousness of students (Duncan-Andrade, 2010). School is not just about facts and figures, school to work connections; it is about creating students to engage in and change the world (Gillen, 2014). Students need to be challenged. To recognize and grow their agency, students need to be made uncomfortable in a comfortable space (Sensoy & Diangelo, 2014).

Raising student consciousness, however, cannot be all. Teachers need to know their students' identities, home, and learning contexts to understand the trauma they have or could experience by engaging in difficult content. Teachers need to be aware, planned, observant, and thoughtful about how they engage children in content (Carello & Butler, 2015; Gibbs, 2020). As the stories of Mr. James, Ms. Watson, Ms. Dixon, and Mr. Jones demonstrate, thoughtful trauma-informed instruction with a critical edge is difficult to implement.

Mr. James, attempting to encourage his students to engage in mild civil disobedience, found his students uninterested in participating, remaining passive in wanting to learn and know but without taking action. Ms. Watson, with her use of George Orwell to help her students critique the confederate flag, set up a strong pedagogical approach that led to a strong discussion; it was heading toward a pedagogic disruption until external pressure began. Similar is the experience of Ms. Dixon and Mr. Jones: Both were aware that their students were the children of soldiers, so they sought to create classroom space for critical analysis and reflection about war. Both were military-connected, Ms. Dixon, a veteran herself, and Mr. Jones connected through marriage and understood the wounds with which their children arrived at the school doors. They both engaged in disruptive pedagogy, and both received pressure from the outside, yet kept these wounds in the front of their minds while teaching.

Returning to our pre-service teacher asking about the trauma that school induces, the story is more complicated than one of pedagogy. There are difficult political and ideological pressures that play into the choices that teachers make in engaging them in even the most thoughtful and well-crafted pedagogy and curriculum. The view has to be expanded to see the entire community, specifically how the teaching will be seen and experienced not only by students but the broader community as well. The hanging question that remains is clear: What are teachers willing to endure—professionally, socially, personally, financially—to ensure they engage pedagogy when teaching hard history that is both critical and trauma-informed?

CONCLUSION

Scholar Wendy Kohli begins her essay *Teaching in the Danger Zone: Democracy and Difference* this way: "My assignment... is to say something about democratic education. I accept the assignment with enthusiasm . . . because of the importance it holds at this historical moment when the *rhetoric* of *democracy* is used by many for all sorts of *contradictory ends*" (Kohli, 2000). Kohli wrote those words over 20 years ago, but they are more apt and even more accurate today. In the run-up to the 2016 presidential election, candidate Trump-inspired legions of followers with his "straight talk" and "truth-telling" promising to destroy ISIS, end the wars in Iraq and Afghanistan, grow the economy by more than 3% a year, build a wall, move the American embassy to Jerusalem, and most recently end the North Korean nuclear threat. Trump argued that he was fighting for the forgotten man in America, the White, blue-collar, Christian American who at one time had plentiful and well-paid factory jobs that had since fallen as the world markets' needs had shifted.

Trump's overt racist, sexist, and homophobic racist statements drew support in defense of confederate monuments and statues, more strict immigration laws, and the ability to refuse service to same-sex couples (amongst many other things) these groups have attempted to grasp the high ground on resistance, casting themselves as the oppressed, the unfree, the trodden upon. Freedom, equality, equal protection, rights and privileges, the same language that was used to fuel and empower the many fights for rights and justice for women, LGBTQAI groups and people of color have now been captured, re-engineered and deployed by White supremacists to threaten minorities, immigrants, women, members of the LGBTQAI community and to roll back their rights.

What does this have to do with schools? Everything. In our media-saturated society, students and their families hang(ed) on Trump's every word and outrageous deed. They are empowered, reviled, or overwhelmed. How students feel, what they see, and the anger and anxiety engendered by Trump's speeches and Tweets are carried into school as toxins. The president's words and actions encourage students to speak about their classmates and members of their community as they never have before. Schools became more dangerous spaces for the students forced to endure the name-calling and bullying, and the teachers attempting to teach authentically through it.

Teachers everywhere who educate the children of soldiers about the horrors of war and racial violence associated with war—but particularly teachers like those in this study in a rural Southern state without collective bargaining or tenure protection—are particularly exposed. They feel threatened, unsafe, and unprotected. To teach critically for social justice, to raise contentious or controversial issues, to teach in a way that gives students more control, could all lead to the loss of a job, the loss of community standing, and the end of their professional lives. Research needs to be done, tactics discovered, and protections ensured to keep teachers safely active in raising critical questions that students in complex pedagogy, and help students to fully understand their rights, their abilities, and the possibilities they have for engaging in a true resistance to change the world. When asked if Mr. Jones would ever return to teaching resistance, he replied, "Well...we're still here...aren't we?" He seemed to be saying he was waiting for his moment of return. May the moment come quickly and loudly and with much success.

NOTES

1. Hard history or difficult content is history that raises questions of race, of violence, of rape, content that is too often passed over quickly or commented on not at all in social studies classrooms.
2. Though more than four teachers were interested in being observed while they taught the history of lynching, only two were permitted by the district. Reasons given for this denial focused on their fear of blowback if it was revealed that lynching was being taught and studied.
3. Though we were interested in interviewing students individually and to engage more students in focus group interviews both of these were denied by the districts in which the study took place.

REFERENCES

Achinstein, B., & Ogawa, R. (2006). (In)fidelity: What the resistance of new teachers reveals about professional principles and prescriptive educational policies. *Harvard Educational Review, 76*(1), 30–66.

Adler, M. (1981). *The paideia proposal.* New York, NY: Touchstone.

Apple, M. (Ed.). (2003). *The state and politics of knowledge.* New York, NY: Routledge.

Apple, M. (2006). *Educating the "right" way: Markets, standards, god, and inequality* (2nd ed.). New York, NY: Routledge.

Barton, K. (2015). Elicitation techniques: Getting people to talk about ideas they don't usually talk about. *Theory and Research in Social Education, 43*(2), 179–205.

Carello, J., & Butler, L. (2015). Practicing what we teach: Trauma-informed educational practice. *Journal of Teaching in Social Work, 35*(3), 262–278.

Catone, K. (2016). *The pedagogy of teacher activism.* New York, NY: Routledge.

Costello, M. (2016). *The Trump effect: The impact of the presidential campaign on America's schools.* Retrieved from https://www.splcenter.org/sites/default/files/splc_the_trump_effect.pdf

Creswell, J. (2008). *Research design: Qualitative, quantitative, and mixed methods approach* (3rd ed.). Thousand Oaks, CA: SAGE.

Duncan-Andrade, J. (2010). *What a coach can teach a teacher: Lessons from a successful sports program.* New York, NY: Peter Lang.

Emdin, C. (2016). *For White folks who teach in the hood and rest of y'all too.* Boston, MA: Beacon Press.

Evans, R. (2015). *Schooling corporate citizens: How accountable reform has damaged civic education and undermine democracy.* New York, NY: Routledge.

Fraenkel, J. K., & Wallen, N. G. (2006). *How to assign and evaluate research in education* (6th ed.). Boston, MA: McGraw-Hill.

Freire, P. (1970). *Pedagogy of the oppressed.* New York, NY: Continuum.

Gibbs, B. C. (2018). Las traviesas: Critical feminist educators in their struggle for critical teaching. In L. Jewett, F. Calderon-Berumen, & M. Espinosa-Dulanto (Eds.), *Curriculum and pedagogy collection 2018* (pp. 111–135). Charlotte, NC: Information Age.

Gibbs, B. C. (2019). Violence, horror, and the visual image: How teachers speak about the difference between the use of photographs of war and photographs of lynching. In S. Lena Raye, S. Masta, S. Taylor Cook, & J. Burdick (Eds.), *Curriculum and pedagogy collection 2019* (pp. 120–134). Charlotte, NC: Information Age.

Gibbs, B. C. (2020). The foot and the flag: Patriotism, place, and the teaching of war in a military town. *Democracy and Education, 28*(1), 1–14.

Gibbs, B., & Papoi, K. (2020). Threading the needle: On balancing trauma and critical teaching. Possibilities and problems in trauma-based and social emotional learning programs. *Occasional Paper Series, 2020*(43). Retrieved from https://educate.bankstreet.edu/occasional-paper-series/vol2020/iss43/13

Gillen, J. (2014). *Educating for insurgency: The roles of young people in schools of poverty.* Oakland, CA: AK Press.

Giroux, H. (1988). *Teachers as intellectuals: Towards a critical pedagogy of learning.* Westport, CT: Bergin and Garvey Press.

Giroux, H. (2011). *Education and the crisis of public values: Challenging the assault on teachers, students, and public education.* New York, NY: Peter Lang.

Harvey, D. (2005). *A brief history of neoliberalism.* Oxford, England: Oxford University Press.

Hess, D. (2009). *Controversy in the classroom: The democratic power of discussion.* New York, NY: Routledge.

Hess, D. (2016). No time to take a pass: Why schools should teach young people about the 2016 elections. *Social Education, 80*(5), 232–233.

Hess, D., & McAvoy, P. (2015). *The political classroom: Evidence and ethics in democratic education.* New York, NY: Routledge.

Kohli, W. (2000). Teaching in the danger zone: Democracy and difference. In D. Hursh & E. W. Ross (Eds.), *Democratic social education: Social studies for social change* (pp. 23–42). New York, NY: Falmer.

Ladson-Billings, G. (1994). *The dreamkeepers: Successful teachers of African-American children.* Jossey-Bass.

Levy, S., & Sheppard, M. (2018). "Difficult knowledge" and the Holocaust in history education. In S. Metzger & L. Harris (Eds.), *The Wiley international handbook of history teaching and learning* (pp. 365–388). Hoboken, NJ: Wiley.

McLaren, P. (1998). *Life in schools: An introduction to critical pedagogy in the foundations of education* (3rd ed.). New York, NY: Longman Printing.

Miles, M., & Huberman, A. (1994). *Qualitative data analysis: An expanded sourcebook.* New York, NY: SAGE.

Mills, M. (1997). Towards a disruptive pedagogy: Creating spaces for student and teacher resistance to social injustice. *International Studies in Sociology of Education, 7*(1), 35–55.

Morgan, D. L. (2002). Focus group interviewing. In J. Gubrium & J. Holstein (Eds.), *Handbook of interview research: Context and method* (pp. 161–176). Thousand Oaks, CA: SAGE.

North, C. (2009). *Teaching for social justice? Voices from the front lines.* Boulder, CO: Paradigm.

Overstreet, S., & Chafouleas, S. (2016). Trauma-informed schools: Introduction to the special issue. *School Mental Health, 8,* 1–6.

Paris, D., & Alim, H. S. (2017). *Culturally sustaining pedagogy: Teaching and learning in a changing world.* New York, NY: Teachers College Press.

Parkhouse, H. (2017). Pedagogies of naming, questioning, demystification: A study of two critical U.S. History teachers. *Theory and Research in Social Education, 46*(2), 277–317.

Patton, M. Q. (2002). *Qualitative research and evaluation methods* (3rd ed.). Thousand Oaks, CA: SAGE.

Picower, B. (2011). Resisting compliance: Learning to teach for social justice in a neoliberal context. *Teachers College Record, 113*(5), 1105–1134.

Roberts, T., & Billings, L. (1998). *The paideia classroom: Teaching for understanding.* New York, NY: Routledge.

Roberts, T., & Billings, L. (2011). *Teaching critical thinking: Using seminars for 21st century literacy.* New York, NY: Routledge.

Rogers, J., Franke, M., Yun, J., Ishimoto, M., Diera, C., Geller, R., Berryman, A., & Brenes, T. (2017). *Teaching and learning in the age of Trump: Increasing stress and hostility in American high schools.* Los Angeles, CA: UCLA's Institute for Democracy, Education, and Access.

Ross, E. W. (2016). The courage of hopelessness: Creative disruption of everyday life in the classroom. In W. Journell (Ed.), *Reassessing the social studies curriculum: Preparing students for a post-9/11 world.* Lanham, MD: Rowman & Littlefield.

Sensoy, O., & DiAngelo, R. (2014). Respect differences? Challenging the common guidelines in social justice education. *Democracy and Education, 22*(2). Retrieved from http://democracyeducationjournal.org/home/vol22/iss2/1/

Shor, I. (1992). *Empowering education.* Chicago, IL: University of Chicago Press.

Shor, I. (1997). *When students have power: Negotiating power in a critical pedagogy.* Chicago, IL: University of Chicago Press.

Sleeter, C. (2014). Deepening social justice teaching. *Journal of Language and Literacy Education.* Retrieved from http://jolle.coe.uga.edu/

Sondel, B., Baggett, H., & Hadley-Dunn, A. (2018). For millions of people this is real trauma: A pedagogy of political trauma in the wake of the 2016 U.S. presidential election. *Teaching and Teacher Education, 70,* 175–185.

Swalwell, K. (2013). *Educating activist allies: Social justice pedagogy with the suburban and urban elite.* New York, NY: Routledge.

Venet, A. S. (2019). Role-clarity and boundaries for trauma-informed teachers. *Educational Considerations, 44*(2), Article 3.

Vinson, K., & Ross, G. W. (2010). Social control and the pursuit of dangerous citizenship. In J. DeVitis (Ed.) *Critical civic literacy: A reader* (pp. 155–169). New York, NY: Peter Lang.

Winn, M. (2018). *Justice on both sides: Transforming education through restorative justice.* Cambridge, MA: Harvard Education Press.

Wright-Maley, C. (2015). On "stepping back and letting go": The role of control in the success or failure of social studies simulations. *Theory and Research in Social Education, 4*(2), 206–243.

Yin, R. (1989). *Case study research: Design and methods* (Revised ed.). Thousand Oaks, CA: SAGE.

Yin, R. (2003). *Applications of case study research* (2nd ed.). Thousand Oaks, CA: SAGE.

Zembylas, M. (2014). Theorizing "difficult knowledge" in the aftermath of the "affective turn": Implications for curriculum and pedagogy in handling traumatic representation. *Curriculum Inquiry, 44*(3), 390–412.

CHAPTER 23

SOCIETY'S GATE KEEPERS

Jose Cordon
Independent Scholar

I think teachers deserve a higher starting salary.

Well actually, I think they deserve more in general annually.

I mean we give millions to individual athletes ...

So, I'm sure we can afford to give more to those who we trust to teach,

our children how to write and read.

I mean, to me, it's obvious and honestly it boggles me how we don't place a higher value on teachers in our society.

Literally in those seats, sit future leaders of education and microbiology.

Potentially a student with a future presidential candidacy.

And that's why I believe no teacher should have to moonlight.

You can't double shift and come back to teach 35 kids in the same room right.

I feel like we should make the teaching profession more appealing.

Making a Spectacle, pages 249–250
Copyright © 2021 by Information Age Publishing
All rights of reproduction in any form reserved.

But honestly, I don't know how just yet, it's just a feeling.

I remember dealing with my inner villain, sitting with my teachers asking
  them for their honest opinions.

And they'd tell me about the time I was killing with certain decisions.

It took me a minute but finally I listened and hope was arisen.

You see teachers save lives, they often do it with no recognition.

That's why I made it my mission to do this...

and through this, say thank you from all of your students.

Thank you for being so prudent and spending your time and your money,

investing in us even though sometimes we aren't very lovely

I want to say thank you, we need to say thank you

I am genuinely grateful for everything that you do.

In conclusion,

I've heard it said, that education is the key to freedom.

Our students are freedom fighters, freedom writers, but who will lead them?

Our teachers are tired, overworked, underpaid, and many are leaving.

We're losing our teachers; society's gate keepers and we desperately need
  them.

Especially now, now more than ever.

SECTION VI

MORE THAN A LABEL: EMPOWERMENT IN CREATING
SPACE IN HIGHER EDUCATION

CHAPTER 24

BLACK ACADEMIC RESISTANCE

A Visual Arts Approach to Empirical Research

Asha Omar
University of Minnesota–Twin Cities

ABSTRACT

Despite a growing diversity in the K–12 student population, Black educators remain disproportionately underrepresented. Studies have shown that the burnout rates of Black educators are higher than their White peers. This chapter uses arts-based methods to explore the ways Black educators are experiencing either working at or attending a predominantly White institution. Through using arts-based methods, the author details the process of creating an art piece that was informed by the experiences of Black educators. Implications for how arts-based research can serve as a tool of resistance as well as how the final painting functions as a form of empowerment and resistance for Black educators in a space where they may otherwise feel silenced is explored. The author further discusses the ways the art piece may promote a sense of belonging within Black educators. Implications for further supports that are needed to promote retention of Black educators are also expressed.

Making a Spectacle, pages 253–269
Copyright © 2021 by Information Age Publishing
253

Figure 24.1 "Ms. Resist" (2019), acrylic and mixed media on canvas. "As Black educators, our mere presence in Academia is likened to an act of political resilience." —Anonymous

The first time I had a Black educator I was in 7th grade. I remember Mr. R's course vividly. It was the first time I had a teacher who talked about my excellence. He vocalized the challenges that I faced, and articulated some of the obstacles that I may face in the future. He related this to math, showing ways to work through the problems. It was having this representation that solidified my passion to become an educator. I wished to create curriculum that represented my Black, Brown, and Indigenous students. I wanted to elevate their voices and be that representation for that student who needed to see themselves in the position. While I taught for over three years, I ultimately left the field due to various issues that I encountered in classroom instruction, school policies, and overall support. This has been the case for many of my Black colleagues, but for those that have stayed, their stories present opportunities for improving retention.

Literature highlighting the experiences of Black educators, from their curricular contributions to their teaching in public school classrooms has increased over the past 40 years (Farinde, Allen, & Lewis, 2016; Hudson & Holmes, 1994). This work has extended to explore the experiences of Black educators in teacher preparation programs, and higher education as a whole (Ladson-Billings, 1996; Jay, 2009; Tillman, 2004). Despite a growing diversity in the teaching profession, Black educators remain disproportionately underrepresented (Ingersoll & Merrill, 2017). According to the *National Center for Education Statistics*, in the 2017–2018 school year, about 80% of teachers identified as White while only 48% of students identified as White. Only 7% of these teachers identified as Black. Several factors have been attributed to the recruitment and retention of Black educators such as their experiences in preservice teaching programs (Redding & Baker, 2019), lack of administrative support (Farinde et al., 2016), and other forms of licensure/hiring discrimination (Carter Andrews et al., 2018).

Researchers have identified several critical reasons Black educators are crucial in the workforce. First, Black educators have been credited with improving the school experiences and academic outcomes of students of color (Villegas & Irvine, 2010). Villegas and Irvine (2010) described the positive impact having a Black teacher has for Black students. Black educators are also more likely to fill teaching positions in lower socioeconomic districts where positions may be more difficult to fill (Villegas & Irvine, 2010). Black educators can also bring rich knowledge from their experiences and perspectives that are historically silenced when it comes to teaching and learning (hooks, 1994). However, Black educators have expressed feeling voiceless and underrepresented in urban, rural, and suburban districts leading to teacher burnout (Ladson-Billing, 1996). Considering the important role Black teachers play in the workforce, it is essential to identify ways to increase the retention of Black educators in classrooms.

The following questions guide this chapter:

1. How can arts-based research be used as a tool to challenge Whiteness?
2. How can the experiences of Black educators attending or teaching at a predominately White institution inform us about the current work/learning environment?
3. How can we use visual art to showcase these experiences?
4. How can art-based inquiry engage Black educators to reclaim spaces that have traditionally excluded them?

This chapter has two goals in addressing the previously stated questions: I aim to first showcase how arts-based methods can be used to empower and resist structures of Whiteness. This project gathered narratives and anecdotes that demonstrated some ways that Black educators have responded to instances of racialization and actively chosen to disrupt and push back against structures of Whiteness. By engaging in the arts-based process, this chapter aims to articulate how this methodology can be used to convey human experiences, as well as ultimately serve as a form of resistance as a physical installation in the education building at a top university. My second aim is to provide insight into the experiences of Black educators to reveal and showcase coping strategies, and ways that community plays an integral role in retention. Understanding the experiences of Black educators and the ways they have disrupted these spaces is necessary to explore strategies to reduce turnover rates among educators of color and to show how the process of creating a visual art piece can empower Black educators within predominantly White spaces. I use the term Black to refer to individuals who identify as African, African American, Black American, or within the Black diaspora.

LITERATURE REVIEW: RETENTION OF BLACK EDUCATORS

Black people historically and presently experience adverse environments where racism, discrimination, tokenism, and outright exclusion have been institutionally perpetuated. This is especially prevalent in educational institutions where Black educators have experienced adverse effects on their professional identity development (Spencer, 2006). In 1954, the year of the Supreme Court's decision in *Brown v Board of Education*, there were about 82,000 Black educators responsible for teaching Black public school students (Hudson & Holmes, 1994). After the decision to desegregate the schools, Black educators were perceived to be inferior, and through discriminatory practices such as firing Black educators who were registered voters, standardized tests for recertification, and penalizing involvement in "civil rights activity," Black educators began to lose their jobs (Tillman, 2004). Between 1954 and 1985, over 60,000 Black educators lost their jobs. The decline affected not only teachers, but also Black students considering education as a career. By 1985 the number of Black students pursuing a career in education had declined 66% (Hudson & Holmes, 1994).

Despite the importance of representation of Black educators and educators of color (Achinstein & Aguirre, 2008; Milner, 2006), the teaching profession remains dominated by White, suburban, middle-class women (Zumwalt & Craig, 2008) despite White students making up only 48% of the public school population. This speaks to the need of recruiting more teachers of color. Surprisingly, studies show that the issue is not in recruitment, but rather in the retention of Black educators (Ingersoll & May, 2011). Ingersoll et al. (2019) assert that in the past 2 decades, teachers of color have been entering the profession at higher rates than their White colleagues; the majority working in underserved urban schools. Farinde et al. (2016) describes the preference Black educators have to teach in more urban districts due to the feeling of a sense of belonging and cultural understanding. However, teacher burnout is higher for Black educators (Ingersoll & Merrill, 2017). Researchers have attributed this lack of retention to teacher preparation programs (Achinstein, Ogawa, & Sexton, Freitas, 2010). The decision to pursue a degree in education can be swayed due to the adverse experiences Black students may have in their university teacher preparation programs (Darling-Hammond, 2010). While efforts have been made to improve teacher preparation programs to increase recruitment and retention of college students of color (Darling-Hammond, 2010), the preservice programs are disproportionately catered to meet the needs of White female educators (Gay, 2000). Farinde-Wu, Griffen, and Young (2020) describes how prospective Black educators in preservice programs are not met with a curriculum that is relevant or reflective of their experiences or commitments as educators. This may contribute to the retention of Black students who end up graduating from these preservice programs.

Recent research has also articulated how Black students interested in becoming educators may decide otherwise due to the overt and/or covert racism they experience attending a predominantly White institution (PWI; Carter Andrews et al., 2019). This demonstrates a need for preservice programs to support their Black students to ensure that their experiences are not harmful but rather fruitful and productive. Such hostile treatment has been associated with the high turnover rates and low retention of Black educators in PWIs (Farinde et al., 2016). Black educators have reportedly felt isolated, hypervisible, and excluded when asked about their work experiences at PWIs (Alexander & Moore, 2008). Sheets (2004) affirms that Black educators need to feel that they are acknowledged and that their strengths are supported in preparation programs in order to apply them pedagogically. Black educators that feel supported on an administrative level, work in more positive environments, have teacher collaboration, and access to teacher resources have been associated with higher retention rates (Borman & Dowling, 2008). This provides some insight into specific factors that schools can try to foster in order to retain their Black educators. Absent in the literature is work explicitly examining Black teacher's perceptions of their preparation and how that affected their retention. Literature that explores existing strategies that Black educators employ in order to survive and thrive in PWIs is also needed.

METHODOLOGY: WHY ARTS-BASED RESEARCH?

Knowledge is not limited to the intellectual. Humans are complex beings that experience knowledge in the mind as well as the body. The world as we know it is an embodied experience, informing us about our lived experiences, performance, and bodily intelligence (Wilcox, 2009). Shange (2019) discusses Black embodiment in schools as what one experiences through the flesh. Our lived experiences are always embodied, it is through our bodies that are racialized and sexualized that we interact with the world (Grosz, 1994). This tells us that when we *know* things, we can *know* in ways other than just the intellectual. Eisner (1998) reminds us that art invokes multidisciplinary responses from the producer and the consumer. This allows responses and participation from both audience and maker that engages the whole human being. Utilizing arts-based approaches to research has grown from the desire of researchers to elicit and share these understandings of human experiences that are not accessible or completely transcribable through more traditional methodologies.

Arts-based research is a field that has grown significantly in the past 3 decades (Barone & Eisner, 2011). It allows a platform where academics can reimagine many aspects of the relationships and responsibilities social science researchers have within the context of their work, their data, and the questions that are generated (Leavy, 2009a; Rolling, 2013). While there is still some push back to the use of an arts-based approach as it disrupts the historical dominance of the positivist structural paradigm, it is becoming more recognized and respected as a valid form of presenting data in academia. Langer (1957) discusses how it is inappropriate to use traditional conceptions of inquiry for evaluating artistic inquiry as arts-based practices and expressions produce meaning, emotion, and contextual truths rooted in human experience. Utilizing arts-based approaches allows the researcher to work in a third space where they are able to tap into their researcher, artist, and teacher sides simultaneously. Pinar (2004) states that A/r/tography is recognized by which merges from "knowing, doing, and making" (p. 9). Operating in this third space and acknowledging one's role as an artist, researcher, and educator requires a reflective, critical approach. This approach challenges the ways researchers have traditionally been trained to separate themselves from their work. Arts-based approaches require the conversation between the researcher and the methodology, admitting the myth of objectivity historically claimed by many ethnographers (Leavy, 2009b). Not only does an arts-based approach require more accountability from the researcher to place themselves into their work, but Leavy (2009a) argues that it is also a way for researchers to access and represent voices that may otherwise be silenced, ignored, or unrepresented in traditional research methods.

However, despite the appeal arts-based research holds for this project, there is pushback and hesitations from researchers to utilize arts-based methods to meet academic conventions. Barone (1995) discusses some pushback to the use of storytelling approaches as it disrupts the historical dominance of the positivist structural paradigm, but goes on to discuss it becoming more recognized and respected as a valid form of presenting data in academia. Leavy (2015) outlines the struggles of the methodology to meet "scientific" notions of "validity" which developed out of positivism. Foster (2012) elaborates stating that arts-based approaches produce less tangible forms of knowledge than more traditional methodologies. Traditional work produces data that can be easily tested for objectivity, reliability, and validity whereas arts-based approaches are more embodied and can be rooted in emotional ways of knowing. This is an example of the gatekeeping that goes on in academia of who can *do* and *engage* with research. This can make it more difficult for researchers to secure funding, find support for their research, and/or get their work published (Foster, 2012; Lawrence, 2008).

The disciplining of arts-based methods moves in ways similar to the way dominant methodologies silence and continue to marginalize the epistemologies of people of color. Denying human experience as valid/truthful forms of knowledge and what someone knows and experiences in their body is anti-Black. To resist this, I drew on arts-based methods for the opportunity the methodology creates to act as a form of social justice, by allowing traditionally marginalized groups to have space in academia—an intentional move against anti-Blackness. Arts-based approaches work to resist categorical or binary thinking and critique the intentions of research entirely (Leavy, 2009a). It is not a field that allows a simplistic, neat, solid explanation with scientific backing; it can, but it also offers a more messy process that allows continuous participatory inquiry on the part of the researcher and the participants, renegotiating what it means to engage in research. By pulling from more creative methods this chapter is able to showcase and engage with human experience and emotion work more accurately.

POSITIONALITY

Educational spaces are institutionally anti-Black. From methodologies that are limited to Western epistemologies, curricular disparities, to anti-Black policies (Morris, 2016). Based on my personal experiences attending a PWI, I have experienced numerous microaggressions and struggled with imposter syndrome. This led to a deep reflection on my part in regard to my intentions at the university, my work, and who I ultimately wanted to represent. How was I going to best serve my community and stay authentic within my work while also navigating this academic space? As a researcher, an artist, an educator, a Biracial/Black woman these identities mean different things for me in the spaces that I am in. Fortunately, I have a community of Black scholars who are either attending or working at a PWI that I can share my experiences with and lean on for advice. Realizing we shared similar emotions and experiences lead me to create the questionnaire for this project. It was a way to document some of the conversations that we were having and the idea for creating an art piece to articulate these experiences was formed.

DATA COLLECTION AND ANALYSIS

Greenwood (2012) asserts that there are two overarching approaches to arts-based research. In the first, art is used as a tool to inquire and study a specific issue. In this case, art can be used for "collecting data, for analyzing it, for presenting findings, or for several of these purposes" (p. 3). The second approach is investigating the arts themselves. It serves as a way for the researcher to "understand and describe the complex layers of meaning within an artwork or an art form" (p. 3). While in some cases both approaches can be utilized in conducting research, this project fits into the first approach. I was involved in the process of art-making due to my 10 plus years as an artist. I assumed the role of an artist-researcher by facilitating conversations and collaboration with the participants to create a visual piece. This was utilizing the "insider perspective" (Wang et al., 2017, p. 15) which Wang et al. (2017) describe as artist-researchers who are actively involved in designing and using artistic methods in the research.

Data was collected during the Spring 2019 semester (January–April). I created a questionnaire on Google Forms to share with colleagues, associates, and friends who identified as Black and were working in predominantly White spaces doing work in education. The survey was sent to 17 individuals and received 12 responses. The questionnaire included the five following questions:

1. Share a specific experience where you can recall feeling targeted for your racial identity.
2. What are some words of encouragement you would share with future Black educators?
3. How have you chosen to cope and/or resist the status quo of your school/institution?
4. Describe your school/institution and share more about your frustrations with that space you exist within.
5. Describe how your racial and/or ethnic identities are or are not affirmed and celebrated at your school/institution.

The analysis portion was collaborative. Initially, I read through the interviews several times, focusing on different aspects of the interviewee's experience and coding themes within the interviews. Then I discussed with the participants the ways I was visually coding to represent their experiences to ensure that I was understanding and conveying the takeaways of their interviews to fidelity. Denzin (1998) asserts that by engaging in dialogue and spending time with each narrative, one is engaging with an inquiry that is "multivocal, collaborative, naturalistically grounded in the worlds of lived experience, and organized by a critical, interpretive theory" (Denzin, 1998, p. 332). This assisted me in ensuring that my work was ethical and representing the participants' experiences appropriately.

READER EXERCISE

So much of the human experience is difficult to convey through words. Thus, when I was deciding how to represent the data I collected, I was drawn to arts-based methods. Art offers that platform to share an experience. Before I describe the process of creating and representing the narratives, go back to the beginning of the chapter and look at the painting that I created. *Name what you experience as viewers (jot down your reaction—could be strong feelings, phrases, memories . . .). Let this sit with you for a moment before coming back to this section.*

McNiff (1998) defines arts-based research as, "The systematic use of the artistic process, the actual making of artistic expressions as a primary way of understanding and examining experience by both researchers and the people that they involve in their studies" (p. 103). The purpose of this exercise and to name your experience is to bring you into the arts-based process. Some experiences are difficult to articulate using words but by using art, especially work that has strong visuals like this one, the artist can usually evoke a strong reaction. Any reaction, strong emotion, perhaps a memory that was sparked from viewing the painting gives you an experience of your own. This is a glimpse into the experiences of those who participated in creating this piece.

PAINTING

The survey was used to explore the nuances within the narratives that would reveal how Black educators were navigating and disrupting systems of Whiteness and making intentional moves to social justice and liberation. Due to this, there were specific patterns and relationships that I was looking for as I coded the narratives. The first pattern that I was looking for was the way Black educators used *resistance*. This appeared as resisting Whiteness as a structure, resisting historical dominant narratives of epistemologies and history, and resisting forms of self-doubt. The second pattern I coded for was *anger*. People expressed this anger through feelings of being tokenized, invalidated, and working twice as hard to prove that they were deserving of the space they are taking up. The third code was narratives that represented *healing*. This was demonstrated in participants expressing knowledge of one's power to change spaces, but also looking for communities to support healing along the journey.

Leavy (2009b) described the process of collecting narratives through interviews and including the participants' voices in the data by looking at the themes and recurring language, then using this language as a framing for a poem. While I did not write a poem, I did a similar process where I used my own positionality as a Black educator and personal experiences, and the narratives from the 12 participants to inform how I would be able to represent this visually. Leavy (2009b), writes that "poetry is an *engaged* method of writing that evokes emotions, promotes human connection and understanding, and can be politically charged" (p. 67). Instead of using a poetic style to convey and evoke emotion, I approached it visually. As the researcher I was involved in the process entirely, from my commitments, positionality, experiences—it all informed the idea for the piece. Arts-based practices take on a more embodied, collaborative approach. Lawrence-Lightfoot and Davis (1977) describes the relationship between the portraitist and the subject, articulating that collaboration has to be made in order to truly capture the subject's essence.

First I created a visual image that resonated with my experience. Then, I shared it with my participants to ensure that they felt like the painting was able to promote the human connection and stir emotions that resonated with their experiences. This was done by sharing a sketch of the painting with the participants and this is where some stylistic changes were made. The final product is the painting at the beginning of this chapter. The name tag that says "Ms. Resist" was a suggestion from one of the participants as they felt that it represented a major theme in their experience as an educator at a PWI and wanted it to be more boldly conveyed in the piece. The pink background color was also a choice from one of the participants who wanted it to draw attention and hold a bold message. The following stylistic choices made with the painting were based directly on the ways quotes were coded or a specific narrative itself. Additionally, all of the visuals representations explained below were communicated and altered with input from the participants to ensure that their experiences were portrayed to fidelity.

DISCUSSION

The relationship between visual arts and empirical research is rarely explored. This project gathered narratives and anecdotes that demonstrated how Black educators have responded to instances of racialization and actively chosen to disrupt and push back against Whiteness. Without using arts-based practices, it would have been difficult to convey the emotion and experiences of my participants if limited to traditional methodologies. The visual art that was produced as a result of these narratives allows the viewer insight into the human experiences and emotions that the participants shared. By using art, we are able to relay some of the ways that Black educators have pushed back against existing power structures and the gaps that remain in making sure that support systems are in place to retain Black educators. From the narratives expressed, the participants were seeking out the support networks on their own, rather than having those in place already in their institution. There were also implications that work needs to be done within PWIs to make sure that Black educators are feeling a sense of belonging and value in their contributions. The continuation of using visual arts to do empirical research also needs to be explored further.

Radical self-care (Ware, 2016) is the need to take care of yourself before you can take care of someone else. When self-care is inconsistent, from neglecting health, fitness, or stress management, it can lead to a physical or emotional crisis. Ware (2016) describes this crisis as ones' inability to function in a professional or personal manner. My participants emphasized their necessity for self-care, one specifically stating that sharing her stories with two other Black educators at her school was an intentional way to heal. "We meet monthly to share our experiences and connect. This has been so important for my health and well-being." Healing for women of color and indigenous people has been attributed to the process of sharing their oral stories (Starks, Vakalahi, Comer, & Ortiz-Hendricks, 2010). Since these spaces do not already exist in their school, my participants have begun creating them by finding a sense of community. This is a way of pushing back in order to survive in the space. Another participant shared her struggles with imposter syndrome but how they have had to fight to overcome these insecurities to continue working in her school. They shared, "I have pushed back more than ever before. I am at an age and place where I am more confident in myself than I have ever been and I am not afraid to be me." Intentionally working on self-care from finding community, to finding positive affirmations within oneself has been crucial to the retention of some of my participants. I decided to showcase this visually by adding jewels on the nails to represent the healing aspect and dedication to self-care. Nail art has been linked to self-expression, as well as an important aspect of self-care to Black Americans (Davis, Khoza, & Brooks, 2019). My participants agreed with the visual—one even asking me to use real jewels on the nails.

Conformity was another important aspect of these narratives. Some of the participants expressed that their culture and funds of knowledge were not valued in the predominately White spaces in which they worked or attended. As a result, some felt pressured to adjust or change certain aspects of who they were in order to satisfy the demands of the school. One of the participants shared their experience with the dress code. They enjoyed wearing their hair in different styles, sometimes wearing it natural or having more protective styles. When they decided to put braids in their hair, "I was confronted with the "dress code" for the research group I worked for. I was reminded that I need to look professional as I was entering the school. My hair is my identity and does not make me professional or unprofessional." Research has shown that Black educators are aware of their appearances in PWIs, and feel pressure to act in a specific way to navigate social interactions (Evans & Moore, 2015; Wingfield, 2007). Pearls were used to showcase the performative element of having to adjust to specific spaces.

Several educators shared that they felt a moral imperative to more emotional labor. One participant even shared how their White colleagues would pass their own responsibilities to them because they were a Black educator. It was assumed because they shared the same racial identity as some of the students, that they should support them. While they would take the kids into their room and work on building a relationship, it was evident that they were frustrated. "I was the only Black teacher. I became the spokesperson for the Black students, as well as the 'Black child whisperer' (along with other Black support staff)." Building relationships takes work, it was evident in this narrative that the assumption was that educators of color will do this work for White staff rather than taking it on themselves. Studies have shown that teachers from any ethnic background can be effective and successful with their Black students (Gay, 2000; Ladson-Billings, 1994). To pass this work over to Black educators is one way that White educators can be increasing the workload of their Black colleagues. Gay (2000) discusses the "professional racism" (p. 205) that this participant was experiencing around the assumption that Black teachers must teach Black students. This undertone of anger for doing more emotional labor that was expressed in the narratives was visualized by the repetition of the bejeweled middle fingers.

A social justice approach to teaching was expressed in the narratives. Many participants discussed their experiences in schools not being very relevant to their cultural or ethnic backgrounds. This was sourced as a reason for pursuing education for several participants. Two participants detailed the way they try to make their curriculum more culturally relevant. One stating that "I try to push the boundaries to make way for those who will come after me. The future is relying on us." Another detailed that "I go out of my way to teach the American experience of minorities and other underrepresented groups. I purposely do not teach about a lot of dead White men. We are overloaded with that information our whole lives and I feel as though students need to know other people can and did succeed in this country and that their history didn't start with slavery." African fabric was used to represent these sentiments. The direction the educator's head was facing in the painting was a way of signifying pushing back against traditional structures of Whiteness. This was also a recommendation from one of the participants who thought it would portray an *unbothered, untraditional* demeanor that countered the hegemonic framing of education today.

The "drinking" of the White tears represents the resistance Black educators exercise in order to push back against structures of Whiteness. This was used to represent my own experience teaching an undergraduate course at my university. I had a student question how I was "qualified" to teach the course and wanted to know how I obtained the position. After I had my supervisor come in and talk to them, they approached me after class apologetic and cried about how they grew up in a small town where there wasn't much diversity. Liebow and Glazer (2019) assert that White tears are a way White people are able to relieve responsibility for having meaningful conversations about race. When confronted with issues about their White privilege, and the ways they have upheld and participated in maintaining structures of Whiteness, "emotional White fragility" is a way for White people to remove responsibility for their commitments.

The painting is hanging in the education building at my school. It takes up a lot of space, it is bright, and it is bold. The viewer cannot escape it when they are in the room and it has received many different reactions. For my Black colleagues, I have seen them taking pictures with it, excited that it is in the space, but I have also seen White students who while meeting in the room glance at it awkwardly, sometimes even laughing uncomfortably. Discomfort with the piece is a stark reaction to being confronted with Whiteness. This is an example of how this type of research can empower Black educators. Having work like this hanging in the education building of a PWI pushes back against dominant methodologies, confronts Whiteness, and stirs an emotional reaction from the viewer. This reveals how creating a visual art piece based on Black experiences can be empowering to showcase in the very spaces where they may feel marginalized. It showcases their experiences and can make them feel seen in a space where they can traditionally be silenced. The painting itself functions as a tool of resistance and was brought to life through the resistive narratives collected from Black educators that informed and guided my artistic process.

CONCLUSION

The retention of Black educators is a prevalent issue facing American public schools today. Through the use of arts-based methods, this chapter explored some of the causes and strategies Black educators have employed in order to work in PWIs. Fostering a sense of community and adopting a

social justice approach to the curriculum were some of the coping strategies articulated through the narratives that reveal ways to support Black
educators in PWIs. Implications on the ways emotional labor is distributed,
anti-Black policies and dress codes are also highlighted as exclusionary
tactics that schools should avoid. The arts-based process as well as the final
painting provides a concrete example of how Black educators can use art-
based methods to reclaim and make space in institutions that have marginalized them.

REFERENCES

Achinstein, B., & Aguirre, J. (2008). Cultural match or culturally suspect: How new
teachers of color negotiate sociocultural challenges in the classroom. *Teachers
College Record, 110*(8), 1505–1540.

Achinstein, B., Ogawa, R. T., Sexton, D., & Freitas, C. (2010). Retaining teachers of color: A pressing problem and a potential strategy for "hard-to-
staff" schools. *Review of Educational Research, 80*(1), 71–107. https://doi.
org/10.3102/0034654309355994

Alexander, R., & Moore, S. E. (2008). The benefits, challenges, and strategies of
African American faculty teaching at predominantly White institutions. *Journal of African American Studies, 12*(1), 4–18. https://doi.org/10.1007/s12111
-007-9028-z

Barone, T. (1995). Persuasive writings, vigilant readings, and reconstructed char-
acters: The paradox of trust in educational storysharing. *International Journal of Qualitative Studies in Education, 8*(1), 63–74. https://doi.org/10.1080/
0951839950080107

Barone, T., & Eisner, E. (2011). *Art based research.* Thousand Oaks, CA: SAGE.

Borman, G. D., & Dowling, N. M. (2008). Teacher attrition and retention: A meta-
analytic and narrative review of the research. *Review of Educational Research,
78*(3), 367–409. https://doi.org/10.3102/0034654308321455

Carter Andrews, D. J., Castro, E., Cho, C. L., Petchauer, E., Richmond, G., & Floden,
R. (2018). Changing the narrative on diversifying the teaching workforce: A
look at historical and contemporary factors that inform recruitment and retention of teachers of color. *Journal of Teacher Education, 70*(1), 6–12. https://
doi.org/10.1177/0022487118812418

Darling-Hammond, L. (2010). Teacher education and the American future. *Journal of Teacher Education, 61*(1–2), 35–47. https://doi.org/10.1177/002248
7109348024

Davis, L., Khoza, L., & Brooks, J. (2019). Nail art, nail care, and self-expression: Gender differences in African Americans' consumption of nail cosmetics. *Fashion,
Style, & Popular Culture, 6*(2), 159–174.

Denzin, N. K. (1998). The art and politics of interpretation. In N. Denzin & Y. Lincoln (Eds.), *Collecting and interpreting qualitative materials* (pp. 500–515). London, England: SAGE.

Eisner, E. W. (1998). Does experience in the arts boost academic achievement? *Journal of Art & Design Education, 17*(1), 51–60. https://doi.org/10.1111/1468-5949.00105

Evans, L., & Moore, W. L. (2015). Impossible burdens: White institutions, emotional labor, and micro-resistance. *Social Problems, 62*(3), 439–454. https://doi.org/10.1093/socpro/spv009

Farinde, A. A., Allen, A., & Lewis, C. W. (2016). Retaining Black teachers: An examination of Black female teachers' intentions to remain in K–12 classrooms. *Equity & Excellence in Education, 49*(1), 115–127. https://doi.org/10.1080/10665684.2015.1120367

Farinde-Wu, A., Griffen, A. J., & Young, J. L. (2020). Black female teachers on teacher preparation and retention. *Penn GSE Perspectives on Urban Education, 16*(1), 1–17.

Foster, V. (2012). The pleasure principle: Employing arts-based methods in social work research. *European Journal of Social Work, 15*(4), 532–545. https://doi.org/10.1080/13691457.2012.702311

Gay, G. (2000). *Culturally responsive teaching: Theory, research, and practice.* New York, NY: Teachers College Press.

Greenwood, J. (2012). Arts-based research: Weaving magic and meaning. *International Journal of Education & the Arts, 13*(1), 20.

Grosz, E. A. (1994). *Volatile bodies: Toward a corporeal feminism.* Bloomington: Indiana University Press.

hooks, b. (1994). *Teaching to transgress: Education as the practice of freedom.* New York, NY: Routledge.

Hudson, M. J., & Holmes, B. J. (1994). Missing teachers, impaired communities: The unanticipated consequences of Brown v. Board of Education on the African American teaching force at the precollegiate level. *The Journal of Negro Education, 63*(3), 388–393. https://doi.org/10.2307/2967189

Ingersoll, R., & May, H. (2011). *Recruitment, retention and the minority teacher shortage.* Consortium for Policy Research in Education.

Ingersoll, R., May, H., & Collins, G. (2019). Recruitment, employment, retention, and the minority teacher shortage. *Education policy analysis archives, 27*, 37. https://doi.org/10.14507/epaa.27.3714

Ingersoll, R., & Merrill, L. (2017). *A quarter century of changes in the elementary and secondary teaching force: From 1987 to 2012.* Statistical Analysis Report (NCES 2017-092). Washington, DC: U.S. Department of Education, National Center for Education Statistics.

Jay, M. (2009). Race-ing through the school day: African American educators experiences with race and racism in schools. *International Journal of Qualitative Studies in Education, 22*(6), 671–685. https://doi.org/10.1080/09518390903333855

Ladson-Billings, G. (1996). Silences as weapons: Challenges of a Black professor teaching White students. *Theory Into Practice, 35*(2), 79–85.

Langer, S. K., (1957). *Problems of art; ten philosophical lectures.* New York, NY: Scribner.

Lawrence-Lightfoot, S., & Davis, J. H. (1977). Perspective talking: Discovery and development. In *The art and science of portraiture* (pp. 19–38). San Francisco, CA: Jossey-Bass.

Lawrence, R. (2008). Powerful feelings: Exploring the affective domain of informal and arts-based learning. In J. M. Dirkx (Ed.), *Adult learning and the emotional self. New directions for adult and continuing education, number 120* (pp. 65–77). San Francisco, CA: Jossey-Bass.

Leavy, P. (2009). Social research and the creative arts an introduction. In, *Method meets art: Arts-based research practice* (pp. 1–24). New York, NY: Guilford Press.

Leavy, P. (2009b). Poetry and qualitative research. In, *Method meets art: Arts-based research practice* (pp. 63–99). New York, NY: Guilford Press.

Leavy, P. (2015). *Method meets art: Arts-based research practice* (2nd ed.). New York, NY: Guilford Press.

Liebow, N., & Glazer, T. (2019). White tears: Emotion regulation and white fragility. *Inquiry,* 1–21. doi:10.1080/0020174x.2019.1610048

McNiff, S. (1998). *Art-based research.* London, England: Jessica Kingsley.

Milner, H. R. (2006). Preservice teachers' learning about cultural and racial diversity. *Urban Education, 41*(4), 343–375. https://doi.org/10.1177/0042085906289709

Morris, M. (2016). *Pushout: The criminalization of Black girls in schools.* New York, NY: The New Press.

Pinar, W. F. (2004). Foreword. In R. L. Irwin & A. de Cosson (Eds.), *A/r/tography: Rendering self through arts-based living inquiry* (pp. 9–25). Vancouver, BC: Pacific Educational Press.

Redding, C., & Baker, D. J. (2019). Understanding racial/ethnic diversity gaps among early career teachers. *AERA Open, 5*(2). https://doi.org/10.1177/2332 858419848440

Rolling, J. (2013). Arts-based research as critical-activist research practice. In, *Arts-based research primer* (1st ed.; pp. 107–130). New York, NY: Peter Lang.

Shange, S. (2019). Black girl ordinary: Flesh, carcerality, and the refusal of ethnography. *Transforming Anthropology, 27*(1), 3–21. https://doi.org/10.1111/traa.12143

Sheets, R. H. (2004). Preparation and development of teachers of color. *International Journal of Qualitative Studies in Education, 17*(2), 163–166.

Spencer, M. B. (2006). Phenomenology and ecological systems theory: Development of diverse groups. In R. M. Lerner & W. Damon (Eds.), *Handbook of child psychology: Theoretical models of human development* (pp. 829–893). Wiley.

Starks, S., Vakalahi, O., Comer, J. M., & Ortiz-Hendricks, C. (2010). Gathering, telling, preparing the stories: A vehicle for healing. *Journal of Indigenous Voices in Social Work, 1*(1), 1–18.

Tillman, L. C. (2004). (Un)intended consequences? *Education and Urban Society, 36*(3), 280–303. https://doi.org/10.1177/0013124504264360

Villegas, A. M., & Irvine, J. J. (2010). Diversifying the teaching force: An examination of major arguments. *The Urban Review, 42*(3), 175–192. https://doi.org/10.1007/s11256-010-0150-1

Wang, Q., Coemans, S., Siegesmund, R., & Hannes, K. (2017). Arts-based methods in socially engaged research practice: A reclassification framework [Abstract]. *Arts-based Methods in Socially Engaged Research Practice5, 2*(2).

Ware, F. (2016, October 25). *Radical self-care, elements of a culturally responsive practice.* Live performance in Scholars Unlimited Training, Denver, Colorado.

Wilcox, H. N. (2009). Embodied ways of knowing, pedagogies, and social justice: Inclusive science and beyond. *NWSA Journal, 21*(2), 103–120.

Wingfield, A. H. (2007). The modern mammy and the angry Black man: African American professionals' experiences with gendered racism in the workplace. *Race, Gender, & Class, 14*(2), 196–212. https://doi.org/10.1080/10646175.2018.1471755

Zumwalt, K., & Craig, E. (2008). Who is teaching? Does it matter? In M. Cochran-Smith, S. Feiman-Nemser, & D. J. McIntyre (Eds.), *Handbook of research on teacher education: Enduring questions in changing contexts* (pp. 404–423). New York, NY: Routledge.

CHAPTER 25

A MIRROR[1]

Sarrah Grubb
Indiana University Kokomo

She said she
Had never seen herself
In a book
Read in the front
Of the class

So after fifteen years of classrooms
when Woodson's[2]
words sang
　　　　"the curl of my hair"
Into the air
And Lopez's image
　　　　Danced to the rhythm

She gasped
Involuntarily

And passed me a note after class
Her tears
Weren't because she was sad
    Or embarrassed
Just happy

There was a book!

Other little girls
Needed to hear it—could get to hear it
And see their reflection

In a book
In a book being read
    In a book being read
        !At the front of the room!
To the whole class.

NOTES

1. Sims Bishop, R. (1990). Mirrors, windows, and sliding glass doors. *Perspectives*, *1*(3), ix–xi.
2. Woodson, J., & López Rafael. (2018). *The day you begin*. New York, NY: Nancy Paulsen Books.

CHAPTER 26

REFLECTION

Inertia and *Pa'delante*

Freyca Calderon-Berumen
Pennsylvania State University, Altoona

Miryam Espinosa-Dulanto
University of Texas–Rio Grande Valley

I pain
relentless ongoing flux of reality
in a society where
power hails 1ton trees plan
ignoring environmental disasters
fossil fuels roots of problems
in a universe of constant flux
I pain
for fixed moments to anchor
searching for endings to become openings
to find walls, barbed wire, biometric screenings
trying to stop

Making a Spectacle, pages 273–276
Copyright © 2021 by Information Age Publishing

> ugliness entering the first world
> poverty faces
> become homes and classrooms
>> I pain and I begin to hope

This shift in perception increases the ability and effectiveness with which we—simple humans—people of color—POC—may adapt and change. In a world such as ours, in which change of such enormous magnitude is called urgently, this perspective is invaluable. Exposed to, while experiencing U.S.A. power structures in the normativity supported by (in)equity of daily interactions, those of us—deemed foreigner—POC—are posed under more scrutiny, called attention to, and differences are emphasized as flaws. As such, in our U.S.A. world, being different—than an idealized norm—is enough reason to be labeled, minoritized, and/or diminished. In other words, demonized.

> no point for wants and feels
> having already a label
> that made me less
> that made me incomplete
> a hyphened american
>> almost good
>> almost enough
>> less than you
>> less than me

The environment created by the 45th U.S. president with his "Make America Great Again" campaign, has brought back an archetypal group member, *American* identity, as "a person who respects political institutions, who is part of a Judeo-Christian religion, speaks English, a member of [the White] racial group. Certainly, some people define the prototypical American as White, Christian, and/or born in the U.S." (Gidda, 2016, n.p.). In addition, this GOP-*American* longs for a time when ethnic minorities weren't in powerful positions or weren't as successful as working- and middle-class Whites. This sentiment is fueled by how the 45th has exploited those racialized beliefs by repeatedly playing on their supporters—GOP Americans' prejudices against non-Christian—especially Muslims, immigrants, and minorities. Thus, individual rights and freedom are given yet sort of questionable for hyphened, undefined, different peoples. It permeates everything and academia is not an exception.

> Our rights
>> as long as I use your words
>> as long as I follow your rules

> as long as I fit in your mold
> as long as I checked the mainstream boxes
> as long as I act like you{/POEM}

Regardless that POC may not be granted the same opportunities as White scholars or as someone who acts like one. We—POC have coined a word, *resilience* because we dare to center our efforts into decolonizing academia (Rodriguez, 2018), completely aware about the risks and empowered by knowing that education is a political act (Freire, 1970/2000). We—POC are passionate with bringing the ideas of social justice and equity into our teaching, research, and service in academia. As we embark in this journey, we heed Marcos' (2002) suggestion that "our word is our weapon." Comandante Marcos is both a leader of *the Ejército Zapatista de Liberación Nacional,* and a writer whose work is probably one of the most poignant critiques of contemporary neoliberalism. Marcos, together with indigenous Mexicans, fought against all the colonial powers in the continent—Canada, the United States, and Mexico—to be seen and to be left alone. These indigenous Mexicans are an example of a decolonizing project. They did not ask for anything but to create and design a space for the marginalized, the subaltern, the unseen, the indigenous people. As such, we are carving a space here, we are using our words.

> the power of accented english
> loudly tells
> *soy bilingüe*
> no shame
> *la lengua que tu tratas de borrar*
> > *cortar/eliminar/callar/olvidar*
> it won't be silenced
> these are my words,
> decolonizing tools
> > that fight attempts to tame our tongues
> > they describe
> > > pain, resistance, survival, resilience
> > while they defend
> > > our voices, our place, our rights
> > to be, to exist

"Academic spaces are not precisely adorned by safety, nor are they where freedom of speech is truly welcome. Not all of us have the luxury to speak freely without getting penalized by being called radicals, too emotional, angry, or even not scholarly enough" (Rodriguez, 2018, p. 3). A big component of the academic job is teaching. When teaching teachers, it becomes imperative to engage and embrace social justice and equity. These are our words, our decolonizing tools.

> living and working in a red state
> compels me to speak up/out/loud and clear
> but once again I withhold
>> my words
>> my thoughts
>> my body language
>>> my body screams
> very carefully I select my words
>> to convey the message—not really a weapon
>> to present different viewpoints—always "otherizing"
>> to try to exist as myself
> I have to share my story
> unique
> yet another immigrant story
>> who cares?

We dare to think, to speak up, to name, to recognize our sociopolitical context, our individual situations, our multiple positionalities, and the implications and traumas associated with these issues.

> enduring the pain
> resisting erasure
>> shining
>> standing up

REFERENCES

Freire, P. (2000). Pedagogy of the oppressed (30th anniversary ed.; trans. M. B. Ramos). New York, NY: Continuum. (Originally published in 1968, English translation 1970)

Marcos, S. (2002). *Our word is our weapon: Selected writings.* New York, NY: Seven Stories Press.

Gidda, M. (2016, November 15). How Donald Trump's nationalism won over white Americans. *Newsweek U.S.* Retrieved from https://www.newsweek.com/donald-trump-nationalism-racism-make-america-great-again-521083

Rodríguez, C. O. (2018). *Decolonizing academia: Poverty, oppression and pain.* Toronto, Canada: Fernwood.

ABOUT THE CONTRIBUTORS

Vonzell Agosto, PhD, is an associate professor of curriculum studies in the educational leadership and policy studies program at the University of South Florida. Her primary line of inquiry asks how educational contexts can be (more or less) oppressive especially with regard to culture, race, gender, and dis/ability. This research is published in handbook chapters, articles, and journals including *Teachers College Record, Educational Researcher, Review of Research in Education, Journal of Curriculum Theorizing, Journal of Curriculum and Pedagogy,* and the *Journal of School Leadership.*

Michelle Angelo-Rocha is a Brazilian PhD student in the educational leadership and policy studies program at the University of South Florida (USF). She earned her master's degree in Latin American and Caribbean studies with a concentration in sociology and human rights at USF, and journalism at the Universidade Católica de Brasília. Michelle's research agenda focuses on social justice issues such as human trafficking, femicide, indigenous education in Brazil, multilingual education in the United States, and media analysis. Her study efforts are on underprivileged Latinx immigrant families in the United States and Latin America. Michelle has experience working as teacher assistant helping adult refugees and K–12 English as a second language (ESL) learners in the Tampa Bay area. She conducted ethnographic research with immigrant victims of human trafficking in Florida, and with women victims of femicide in Argentina. Michelle worked with service providers, nongovernmental organizations, human rights activists, educators, policymakers, and law enforcement that work directly with Latinx trafficking victims and refugees.

Making a Spectacle, pages 277–288
Copyright © 2021 by Information Age Publishing
277

Lisa Armstrong is a third-year doctoral student in the applied cultural anthropology program with a heritage concentration at the University of South
Florida. She earned a master's degree in Africana studies at the University
of South Florida researching the stability of Black families through kinship
and community networks for her thesis project *Family Life in Carver City–
Lincoln Gardens* (2016). This study is on a historically (traditional) Black
middle-class community in Tampa, Florida. She has also studied abroad in
Bahia, Brazil, where she focused on Afro-Brazilian culture and language.
She has worked on several service projects. Most recently, her work relates
to the resettlement and transition of African refugees in Tampa communities and schools. Her research aims to apply ethnographic methods to create alternative historical narratives that empower under-documented Black
experiences. Lisa has presented her research in national and international
academic conferences that include: USF Institute for Black Life, Association for the Study of African American Life and History, American Anthropological Association, Society for Applied Anthropology, Association
for the Study of Worldwide African Diaspora, and Collegium for African
American Research.

Matthew Bradley as an experienced elementary school principal who began
his career teaching students with disabilities in a high school setting. He
worked for a number of years as a behavior consultant for preschool to Year
12 across a region of schools supporting whole school systems, teacher behavior and pedagogy, and individual student intervention. Matthew moved
into an executive position in a clinical elementary setting supporting students with significant emotional disturbance including a locked psychiatric
ward. This was where he first began as a principal and developed models for
working with staff, families, and students experiencing trauma. He spent 7
years as principal of an elementary school that supported significant numbers of students with refugee backgrounds and was focused on future focused pedagogies. This led to him speaking at conferences and supporting
other schools from across the State in both areas. It was at this setting that
Matthew worked closely with the university in regards to leadership, refugee education, pedagogy, and belonging. Currently Matthew is the principal of a demonstration school that works closely with the local university in
the preparation of preservice teachers.

Freyca Calderon-Berumen works as an assistant professor in elementary
and early childhood education at Penn State Altoona. She completed her
PhD in curriculum studies at Texas Christian University. Her research interests are around critical multicultural education and critical pedagogy as
an avenue to address social equity and justice, and as tools to a decolonizing praxis in education. Her work privileges qualitative methods exploring
possibilities for community building for marginalized and under-theorized

groups and contributing to the teacher education field by linking theoretical perspectives with everyday experiences and developing culturally relevant understandings. Particularly, she is interested in exploring the ways immigrant women shape their identity and their survival strategies in educating bilingual and bicultural children in the United States as they create their cultural curriculum of the home.

Larisa Callaway-Cole is an assistant professor in the Department of Human Development and Family Science in the College of Education and Human Sciences at Oklahoma State University. Prior, Larisa spent several years teaching in early childhood and higher education contexts throughout California. She has an EdD in educational leadership from a joint doctoral program between California State University Channel Islands and Fresno State University. Larisa's research interests focus on the dynamic counternarratives of minoritized children and families in her community, specifically regarding the power of storying and prioritizing loving-relationality in research methodologies. She is currently engaged in research that posits love as a resistant and transformational response to raising young children.

Ivan Cantu is an undergraduate student in art education at the University of Texas Rio Grande Valley (UTRGV). He is from Edinburg, TX and has always lived in the Rio Grande Valley. Cantu has worked with a variety of art media, ranging from ink, photography, and jewelry.. He is interested in making art work that pushes against his comfort zone and breaks boundaries. He has taught at the UTRGV Recreation Facility as a summer camp art instructor. He also has taught art classes at St. Matthews Episcopal School in Edinburg, TX. Cantu's goals are to teach art at a high school and continue developing both his body of work as well as facilitating his students' art making.

Maricela Casas is an undergraduate student in art education at The University of Texas Rio Grande Valley. Born and raised in the Rio Grande Valley in the city of Pharr, Casas taught art at St. Matthew's Episcopal School for two semesters. Currently, Casas works in the special education department at IDEA Public Schools. She studied abroad in Spain while working on her associate's degree at South Texas College. She is fluent in both English and Spanish, has two younger brothers, and one younger sister. Casas' goals include completing her undergraduate studies to become an art teacher for IDEA Public Schools. She wants to continue sharing her knowledge and beautiful art.

Jose Cordon has been using poetry to deliver messages and connect with people since he was 14 years old. Over the years he has been able to share his passionate poetry with organizations such as the One Day at a Time program, AltaMed, La Luz Center, the Latino Community Foundation, Monument Impact, and more. Currently he is working on creating a nonprofit connecting rescue dogs with under-severed youth in Contra Costa County, California. Using the human-canine bond to encourage positive behavioral changes. He is also developing a special one-hour poetic presentation combining spoken word poetry, humor, and his life's lessons to create a unique, moving, and personal experience.

Dionne L. Davis is a doctoral candidate at the University of South Florida. She is originally from North Carolina and has resided in Tampa, Florida since 2010. She earned her bachelor's degree in Elementary Education and Afro American Studies and her master's degree in School Administration from the University of North Carolina at Chapel Hill. Dionne has dedicated her 20-year professional career in public education as a teacher and school administrator to equitable schooling for all children and believes her current research interests relative to diversifying site-based leadership amongst women in two-way immersion schools will aid in serving future generations of scholars.

Emily Marie Passos Duffy is a poet, teacher, and ecdysiast. Her written work has been published in *Boulder Weekly, Portland Review, Cigar City Poetry Journal, Spit Poet Zine,* and *Iron Horse Literary Review.* She is a contributing member of *The Daily Camera*'s Editorial Advisory Board and a 2020 artist-in-residence at Boulder Creative Collective. She earned her MFA in Creative Writing and Poetics from Naropa University in 2018, and she teaches in the English department at Red Rocks Community College.

Erin Dyke, PhD, is an assistant professor of curriculum studies at Oklahoma State University. Erin's research interests include pedagogies of social movement spaces; activist research methods; social justice, abolitionist, and decolonial movements in education; and gender/sexuality and education. Her work has appeared in the *Journal of Curriculum Theorizing, Urban Education, The International Handbook of Indigenous Education, Berkeley Review of Education,* and *Transformations: A Journal of Inclusive Pedagogy.* Her latest work is focused on studying the 2018 teacher uprisings and their impacts on labor and intersecting social justice issues in education. Co-authored with Brendan Muckian-Bates, her forthcoming book, *Rank-and-File Rebels: Theories of Power and Change in the 2018 Education Strikes* (Colorado State University Open Press) examines how gender, race, class, and emergent forms of solidarity and social movement unionism shaped the spring 2018 statewide public education walkouts.

Miryam Espinosa-Dulanto is a faculty member at The University of Texas–Rio Grande Valley, Teaching and Learning Department. Dr. Espinosa-

Dulanto holds a PhD in curriculum theory and educational policies for linguistic minorities from the University of Wisconsin-Madison. Dr. Espinosa-Dulanto's writing as well as her academic research departs from identifying herself as a woman of color, a Borderlands Mestiza, and a nonmainstream person in the United States. From that perspective, her research explores the construction, access, and transmission of knowledge especially for minorities in U.S. schools. Dr. Espinosa-Dulanto is a veteran teacher, she has taught in urban and rural settings, in the United States, Latin America, Europe, and Asia. In addition, Dr. Espinosa-Dulanto is an avid ethnographer who uses testimonios, narrative inquiry, photography, and poetry as tools to learn and communicate.

David R. Fisher currently works in educational administration and was a public school music teacher for 10 years. His research interests involve charter school policy, organizational theory, and critical arts-based inquiry. Through the use of the qualitative methodologies of narrative inquiry and autoethnography, David examines the impact of educational competition and choice on communities and its relation to Indigenous and structural issues in the United States. In order to combat these and other oppressive policies, David offers the arts as a means of practicing empathy and resisting political oppression. His degrees include a PhD in educational leadership and a master's and bachelor's degree in music.

Kiara Flores is a high school student in Northwestern Florida. She enjoys engaging with and creating artwork, especially within the context of social in/justice. While history is one of Kiara's favorite subjects, she also is interested in how other subjects, like science and language arts, contribute to her understanding of the world.

Christen Sperry García is originally from the San Diego-Tijuana borderlands. Christen is a visual and performance artist, writer, and educator. She is cofounder of Museo Me Vale and the Nationwide Museum Mascot Project (NWMMP). Examining the borders that exist between the public, communities, and art institutions, NWMMP has mascotted and performed at over 40 venues including the Museo de Arte Contemporáneo Lima, Peru; Fowler Museum at UCLA, Los Angeles, CA; Museo Jumex, Mexico City; Museum of Contemporary Art San Diego, CA; Hammer Museum, Los Angeles, CA; and Museo de Arte Moderno, Bogotá, Colombia. For 6 years, she worked for the studio of internationally known video artist Bill Viola in Long Beach, CA. She coordinated worldwide exhibitions, publications, artist lectures, museum collections, and collaborated with the artist's galleries in New York, London, and Seoul. García received her PhD in Art Education at The Pennsylvania State University. She earned an MFA in Studio Art (Sculpture/4D) from California State University, Long Beach, and BS in Studio Art at the University of Wisconsin-Madison. An assistant professor of Art Education in the School of Art at the University of Texas Rio Grande Valley, she lives between South Texas and Los Angeles with her two young boys.

Brian Gibbs taught social studies in East Los Angeles, California for 16 years. He is currently a faculty member in the school of education at the University of North Carolina at Chapel Hill. He researches critical teaching in complex social contexts, most recently how war is taught to the children of soldiers, how lynching is taught in schools near historic lynching sites, and a longitudinal study examining how teachers teach for social justice in unjust school spaces.

Sarah R. Gordon, PhD is an associate professor of educational leadership at Arkansas Tech University. She holds her PhD in research, evaluation, measurement, and statistics (REMS) from Oklahoma State University (OSU). Dr. Gordon worked in Student Affairs at Oklahoma State for 8 years and spent 3 years as the director of University Assessment and Testing at OSU. She was also a faculty member at OSU before coming to Arkansas Tech University. Dr. Gordon has taught courses and published work in the areas of program evaluation, research methods, and assessment. Her research interests include perceptions of evaluation and assessment in P–12 and higher education, effective assessment practices in higher education (in both academic and student affairs), and diversity as a concept and learning outcome in higher education.

Sarrah Grubb serves as an assistant professor of education at Indiana University, Kokomo. She earned her PhD in educational administration from the Department of Educational Leadership at Miami University in Oxford, Ohio. She has varied experience in education, including teaching at the elementary, middle school, and high school levels, and coordinating curriculum, instruction, and professional development across all levels of schooling. She rediscovered teaching as soul work through an appointment at a rural work college in the hills of eastern Kentucky, where she became dedicated to collaborating and co-creating curriculum with preservice teachers as they develop their teacher hearts.

Mark Hickey is a PhD student in curriculum studies at Oklahoma State University. Previously, Mark was a high school English teacher, having taught Grades 8–12 in Philadelphia, PA and Brooklyn, NY. Mark's research and work focuses on the intersections of authority relations in classroom spaces and is informed by post-structuralist and queer theory.

Michaela Inks is an applied anthropologist who does research with the local refugee population on issues such as social services, education, nutrition, and media. She is attending the graduate program in applied anthropology at the University of South Florida as a master's student. She is also an active member of the Tampa Bay Refugee Task Force and has taken a short-term position with Americorp Vista to continue building refugee community resources. Her goal as an anthropologist is to go beyond what the discipline expects from its researchers and establish changes that uplift those in her community who need it most. With her research she wishes to show how refugees live complex, multifaceted lives and use her platform to share experiences beyond those described as "surviving."

Jennifer Job, PhD, is an on-the-ground organizer, fundraiser, and digital strategist for nonprofit groups advocating for social justice. She graduated with her PhD in culture, curriculum, and change from the University of North Carolina at Chapel Hill and was assistant professor of curriculum studies at Oklahoma State University before deciding to return to North Carolina and work on the front lines of the political social justice movement. She is a previous editor of this volume and has articles published in *The High School Journal*, *Youth Voice Journal*, and *Journal of Curriculum Theorizing*, among others.

Nadia Khan-Roopnarine is a New York City public school teacher. She teaches high school English in Brooklyn. As a founding teacher at Spring Creek Community School she has served as the English department chairperson since 2013. She is also a contributing writer to the New York City, "AP for All" curriculum in English literature and composition. She is currently completing her doctoral dissertation at Molloy College. Her work examines the legacy of colonialism in advanced placement English curriculum and pedagogy. Her forthcoming publications address the importance of interrogating critical pedagogy through radical love. Her work with the Paulo Freire Graduate Student Council also examines the notion of femtorship and the critical organizing process.

G. Dean McBride is an adjunct assistant professor of theater arts at the University of Texas at Arlington. He holds an MFA in arts administration from Texas Tech University and is currently pursuing the PhD in art education from University of North Texas. As a long-term survivor of HIV/AIDS and addiction, his ongoing project is primarily concerned with queer dis/ease and explores learning selves in the making through uncanny arts-based pedagogies and curricula as forms of social and political action and recovery.

Eleni Mousena, PhD, is an assistant professor in the Department of Early Childhood Education at the University of West Attica. She worked (2007–2017) as a school supervisor for the Ministry of Education, and as a national expert in the European Commission on quality education project

(2011–2014). Her research interests focus on pedagogy, literacy and curriculum, citizenship education, and educational linguistics. She took part as a research group member in many projects, related to educational reforms. She has participated in many international conferences as a speaker and has written articles in books and scientific journals. Member of ASCD (Association for Supervision and Curriculum Development), member of EECERA (European Early Childhood Research Association), member of Capacity Building for LLP (Lifelong Learning Program), Consortium, member of Hellenic Association of Political Science, and member of Hellenic Educational Association.

Ann Marie Mobley was born and raised in Tampa Florida and is a product of Hillsborough County Public Schools. She is a graduate of Howard W. Blake High School. After completing high school, Ann Marie pursued higher education and went on to attend Florida Agricultural and Mechanical University (FAMU) a well-known HBCU in Florida. While at FAMU she earned a bachelor's degree in 6–12 secondary social science and a master's in applied social science with a concentration in history. Following her departure from FAMU, Ann Marie was immediately accepted and enrolled in The University of South Florida's PhD Educational Leadership program where she currently studies. Ann Marie has a passion for education and has prided herself on being a public school classroom teacher as well as a lifelong learner. Her experiences throughout her school career both as a student and teacher help and shape her pedagogical practices and philosophy. It is her greatest belief that everyone has the right to learn.

Mary Newbery recently graduated from Teachers College, Columbia University with a doctorate in curriculum studies from the Department of Curriculum and Teaching. She currently works as an adjunct professor in the School of Education at Quinnipiac University, where she teaches an educational leadership course on designing and leading curriculum and instruction programs in K–12 schools. She also works as a school leader in Connecticut. Her research interests include feminist, poststructural and new materialist theories, and post-qualitative research methods. In particular, she is interested in engaging with critical, posthumanist theories to inform transdisciplinary curriculum experiences across the arts and sciences in K–12 schools. This work is committed to co-creating opportunities for critical and place-based learning experiences with students and educators that are entangled with a posthumanist politics of relationality and connectivity.

Jessica O'Brien is a PhD student studying secondary English education at the University of South Florida. She is an adjunct professor at the University of Tampa and a middle school language arts teacher. Her research interests include the preparation of preservice English teachers, educational technologies, and curriculum development.

Asha Omar is a third year PhD student studying racialization in elementary schools. Before entering academia she taught first grade for 3 years where she observed anti-Black policies, disciplinary practices, and curriculum. Omar's research centers around the ways Black youth experience racialization in schools and how that affects their sense of belonging and identity development in school spaces. Omar is an artist/activist who enjoys pulling from life experiences to challenge dominant narratives represented in art. Using her background as an artist, Omar is specifically interested in the ways arts-based methods can portray truths that have traditionally been marginalized and offer a platform for youth who may not have the words to convey their experiences. Omar centers the participants in her research activities and works to find ways to make her data, the analysis and implications collaborative with participants.

Kristin Papoi, PhD, is a clinical assistant professor and director for the Master of Arts of Teaching program at the University of North Carolina at Chapel Hill. Her research and teaching expertise center on teacher education, language/literacy education (including emergent, early, and multiliteracy approaches), qualitative research methods, and arts integration for diverse learners. Currently, her research and teaching focus on reflective practices of preservice teachers and experiential education as it relates to teacher education and instructional practice within the sociopolitical-cultural context of schools.

Paul Pérez-Jiménez was born in Anáhuac, Tamaulipas (locally known as *El Poblado Anáhuac*) in northern México but attended public schools in McAllen, TX. He graduated from Corpus Christi Minor Seminary; a Jesuit led high school in 1981. Most of his undergraduate preparation was from the University of Dallas; however, he transferred to the University of Texas-Pan American, where he earned a bachelor's degree in Spanish with a minor in English in 2007. He then received a master's degree in English—Rhetoric and Composition in 2010 from the University of Texas Rio Grande Valley, followed by a certificate at the master's level in Interdisciplinary Studies—Young Adult Literature in 2012. Paul was awarded the Stanford Hollyhock Fellowship in 2015 and 2016, where he studied equity in teaching. Paul received a doctor of education degree in curriculum and instruction in higher education with educational technology hours in 2019 and specializing in both cooperative learning and critical theory from the University of Texas Rio Grande Valley. In 1994, Paul married Flor N. González. They reside in Alamo, TX, with their four daughters, Wendy, Sammy, Amy, and Katalina.

Megan Ruby is an advanced doctoral student in curriculum studies at Oklahoma State University. She has taught at multiple grade levels as an elementary teacher in public education from 2010–2018. Megan's research interests include critical Whiteness studies, the emotional aspects of teacher burnout in our neoliberal era, and gender and education. She has presented at numerous national and international conferences, and her work is featured in the forthcoming book *Critical Understandings in Education Encyclopedia: Critical Whiteness Studies*. She is currently working on her dissertation, which explores how the constructs of niceness frustrate White women educators from engaging anti-racist pedagogy in the classroom.

Jinan El Sabbagh is a fourth-year doctoral student at Oklahoma State University. Prior to becoming a full-time student and graduate research assistant, she taught English for 6 years ranging from Grades 9 through 12. Her research interests include mindfulness and social-emotional learning in schools as ways to counter dominant punitive forms of discipline; trauma-informed practices and pedagogies; the school-to-prison pipeline; nature of discipline within schools for teachers and students; abolition practices; and the intersection of race, gender, sexuality in connection to punitive discipline practices in schools. She is also interested in developing professional development that helps teachers engage in reflexivity, culturally sustaining pedagogies, and be equipped with the tools they need to reduce the stress and effects of trauma on students and themselves.

Maritzabel Salinas is an undergraduate student in art education studying at The University of Texas Rio Grande Valley. She was born in Mcallen, TX, but lived in Miguel Aleman, Tamaulipas, Mexico until college. Attending kindergarten through high school in the United States, Maritzabel struggled to adapt between the dualities of U.S. and Mexican culture. Living only minutes away from the U.S. border, her life was very different from her U.S. American peers. Salinas works in the medium of oil paint. She reinterprets master painter narratives (mostly White men) from a Latina perspective. Even though her paintings are very decorative and bright, she contrasts this to tell a darker story. Salinas has taught art at St. Matthew's Episcopal School and Edinburg High School. Maritzabel's goals are to become an art educator and allow *all* students to walk away with something from her art class. For her, art can be technical, art can be creative, and art can be therapeutic.

Joellyn Sanchez is an undergraduate student in art education attending The University of Texas Rio Grande Valley. She was born and raised in McAllen, Texas. Living on the border with a Mexican American identity, she found a passion in art and teaching. Art has always influenced her to be the best version of herself and find different viewpoints for everything. After finishing school, she would love to bring what she knows to her future students. Although having struggled to get where she is, Sanchez is determined, with her heart and mind, to finish her degree, continue making art, and teach.

Kelly P. Staniunas recently completed her PhD in educational leadership and policy studies at the University of Massachusetts Dartmouth. She is an artist, adult educator, translator, and community organizer; she is also an ever aspiring Freirean, a punk, and an adamant anti-capitalist. Previously she studied applied linguistics (MA) at the University of Massachusetts–Boston, and has a BFA from Massachusetts College of Art. Through drawing, photography, research-based and creative forms of both fiction and nonfiction writing, and documentary video, she aims to disrupt conformity and inspire transformative dialogue. She currently serves in a coordinator role with Mexico Solidarity Network (MSN) and the Autonomous University of Social Movements (AUSM) in Chicago.

Maura Sellars, PhD, is a pedagogical leader working towards more inclusive school systems for the most disadvantaged students. She has almost thirty years experience working in schools as a classroom teacher and executive member of staff. She has a research focus that comes from her belief that children from the most disadvantaged backgrounds can contribute a huge amount to an inclusive classroom. She has a particular interest in differentiated classroom practices, working with students' strengths and developing the students' cognitive capacities of executive function within diverse social and cultural communities. Her research takes a holistic look at what it is to be educated and included. Her publications include single authored books, journal articles, and conference papers. She is currently working as a lecturer in the School of Education, University of Newcastle, Australia.

Chantae D. Still is a certified evaluator and a doctoral candidate at the University of South Florida, pursuing the PhD in adult education. Her professional background, which consists of roles across the fields of child development, human services, and student affairs, fuels her broad ranging research interests. From using student and faculty interaction to improve college student engagement, to identifying protective factors in child welfare caseworkers, or giving voice to narrative accounts of systemic racism, Chantae is interested in identifying and increasing contributors of equitable experiences. More recently Chantae's longtime hobby and pastime, poetry writing, has evolved into a desire to merge scholarship and spoken word for curriculum instruction and contemporary adult education. The poem MAGFO, captures her experience of the Make America Great Again slogan, and presents an alternative message.

Caitlin Sweetapple has been working with students on the autism spectrum for over ten years. Caitlin is one of the founding teachers at Shrub Oak International School and is ecstatic about her new role as director of education. Her mission has been simple: foster positive relationships with students in order to lead them into a lifetime of learning and success. Caitlin has taught students aged 3–21 years old in various special education settings. She has also taught undergraduate courses at her alma mater, Manhattan College. Caitlin received her master's degree in Belgium from Katholieke Universiteit Leuven, where she had extensive training from some of the top leaders in the field of special education and adapted physical education. Caitlin is developmental individual-differences relationship-based model (DIR) certified, a Crisis Prevention Institute (CPI) Trainer, and a certified Water Safety Instructor (WSI). She is currently a doctoral candidate at Molloy College, studying educational leadership for diverse learning communities.

Samuel Jaye Tanner is an assistant professor of literacy education in The Pennsylvania State University System. His research concerns issues of Whiteness, improvisation, and arts-based educational research. Sam's most recent book, *Whiteness, Pedagogy, and Youth in America* is about Whiteness pedagogy in K–12 contexts. Sam is also a creative writer.

Monica Varela is an undergraduate student at the University of Texas Rio Grande Valley pursuing a degree in art education and a minor in the expressive arts. She is from the Rio Grande Valley region and most of her family is located right across the border in the state of Tamaulipas, Mexico. She has taught at St. Matthew's Episcopal School. Her current goal is to become an art educator in her community in South Texas. She has studied literature and renaissance art in Florence, Italy and is considering a master's degree in expressive arts therapy. Varela works in ceramics and is interested in critical and anti-oppressive pedagogies, as well as language and its relationship to cultural identity.

Bretton A. Varga is an assistant professor of history-social science at California State University, Chico. His research works with(in) critical theories of race, art, and temporality to explore how visual methods and artistic mediums can be used to unveil historically marginalized perspectives and layers (upon layers) of history that haunt the world around us.

CPSIA information can be obtained
at www.ICGtesting.com
Printed in the USA
JSHW042351021120
9256JS00004B/18